JERUSALEM

 ELISABETH SIFTON BOOKS · VIKING

JERUSALEM
Rebirth of a City
Martin Gilbert

ELISABETH SIFTON BOOKS · VIKING
Viking Penguin Inc.,
40 West 23rd Street,
New York, New York 10010, U.S.A.

First American edition
published in 1985

ISBN 0-670-80789-3
Library of Congress Catalog Card Number: 85-40071

Title page illustration:
An engraving of 'Modern Jerusalem', *c.* 1850
by W. H. Bartlett

Printed in Great Britain by
Butler & Tanner Ltd
Frome, Somerset
Set in 12/15 Sabon

Dedicated to four Leningrad Jews

Misha Beizer
Nehama and Alex Lein
Mike Salman

and to two young Muscovite 'pickles'

Eli and Mati Kosharovsky

in the hope that each of them
  may one day see Jerusalem

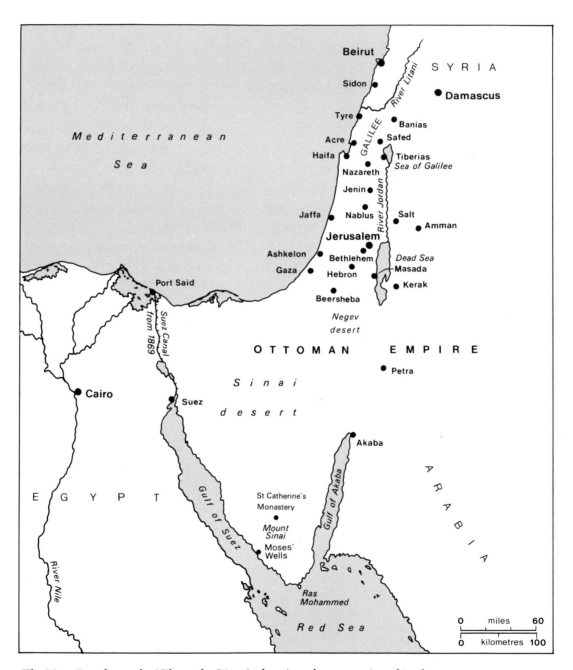

The Near East from the Nile to the Litani, showing places mentioned in the text.

Contents

LIST OF MAPS

ACKNOWLEDGEMENTS

In the preparation of this volume, I should like to acknowledge the gracious permission of Her Majesty the Queen to consult documentary and photographic material in the Royal Archives at Windsor, and to make use of this material both in the narrative and in the illustrations. For their help in consulting this material, I should like to thank Oliver Everett, the Deputy Librarian, Miss Elizabeth Cuthbert, and Miss Frances Dimond, Curator, Photographic Collection.

I am grateful to many individuals for introducing me to the history and by-ways of Jerusalem, since my first visit there in 1971, and above all to my wife Susie who accompanied me on that visit and on more than twelve subsequent annual pilgrimages.

No book on Jerusalem can be written without special thanks to Teddy Kollek, who became its mayor in 1966, and who was mayor of the city throughout the twelve years during which I have been collecting my materials; he not only gave me access to the archives under his mayoral direction but also allowed me to consult his own remarkable private library.

I am also grateful to Shlomo and Irene Gotman, formerly of Leningrad, and to Eitan, Alexandra and Miriam Finkelstein, formerly of Vilna, who, coming to Jerusalem after many years of struggle, allowed me to re-explore the city with them, and to re-tell the stories unfolded in these pages to those for whom Jerusalem's sites and stones had long been but a dream.

In the preparation of this book I am grateful to my secretary, Sue Rampton, who typed the text, and to Helen Gardiner, Christine Harmer and Lisa Hedley for their secretarial help in the last stages of preparation. I am also grateful to those archivists and librarians who allowed me to see and use their materials, and to John and Judy Trotter, booksellers, for making available photographic albums and sets of stereoscopic photographs from their collection. I should like to thank Bodley's Librarian, Oxford, and the librarians of the Jewish Agency, Jerusalem; the Central Zionist Archives, Jerusalem; the Municipality of Jerusalem; the Bibliothèque National, Paris; the Israel Museum, Jerusalem; Mishkenot Sha'ananim (Montefiore Cottages), Jerusalem; the Imperial War Museum, London; and the Palestine Exploration Fund, London, whose archivist, Mrs Gillian Webster, spent several hours showing me the catalogues and photographs of the Palestine Exploration Fund, the foundation of which in 1865 played a conspicuous part both in the exploration of Jerusalem and in the photographing of the city.

I am grateful to Clinton Bailey for his help on all sources relating to the Bedouin in the Jerusalem region; to John Charlton, of Chatto and Windus, for seeing the book through all its stages from inception to publication; and to Ron Costley for his work on the lay-out and design. Many of the photographic reproductions were made from faded and damaged originals by Gerry Moeran and Jean Hunt, of Studio Edmark, Oxford. The maps were prepared specially for this volume by Terry Bicknell.

Finally, I must thank my daughter Natalie, for her help in transcribing material with me at Windsor, and my two sons, David and Joshua, for their continued forbearance of an often desk-bound parent.

MARTIN GILBERT
Merton College, Oxford
20 July 1984

This volume recounts the story of the reawakening of Jerusalem between 1838 and 1898: sixty years during which the city was transformed from little more than a crumbling ruin into a bustling metropolis. In a series of vignettes, drawn decade by decade from the descriptions of residents and visitors, it is my hope to provide not only the facts but also the atmosphere of those sixty years.

During the period covered by this volume, Jerusalem was a remote provincial city of the Ottoman Empire, ruled from Constantinople. A succession of Turkish governors maintained law and order by means of a small military force, while Muslims, Christians and Jews pursued their different, and at times conflicting, courses in the city.

For Christians, Jerusalem had long been a centre of pilgrimage. Each Christmas and Easter, tens of thousands visited the Holy Sites, and followed the Stations of the Cross along the Via Dolorosa. For Muslims it was the plateau of the Haram al-Sharif, or 'Noble Sanctuary', dominated by the Dome of the Rock, which was the centre of their devotion. The Dome, also known as the Mosque of Omar, marked for Muslims the spot from which Mohammed had ascended to heaven. For Jews, that same plateau, once the site of the Temple with its Holy of Holies, served, through the stone grandeur of its one surviving Western or 'Wailing' Wall, as a focal point of prayer and messianic longing. It was on the same rock beneath the Dome, according to both Jewish and Muslim tradition, that Abraham prepared to sacrifice his son.

In 1838 Jerusalem had fewer than 16,000 inhabitants. Of these, 5,000 were Muslim Arabs, 3,000 were Christian Arabs and 6,000 were Jews. Also living in the city were about 100 European missionaries and traders, and 800 Turkish soldiers. By 1860 Jewish immigration, mostly from Tsarist Russia, had turned

Three elderly Jerusalem Jews, a photograph taken by Bonfils in the late 1870s.

the Jews into the largest single group in the city. A decade later, pressure of population led to the creation of houses and suburbs on many of the hills outside the city's sixteenth-century walls. By 1896 the population had risen to 45,300, of whom 28,000 were Jews, 8,700 Christian Arabs, and 8,600 Muslim Arabs.

Following the Crimean War, the European powers had insisted upon a physical presence and increased authority in the city, both through their consuls and through the non-Turkish citizens to whom they could offer the protection of foreign citizenship. European missionary activity, led by Anglican missionaries from Britain and Protestant missionaries from Prussia, likewise brought a substantial influx of Europeans and European activity, focussed upon the conversion of both Jews and Muslims. In the person of James Finn, the British Consul from 1846 to 1863, consular and missionary zeal were combined.

Like moths to a fiercely burning candle, pilgrims, missionaries and visitors added their bustle to the narrow, zigzag alleyways of Jerusalem. No land seemed too distant to be caught by the lure of the beckoning flame. From the United States came two of the earliest archaeologists, Edward Robinson and Eli Smith, as well as the naval expedition which first charted the Dead Sea. Also from the United States, in the last decade of the century, came one of the most imaginative photographers, Alfred Underwood. From almost as far away, from the banks of the Volga and the vast expanses of Tsarist Russia, came tens of thousands of Christian pilgrims, determined to see the Tomb of Jesus, the Tomb of the Virgin, the Mount of Olives, the Garden of Gethsemane, and the site of the Ascension. Also from Russia came thousands of Russian Jews, seeking an escape from the physical persecution of Tsardom, from the threat of twenty-five years' military service, and the violence of the anti-Jewish pogroms of the early 1880s, as well as the fulfilment of their spiritual longings.

Many of the wealthier European and American visitors to Jerusalem spent only a few days in the city. For them, throughout sixty years of turmoil and change, the city seemed dominated only by filth and superstition, by the spectacle of squabbling religious sects and diverse races, and above all by the curiosity or pathos of the Wailing Wall. Most visitors failed to appreciate the changes that were taking place towards the modernization of the city: the paving of roads, the building of hospitals, the establishment of European-style schools, the introduction of modern hotels and, with the building of the railway in 1892, the increase in commercial life and secular prosperity.

The Jerusalem of which such visitors wrote when they returned home, and

to which first the printmakers and then the photographers directed their attention, was in many ways a different Jerusalem from that of the earthly city,
with its community tensions, its religious conflicts, its dedicated reformers and
its growing commercial acumen. For them it was a Jerusalem of holy sites
made famous to generations of school children and adults in their synagogues,
churches and mosques situated hundreds, and even thousands of miles away.

From San Francisco to Vladivostok, from Edinburgh to Cape Town, Jerusalem was known to millions of people who might never think of visiting it.
Some of Jerusalem's scenes and buildings were as familiar to them as the scenes
and buildings of their own cities, sometimes even more familiar.

To a Muslim, whether in Casablanca or in Calcutta, the bold silhouette of
the Dome of the Rock was one of the clearest images of his faith, even though
it was to Mecca that he turned in prayer or went in pilgrimage.

For a Christian, the Church of the Holy Sepulchre, built as it was over the
site both of the crucifixion and of the burial of Jesus, was one of the most
frequent religious images before his eyes, as were the familiar façade of the
Virgin's Tomb and the gentle slopes of the Mount of Olives.

For a Jew, no more poignant image existed than the Western, or Wailing,
Wall, the last relic, according to Jewish legend, of the Great Temple structure
destroyed first by the Assyrians and then by the Romans. There were other
images too, which by the end of the nineteenth century had come to symbolize
Jerusalem for the Jews: among them the lone conical splendour of Absalom's
Tomb, and the view of the former Temple platform as seen from the higher
crest of the Mount of Olives.

These scenes and buildings, recurring in the accounts of all visitors, and
appearing in every artist's print, engraving and photographic study, helped to
fix in the mind and eye of those who would never visit Jerusalem its unique
character as a focal point of the pious aspirations of three religions. Yet these
aspirations bore little relation to the changing pattern of life in the city, except
perhaps for those Jews who, abandoning the concept of Zion as a purely
spiritual idea, began in increasing numbers from the 1880s to think in terms of
a practical return to an earthly Zion: one whose centre would be found inside
and beyond the walls of this provincial Ottoman city.

Among the European visitors to Jerusalem whose impressions are recounted
in this volume were a father and son who visited the city with a twenty-year
interval between them. The father was Albert Edward, Prince of Wales, later
King Edward VII, who came to Jerusalem in 1862. Twenty years later his son,

The Ecce Homo arch and the Via Dolorosa in the 1870s.

The same view twenty years later, showing the Sisters of Zion Convent.

Prince George, retraced his father's footsteps in and around the city. Prince George, the grandfather of the present Queen, was to reign from 1910 to 1935, as King George V. The journals which father and son both kept during their visits to Jerusalem show how much was seen, and how much could be felt, in the few 'Jerusalem' days available during a wider tour of the lands of the Bible. Prince Albert Edward travelled with the photographer Francis Bedford; Prince George, visiting in 1882, also brought back with him a photographic record of his visit, consisting, as it did for most visitors of that decade, of photographic prints prepared by the French photographers, Félix and Adrien Bonfils; prints that were offered for sale to all travellers as a permanent memento of their visits.

In 1865, three months after the visit of the Prince of Wales to Jerusalem, a group of distinguished British scholars, churchmen and public figures gathered in London to establish the Palestine Exploration Fund. This body was to eschew any religious or proselytizing activity, and to sponsor scientific research and exploration into the sites and history of Jerusalem. More than any other single institution, the Palestine Exploration Fund, through its emissaries and publications, discovered and made known the ancient and biblical realities that lay beneath the dust and rubble.

With the substantial increase in European and American visitors to Jerusalem after the Crimean War, two of the most popular guidebook publishers, Karl Baedeker and Thomas Cook, included Jerusalem in their growing selection of travel guides. Both of them concentrated on those places of religious, and in particular Christian religious, interest. As for 'modern' Jerusalem, both guidebooks found little of praise on which to comment, noting again and again 'a somewhat dirty street', 'hideously repulsive lepers', the 'modern crust of rubbish and rottenness', and ruins which typified 'the degraded aspect of the city'.

But however caustic might be the comments of guidebooks on Jerusalem's ugliness, stench and dust, the city remained a place to visit, whether by European princes or by Russian peasants. There was little contact, however, between the visitor and the citizen. Even European Jews who came for brief visits rarely saw much of their fellow Jews of Jerusalem, beyond a brief glimpse of the poorest of the Jewish quarters and a short visit to the Wailing Wall, a visit which sometimes left them with a feeling of disgust, rather than of spiritual uplift. Many of the Jews from western Europe were unfamiliar, not only with the styles and costumes of Russian Jewry, but, even more so, with the manners and customs of the Sephardi Jews, some of whom came from Iraq, Greece and Asia Minor, others from Morocco. There were also Jews from such remote regions as the Central Asian khanate of Bukhara, the mountains of Georgia, and the wildernesses of the Yemen.

The growing Jewish population was also largely an impoverished one, dependent for its survival upon the charity of European Jews. A series of emissaries, often distinguished rabbis, was sent from Jerusalem to seek financial aid. Several European Jews responded by personal visits and substantial contributions; chief among these benefactors was a British Jew, Sir Moses Montefiore, each of whose visits to Jerusalem led to an upsurge of hope among the needy. Even with the growth and modernization of Jerusalem by the end of the nineteenth century, the charity system still predominated, despite growing demands among a new generation of Jerusalem-born, yet at the same time westernized, Jews, for an end to the dependence upon their European brethren.

The visit of the German Kaiser to Jerusalem in 1898 marked a climax of European involvement, the city putting on a great show to entertain him, and the German community in Jerusalem redoubling its building efforts in the city. That same year saw the arrival in Jerusalem of Dr Theodor Herzl, the Zionist leader, whose ideal was a Jewish state in Palestine centred upon Jerusalem, and who advocated the preservation of the Old City as a spiritual centre for all three religions, with the creation around it of a modern Jerusalem which would serve as a focal point for the world-wide aspiration of the Jews for a national centre, and a national home.

In their meeting in Jerusalem, the Kaiser and Herzl had discussed the need for water if Palestine were to become a modern country. Sixty years earlier it had been the discovery of one of the main biblical water sources of the city that had enabled the two American archaeologists, Edward Robinson and Eli Smith, to locate some of the earliest sites of the biblical past.

Until 1854 Jerusalem had been known to those who could not visit it through prints, paintings and engravings. But following the first photographs of the city, taken that year by Auguste Salzmann, its buildings and human scenes quickly became familiar in distant lands. Photographic studios sold sets of pictures to visitors, and the growth of the city was diligently recorded by a succession of photographers, among them, in 1857, James Robertson, who had earlier been the chief engraver to the Imperial Mint in Constantinople; from 1877 the French photographers Félix and Adrien Bonfils; the Italian, L. Fiorillo, from 1886; and the American photographic studio of Underwood and Underwood, whose first set of stereoscopic views of Jerusalem was issued in 1898, the year of the Kaiser's visit.

Despite the transformation of Jerusalem between 1838 and 1898 from a dismal backwater to a modern city, much that was remote, dirty and disagreeable remained; while in the city's success in attracting Jews, Christians and Muslims in ever growing numbers, lay the seeds of future conflict. This conflict was glimpsed twice in the 1880s, and again in 1898, when, as a result of Muslim Arab pressure, the Turkish authorities first suspended, and then imposed strict laws against, Jewish immigration. These laws were soon rescinded. But the pressures that had led to them, and the bitterness which they caused, were to cloud the city's evolution in the years to come.

CHAPTER I

1838–40: Wretched times

In the year that Queen Victoria ascended to the British throne, an American theologian was offered the chair of Biblical Literature at the Union Theological Seminary in New York. He accepted this professorship, on condition that he could first travel to the Holy Land, something he had wanted to do since childhood. His condition was accepted, and in 1838 Edward Robinson left the United States for Palestine. He was 42 years old, determined to survey at first hand the biblical scenes of his academic study, and of his Christian faith.

The Jerusalem which Robinson reached in April 1838 was a city which had for several centuries been submerged in grime and dust. Within its walls, built by the Ottoman Turkish rulers three hundred years earlier, lay a maze of narrow, dirty streets and broken stones. The walls of 1535 were massive, pierced by only a few narrow gates, and holding within their compass less than 16,000 people. Of these 16,000, about 6,000 were Jews, many of them recent immigrants from Russia, 5,000 were Muslim Arabs and 3,000 were Christian Arabs. There were also in the city 100 Europeans and westerners: mostly missionaries and traders.

Guarding these Jews, Arabs and Europeans were 800 Turkish soldiers, representatives of the Ottoman Empire, taking their orders from Constantinople. Each night, at sunset, the gates of the city were closed, and its inhabitants locked in. No one lived outside the walls. The deep valleys at the city's edge, and the stony hills beyond, were the haunt of wild animals, and robbers.

It was during the afternoon of Saturday, 14 April 1838, that Robinson entered Jerusalem for the first time, by camel, through the Jaffa Gate, to be greeted by eight American Protestants, all missionaries, who had gathered that Easter from their various near-eastern missions, including those of Cyprus,

Greek Orthodox monks outside the entrance to the Church of the Holy Sepulchre (1880s).

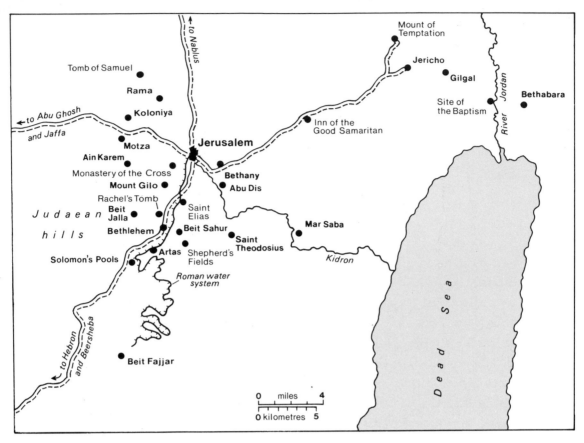

The Jerusalem region, showing places mentioned in the text.

Beirut and Constantinople. They were the guests of the two resident American missionaries in Jerusalem, the Rev. Whiting and the Rev. Lanneau. All eight had been sent to the near east by the American Board of Commissioners for Foreign missions, based in Boston. Four of them had been Robinson's pupils. That night, Robinson noted in his diary that the streets of Jerusalem could 'bear comparison' with those of any other oriental city, 'although if one seeks it here, or elsewhere in the east, for the general cleanliness and thrift which characterize many cities of Europe and America, he will of course seek in vain'.

On reaching Jerusalem, Robinson, like all visitors, took a dragoman – or guide. Robinson's guide in Jerusalem was a Russian Jew who had come to Palestine in 1815, Rabbi David Beth-Hillel. Himself a traveller, Beth-Hillel had set off from Jerusalem in 1824, visiting, at a leisurely pace, Arabia, Kurdistan and Persia before reaching India seven years later. There, in Madras, he published in 1832 an account of his journey. Five years later Beth-Hillel returned to Palestine, in time to serve Robinson as guide and interpreter in his pioneering task.

The Mount of Olives, Absalom's Tomb and the Kidron valley, looking south from Jerusalem.

The two American missionaries in Jerusalem by whom Robinson had been greeted on his first day in the city were soon forced to leave it, Whiting because of his wife's 'declining health', Lanneau because of 'a severe affliction of the eyes'. Within a year, the Mission itself was withdrawn, and Lanneau, who had gone to Beirut for medical treatment, returned to the United States. Robinson remained. He was assisted in his exploration in Jerusalem by a former pupil, Eli Smith, who had earlier served as an American missionary in Malta and Beirut. Smith, a resident of Jerusalem, was a distinguished orientalist, spoke Arabic, and, like Robinson, was eager to identify as many biblical sites as possible. The two men devised a method whereby they found out from local Arabs the current Arabic names for towns, villages, ruins and monuments, and then tried to work out from the sound and meaning of these names their biblical equivalent.

For four months, from March to June 1838, Robinson and Smith travelled through the lands of the Bible. Together they discovered five of the six ruined cities of the Negev desert, identified the Dead Sea fortress of Masada, and, in Jerusalem, found several remains of the ancient walls. The two men realized the significance of their work, commenting that 'for the lapse of more than fifteen centuries Jerusalem has been the abode not only of mistaken piety, but also of credulous superstition, not unmingled with pious fraud'.

It was while they were in Jerusalem that Robinson and Smith decided to walk through an ancient tunnel which entered the rock of the Hill of Ophel at the Gihon spring in the Kidron valley. This tunnel passed under the hill, to emerge from the rock at the Siloam pool. It was at the Gihon spring, according to legend, that the Virgin Mary once drew water; where, according to another tradition, she washed her Son's swaddling clothes: hence its name among Christian pilgrims, the Virgin's Fount.

Robinson and Smith first tried to penetrate the tunnel from the lower, Siloam end, where the rock ceiling was highest. But after walking through it for 800 feet, lighting their way by candles, they found that the ceiling became so low 'that we could advance no further without crawling on all fours and bringing our bodies close to the water. As we were not prepared for this', Robinson later wrote, 'we thought it better to retreat, and to try again another day from the other end.'

To show how far they had reached, the two Americans used smoke from their candles to mark their initials on the rock, together with the figure 800 to indicate the distance in feet from the Siloam pool entrance. Three days later they entered the tunnel again, this time from the Gihon spring. 'Having clothed (or rather unclothed) ourselves simply in a pair of wide Arab drawers', Robinson wrote, 'we entered and crawled on, hoping soon to arrive at the point which he had reached from the other fountain.' Most of the way they proceeded on their hands and knees. But in several places 'we could only get forward by lying at full length and dragging ourselves along on our elbows'.

The two men finally reached their earlier mark, and then emerged into the light of Siloam. The total distance they measured as 1,750 feet. Here, then, was one of the sites of the biblical city, a tunnel under the City of David: a city and a tunnel that lay outside the Turkish walls of 1535, amid dust and ruins.

Robinson and Smith noticed that, as well as a small continuous flow of water, the Gihon spring sent out periodic gushes which lasted for half an hour or more, and emerged at intervals of between four and ten hours. The flow and the gushes between them produced between 7,000 and 40,000 cubic feet of water each day. By this means, the biblical citizens were able to survive in an

The pool of Siloam (*top*) and the Gihon spring or Virgin's Fount (*above*), in the late 1870s (Bonfils).

otherwise arid landscape. As the ancient Greek geographer Strabo had commented: 'Jerusalem is a rocky well-enclosed fortress, well-watered within, wholly dry without.' The water was the water of Gihon. The most ancient part of the tunnel which Edward Robinson and Eli Smith walked through in 1838 was the means whereby this water had been brought into the city in time of siege; drawn up through a shaft of which Robinson and Smith knew nothing.

It was to the Bible that the explorers of 1838 now turned to identify the Gihon spring. 'And I went out by night by the gate of the valley,' declared Nehemia, 'even before the dragon well.' Was the Gihon spring the 'dragon well'? In talking to the Arabs who lived near the spring Robinson and Smith were told of a local legend that beneath the cave from which the water came lived a dragon. When the dragon was awake, he stopped the water. When the dragon slept, the water flowed.

Many Old Testament stories were attached to the Gihon spring. It was through its capture that David had conquered the Hill of Ophel from the Jebusites and secured it for the Jewish capital. It was to Gihon that Solomon had been taken on King David's mule, accompanied by Nathan the prophet, and there anointed with oil by Zadok the Priest. 'And they blew the trumpet,' the Bible recounts; 'and all the people said, God save King Solomon. And all the people came up after him, and the people piped with pipes, and rejoiced with great joy, so that the earth rent with the sound of them.'

This triumphant scene took place at the Gihon spring in about 961 BC. Nearly 250 years later, in 711 BC, one of the Jewish kings of Judah, Hezekiah, decided, in alliance with the rulers of Egypt, Sidon and Ashkelon, to challenge the overlordship of Assyria. For a short while his kingdom maintained a precarious independence. But the Assyrian king, Sennacherib, soon moved against the rebellious Jewish kingdom. As Lord Byron was to describe it in 1815, 'the Assyrian came down like a wolf on the fold'.

During his attack, Sennacherib destroyed forty-six fortified cities and towns, as well as many smaller villages. Then Jerusalem was besieged, and, according to the biblical account, Sennacherib addressed its citizens with the words: 'Does not Hezekiah persuade you to give yourselves to die by famine and by thirst.'

Not by thirst, however, was Jerusalem to be destroyed. Long before Sennacherib's force had reached the city walls, Hezekiah had repaired the Jebusite tunnel, and driven it forward under the Hill of Ophel to the western slope at Siloam. Water was now available both in the city itself, through the Jebusite shaft, and on the sheltered slope. 'This same Hezekiah', the Bible tells us, 'also stopped the upper watercourses of Gihon, and brought it straight down to the west side of the City of David.' Nor is this the sole biblical reference. Hezekiah's 'acts' are elsewhere described, 'how he made a pool, and a conduit, and brought water into the city'.

The 1,750 feet which Robinson and Smith had traversed constituted the complete length of Hezekiah's tunnel, including the section at the Gihon end which had been built by the Jebusites more than 300 years earlier. The two Americans had failed to see the Jebusite shaft. But a miracle of ancient engineering was now known and recorded; a site for European visitors to marvel at, provoking as it did such direct thoughts of biblical events.

As in so many of the city's sites, stories from the Old and New Testaments combined in a single location. But Jerusalem was not merely a monument. Despite its dilapidated condition, it was still a living city, after more than 3,000 years of continuous habitation. Its glories seemed to be, however, in the past. The year 1838, in which Robinson arrived from the United States, marked a low point in the city's history. For Jerusalem, the site of the ancient Temple of the Jews, of David's kingdom, of the crucifixion of Jesus, of early Christian conversion, of Mohammed's ascent to heaven, and of much past prosperity, had fallen into a despondent, almost rural state. Even Robinson and Smith were struck by this aspect, noting, of the north-east corner of the Muslim quarter, that 'the whole slope within the city walls is occupied by gardens, fields, and olive yards, with comparatively few houses or ruined dwellings; the whole bearing more the aspect of a village in the country than of a quarter in a city'. As for the city as a whole, Robinson and Smith concluded: 'The glory of Jerusalem has indeed departed. From her ancient high estate, as the splendid metropolis of the Jewish commonwealth and of the whole Christian world, the beloved of nature and "the joy of the whole earth", she has sunk into the neglected capital of a petty Turkish province; and where of old many hundreds of thousands thronged her streets and temple, we now find a population of scarcely as many single thousands dwelling sparsely within her walls.'

Among those who visited Jerusalem in 1838 was a Jew from Poland, Dr Louis Loewe. When first seen from afar, he wrote, the city was impressive: the Muslim houses of prayer give it 'much beauty'. But as one drew nearer to the city its 'desolation increased, and wherever I looked I saw only caves and ruined stone, where in antiquity, perhaps, glorious palaces had stood – the markets I passed on my way to the Street of the Jews were narrow and horrible as in the cities of Egypt'.

The 'Street of the Jews' towards which Dr Loewe was walking lay in the centre of the Jewish quarter of the city, and was the hub of activity for the 6,000 Jews for whom the quarter offered not only homes and work but security. Each year, Jews arrived to swell the numbers, and the crush: theirs was by far the fastest growing community, even though it was divided into several groups, often hostile to each other, especially across the divide between the Ashkenazi, or 'German', Jews from eastern Europe and Russia, and the Sephardi, or 'Spanish', Jews from the Ottoman Empire and North Africa.

Among the newly arrived Ashkenazi Jews in 1838 was one of the most learned Russian Jews of the time, Joseph Sundel, who had been sent by the Jews of Vilna to be the rabbi of the 'Vilna' Jews in Jerusalem. Sundel had accepted the appointment; but being a man of profound modesty, he refused to support his religious work from communal funds, and soon after his arrival he opened a vinegar factory in the city, in order to be self-supporting.

Three of Rabbi Sundel's daughters married Russian Jews who decided to live in Jerusalem: Uri Shabbetai, who was to become a member of the Jerusalem religious court or Beth Din; Nathan Nata Natkin, one of those Jerusalem Jews who served the community by travelling throughout Europe in search of charitable donations; and Samuel Salant, who was to be Ashkenazi Chief Rabbi of the city from 1878 to 1909.

Within the city walls, the late 1830s had been a time of renewed activity. In 1836, the Ashkenazi Jews bought, from an Arab, the ruins of the eighteenth-century Hurva synagogue, and were given permission to build a new synagogue on the ruins. They were helped in their task of purchasing the site by the Sephardi Chief Rabbi of Jerusalem, Jonah Navon, a member of one of the oldest Jewish families in the city; a family which had come from Turkish Anatolia more than a century before.

In 1837 several hundred Jews reached Jerusalem from the Galilee. They came as refugees, having fled the mountain city of Safed after an earthquake had destroyed the Jewish quarter there, and local Muslims had attacked them. These Jews of Safed, many of whom had come from Russia after the Napoleonic wars, joined a group who had come to Jerusalem from Safed twenty-five years earlier, after the plague of 1812. Their chosen abode was in the north-east section of the city, adjacent to the Muslim quarter. Other Jews remained in Safed, as in several towns in the Galilee, and on the coast. But increasingly, it was to Jerusalem that they looked for refuge, when times were bad.

'Jerusalem Jews at the Wailing Place', 1896 (Underwood and Underwood).

The re-establishment of Ottoman rule, after the brief conquest by Ibrahim Pasha from Egypt in 1836, brought a greater stress on law and order. The most formidable building to be built in Jerusalem in the late 1830s was a prison, the Kishle, established in 1838 just inside the Jaffa Gate. Its low, austere structure has survived to this day, its walls still redolent of a stern master. Opposite the Kishle prison, across the small square, was established in 1839 the first British Consulate in the city. Nearby was the house of a Protestant missionary, John Nicolayson, a Dane by birth who had been living in Jerusalem since 1823.

For the Greek Orthodox Church in Jerusalem, 2 October 1838 saw the election of Hierothos, Archbishop of Tabor, as Patriarch. The election took place while Hierothos himself was in Russia, collecting alms from the poor but devout Russian peasantry and the wealthier patrons of orthodoxy. That same

The outer wall of the Kishle prison, a photograph taken in 1984.

month, a cholera epidemic, beginning among the Jews and then spreading to the Muslims, forced the regular influx of Christian pilgrims from Russia to remain for nearly two months at the port of Jaffa.

When the pilgrims did arrive, it was to a scene of rejoicing, for, on 22 December 1838, the Greek Orthodox community was able to redeem, by a substantial payment in gold, the Patriarch's mitre, crozier and several crosses. These, the Greek Orthodox monk Neophytos of Cyprus noted, 'had been given to a Jew, named Angel, as a surety'. Neophytos added that on December 26 the sacred objects were returned to the Greek Orthodox treasury 'to the great glory of Jesus Christ, born and risen'.

In the late eighteenth and early nineteenth century, individual Jews could be found throughout Europe, urging those Jewish communities through which they passed, for charity. Many of these wandering Jews came from Jerusalem, which, they would recall, had once been the centre of a powerful Jewish kingdom, and which remained, after nearly two thousand years of dispersal, the centre of Jewish spiritual longing.

These travelling Jerusalemites pleaded the cause of their fellow-Jews in the Holy City. It was the cause of poverty, and the cause of kinship. They called themselves 'emissaries', beggars in reality, but in a holy cause, and with persuasive tongue. When successful, they received sums of money sufficient for the sustenance of as many as a thousand needy individuals. Returning to Jerusalem, these itinerant Jerusalemites distributed this charity – known in the city as Halukah – not only to the local poor, but also to Jews who had come to Jerusalem from the northern towns of Safed and Tiberias in order to benefit from Europe's generosity.

This process of charity was observed by an English diplomat, William Tanner Young. In August 1838, while in London, Young had explained to the Foreign Secretary, Lord Palmerston, that those Jews from the northern districts who travelled to Jerusalem both for charity and for worship were 'chiefly European Jews, possessing to a certain extent the germs of civilization'. Young suggested to Palmerston that it might be possible 'by degrees' to give these Jews the courage 'to venture forth from their towns, where they now huddle together for mutual safety – but in idleness and misery – to cultivate a little of that most excellent land, with which they are everywhere surrounded'.

Young's interest was enhanced by his imminent appointment as Vice-Consul at Jerusalem. He was to be the first British 'representative' in Jerusalem since the Crusades, and the only diplomatic representatives in the city of any foreign power. On 31 January 1839 Young received his instructions: it would be a part of his duty at Jerusalem, he was told, 'to afford Protection to the Jews generally'.

The new Vice-Consul arrived in Palestine in February 1839, disembarked at the port of Jaffa, and proceeded at once along the rough unmetalled road that led across the dusty coastal plain to the Bab el-Wad, the narrow pass which marked the only easy entrance to the Judaean hills. From the Bab el-Wad, Young continued up the steep, winding gorge, and across the precipitous hills to the walled city more than two thousand feet above sea level.

Young's first discovery in Jerusalem, as he reported to Palmerston on 14

March 1839, was that there was no Christian cemetery in the city, 'though this privilege', he pointed out, 'is enjoyed by other nations including the Hebrew'. Young thereupon sought, and eventually obtained, Turkish permission for a Christian cemetery just outside the walls, near the summit of Mount Zion. For each such change, not only did the approval of the city's Turkish Governor – the Pasha – have to be sought, but the approval also of the Ottoman authorities in Constantinople: even, at times, of the Sultan himself, ruler of a vast, ramshackle empire, of which Jerusalem, once a flourishing city, was now a mere provincial appendage, far removed from the power, the wealth and the corruption of the Sultan's court.

On 29 March 1839, only two weeks after William Young's first report to Palmerston, another of Queen Victoria's subjects, the painter David Roberts, entered Jerusalem on a sketching journey through Egypt and Palestine. The views of the Holy City which he drew in the course of only a few days were to become as popular for the early-Victorians as picture postcards were to become for their grandchildren. In his sketches of Jerusalem, Roberts portrayed idyllic, soft, pastoral scenes, enlivened by the merest touch of the exotic Orient.

After less than a week in the city, but with a bulging portfolio of sketches, Roberts left Jerusalem in the company of 4,000 Greek and Russian pilgrims – part of the annual influx of Orthodox believers – for Jericho and the Jordan. Then he travelled northwards to the Sea of Galilee and the mountains of Lebanon. In Jerusalem, meanwhile, Vice-Consul Young was carrying out Palmerston's instruction to report on the 'present situation' of the Jewish population in Palestine. Young's first report, dated 25 May 1839, was detailed and eloquent. There were, he said, at least 5,500 Jews in Jerusalem, a further 4,160 elsewhere in Palestine, the second and third largest Jewish communities being the 1,500 Jews of Safed and the 750 Jews of Hebron. Tiberias had 600, Sidon 250, Haifa and Nablus 150 each.

The number of Jews in Jerusalem, Young noted, was on the increase, many families living outside the Jewish quarter. Most of them were 'very poor', and dependent upon charity from Europe. Five hundred of Jerusalem's Jews were 'acknowledged paupers'. Five hundred more received charitable relief 'but are not known openly as paupers'. Young added: 'the want of union among themselves, and their internal caballing – the natural fruits of their poverty – tend much to increase their wretchedness'.

Young reported that the Turkish Governor of Jerusalem had shown 'much more consideration for the Jews' than had his people; and that several Jews

Above: Russian pilgrims in Jerusalem. *Below left:* western European travellers at the Inn of the Good Samaritan, on the road from Jerusalem to Jericho. *Below right:* the site of the baptism of Jesus, pilgrims and priest at the bank of the river Jordan. The woman with the bottle and the woman with the kettle are collecting some of the holy water.

had told him that 'they enjoy more peace and tranquillity under this Government than they ever enjoyed here before'. His report continued, however: 'Still, the Jew in Jerusalem is not estimated in value, much above a dog – and scarcely a day passes that I do not hear of some act of tyranny and oppression against a Jew – chiefly by the soldiers, who enter their houses and borrow whatever they require without asking any permission – sometimes they return the article, but more frequently not. In two instances, I have succeeded in obtaining justice for Jews against Turks – But it is quite a new thing in the eyes of these people to claim justice for a Jew, and I have good reason to think that my endeavours to protect the Jews, have been – and may be for some little time to come – detrimental to my influence with other classes – Christians as well as Turks. If a Jew, My Lord, were to attempt to pass the door of the Church of the Holy Sepulchre, it would in all probability cost him his life – this is not very Christian like, considering Himself was a Jew – And were a Jew here, to fly for safety, he would seek it sooner in a Mussulman's house than in that of a Christian.'

After any report of plague in Jerusalem, Young told Palmerston, Turkish employees in the Quarantine Service, as well as Muslim Arab doctors, 'rob and oppress them to the last degree'. 'What the Jew has to endure at all hands', Young reflected, 'is not to be told,' and he went on to explain how 'Like the miserable dog without an owner he is kicked by one because he crosses his path, and cuffed by another because he cries out – to seek redress he is afraid, lest it bring worse upon him; he thinks it better to endure than to live in the expectation of his complaint being revenged upon him. Brought up from infancy to look upon his civil disabilities everywhere as a mark of degradation, his heart becomes the cradle of fear and suspicion – he finds he is trusted by none – and therefore he lives himself without confidence in any.'

Young saw another side of the Jewish nature. Jews, he told Palmerston, 'are not wanting in any of the best feelings of our nature'. His report continued: 'Gratitude is eminent among the good qualities of their hearts, and if the Protection could everywhere be accorded to the Jews – which Your Lordship has commanded me to afford them here, a short time would, I am persuaded, give sufficient evidence that the Jew is worthier of a higher consideration than it is now his lot generally to find.'

In 1839 a veritable Babel of languages could be heard in the narrow streets of Jerusalem. The Christian and Muslim Arabs spoke Arabic. Their leaders, as well as the Turkish authorities, spoke Turkish. The few hundred Armenians in the city spoke Armenian. Among the westerners, French was the principal language of communication. As for the Jews, as Vice-Consul Young noted, their chief languages were Spanish and Arabic. But contracts among them, 'and their writing generally', were done in Hebrew. The Jews from Russia spoke Yiddish, the mediaeval German dialect of their ancestors.

A diligent and observant diplomat, Young continued to send regular reports to the Foreign Office in London, and to the British Consul-General in Egypt. 'The prejudice of the Christian against the Jew in Jerusalem', he wrote on 19 April 1839, 'amounts to a fanaticism that', if he were even to appoint a Christian interpreter, would 'quite defeat the object of gaining them the protection they require.' And on 25 May 1839 he described the fate of a 28-year-old Jew from Salonica who had been the watchman at a house which had been robbed. The young man had only just reached Jerusalem, and had, a week earlier, applied for a job with Young himself. He was taken before the Governor, Young wrote, 'where he still declared his innocence. He was then burned with a hot iron over his face, and in various parts of the body – and beaten on the lower parts of his body to that extent that the flesh hung in pieces from him. The following day the poor creature died.'

Such a punishment, Young commented, was 'most revolting to human nature'. He had therefore refused to meet with the Governor, as such proceedings 'were quite contrary to the English sense and humanity'; and this sign of British disapproval 'was not', Young reported to Palmerston, 'without its influence in the city – especially in favour of the Jews'.

Young's courageous act made clear to the Jews that, in Queen Victoria's Britain, they had a friend. But it was a Jew from Britain who brought them their principal cause for hope in 1839. Sir Moses Montefiore, a former Sheriff of the City of London, visited Palestine in June 1839, spending several days in Jerusalem. It was his second visit to the city, his first having been in 1827. Not only did Montefiore dispense what Young called 'considerable sums of money in charity'. He also promised, and here his visit made a greater impact than a mere philanthropic gesture could have done, that on his return to England he would 'do something towards ameliorating the condition of the Jews in Palestine'.

Montefiore did not forget his promise. He was to return to Jerusalem five times, with myriad benefits to his fellow Jews. Born in 1784, related by marriage to the Rothschilds, a striking physical presence – he was 6 feet 3 inches tall – he had been knighted by Queen Victoria in 1837, on her first visit to the

Sir Moses and Lady Montefiore enter Jerusalem in June 1839, a contemporary drawing.

City of London. From 1838 to 1874 he was president of the Board of Deputies of British Jews. His hundredth birthday, in 1885, was to be celebrated by Jews all over the world as a public holiday. He died in 1886, at the age of 101.

Sir Moses Montefiore left copious notes of his visits to Jerusalem, as did his wife Judith. Their notes for 7 June 1839 record 'a present of five sheep' from the Governor of the city and 'numerous presents' from representatives of the Ashkenazi and Sephardi congregations 'of choice wines, fruit, and cakes, besides articles of rich embroidery'. On the following day, a Saturday, Sir Moses and his wife went to the Mount of Olives to recite their prayers 'under the shade of an olive tree, directly opposite the spot where stood the Temple of Solomon'. Their 'happy moments' at prayer were, however, 'unfortunately disturbed by the wailing of the Mohammedan mourning women who followed no less than four funerals'. That same Saturday, Sir Moses discussed with

The Dome of the Rock and the Temple Mount (or Holy Sanctuary), from the Mount of Olives (Bonfils). The gate in the wall is the Golden Gate, closed since Crusader times.

Consul Young the employment of Jews in agriculture, Young expressing his 'approval', while Mrs Young gave Lady Montefiore 'some distressing accounts of the poverty of the people and pointed out the necessity of at once finding them some means of earning a livelihood'.

Montefiore spent a week in Jerusalem, camping on the Mount of Olives. On June 9 more than three hundred visitors had left the city to see him. On June 10 he had ridden with his wife around the walls of the city, visited all the 'important tombs and monuments' in the Kidron valley and once more received 'hundreds of visitors' among whom where four clergymen from Scotland who were making a tour in the Holy Land 'to enquire into the state of the Jews there' and intended going through Poland for the same purpose.

On June 11, Montefiore and his wife had visited the Tomb of David on

Mount Zion, and the Tomb of the Kings to the north of the city, spending the night once more on the Mount of Olives in preparation for entering the city on the morning of June 12. A number of Jews spent the night on the Mount of Olives near them in order to join their procession in the morning.

Montefiore entered Jerusalem on the morning of June 12 in procession with the Governor and riding a white Arabian horse which the Governor had sent him the day before. The city's benefactor then visited both the Sephardi and Ashkenazi synagogues, in which prayers were offered up 'for the friends of Zion', and then proceeded to the Wailing Wall for further prayers, returning at 4 o'clock to the Mount of Olives after a visit to the British Consul. June 13 was taken up with receiving 'persons who came with petitions', distributing the money he had brought with him from England, promising to send further money either from Beirut or Alexandria, and preparing for their departure on the morning of June 14 for Rachel's Tomb, Hebron and Jaffa.

While Montefiore was in Jerusalem in June 1839, a poem in his honour was written by a 17-year-old orphan, Jacob Saphir. This young man's parents, disciples of the already legendary Gaon of Vilna, had brought him to Palestine from Russia in 1832, when he was 9 years old. A year after they had arrived, in Safed, his father had died. Then, just as the traditional Jewish year of mourning was about to end, his mother also died. In 1836 Jacob Saphir had fled to Jerusalem from Safed, as a result of one of the periodic outbreaks of Muslim violence against Jews. In Jerusalem his abilities were quickly recognized among the Ashkenazi Jews: he was already fluent in both spoken and literary Arabic, had studied the Koran, possessed a rhetorical mastery of Hebrew, and was quickly appointed to be the scribe of the 'Perushim', or Russian, Jews. A decade later, while a teacher in the Etz Hayyim 'Tree of Life' religious school, Saphir was to serve as an overseas emissary for the 'Perushim', in search of charitable funds.

With so many Jews living in Jerusalem, the work of Christian missionaries was much encouraged by Protestant groups in western Europe. On 23 September 1839 Vice-Consul Young reported to Palmerston that the London Society for Promoting Christianity amongst the Jews had received permission to buy land. This marked a decisive step forward in Anglican and Protestant missionary work in the city. This permission had been granted specifically to John Nicolayson, the Danish-born Protestant who had been living and preaching in Jerusalem for sixteen years. Thus a dual British policy emerged towards the growing number of Jews in the city: official protection through the Consulate, and private conversion through the missionaries.

By contrast to the resident Jews, whose numbers were growing in the late 1830s with the arrival of new immigrants, from Safed, Algiers and Salonica, the Muslim and Christian Arab population was static. But each years tens of thousands of Christian pilgrims, chiefly, as David Roberts had seen, of Greek and Russian Orthodox persuasion, but also Protestants and Roman Catholics, reached the city for short visits: mostly at Easter.

At the centre of all Christian pilgrimage was the Via Dolorosa, or 'Street of Pain'. Each Easter, pilgrims from every country of Christian Europe joined with the Christians living in the city to walk in procession. Their path followed the sites which since the sixteenth century had been 'identified' as the route leading from the place of Jesus' imprisonment to Golgotha, the place of his crucifixion, encompassed by the Church of the Holy Sepulchre, its roof still blackened as a result of a serious fire in 1808.

The Via Dolorosa, a rough road set between ruined walls, poor Muslim dwellings, and bazaars crowded with foodstuffs, clothes, and the carcases of sheep being cut up for meat, was destined to be transformed within a few decades into a fine thoroughfare. The transformation took place only slowly, however, its first step marked in 1839 with the building by the Franciscans of a Chapel of the Flagellation, to commemorate the event, 'And they smote him on the head with a reed, and did spit upon him.'

The Easter pilgrims did not always behave according to western European concepts of Christian decorum. On 28 April 1840 Vice-Consul Young reported that the Russian pilgrims 'are carried by their religious fanaticism, beyond all bounds of order and decency'.

Jerusalem was also, but only just, a part of the European grand tour for tutors and pupils, provided they were wealthy. In 1839 the 25-year-old Albert Cohn, tutor to the children of Baron James de Rothschild, brought three of his pupils to Jerusalem. Later, Cohn, an Austrian-born Jew, was to be put in charge of the Rothschild family's benevolent work in Paris: his return to Jerusalem in the 1850s was to have important repercussions for Jerusalem Jewry.

That winter two Frenchmen visited Jerusalem: the painter Horace Vernet and his friend Frederic Goupil Fesquet, a photographer. Fesquet, a pioneer of the daguerrotype technique of photography, had been commissioned to visit the Holy Land by a French optician, N. P. Lerebours. The photographs which he took were the first ever taken in Jerusalem. They were turned into engravings, and published by Lerebours in Paris in 1840.

Among the Jews who had fled to Jerusalem after the Safed earthquake of 1837 was Israel Bak. Then aged 40, Bak had been born in the Ukrainian town of Berdichev. His name was that of a family of printers of Hebrew religious books since the early sixteenth century, first in Venice, then in Prague; but no link has been found between the young man from Berdichev and his famous namesakes. Bak, however, had already built up his own reputation as a printer in the Ukraine, printing more than thirty books before his press was closed down by the Tsarist authorities in 1821. For ten years he fought to open his printing press, but in vain. Then, in 1831, he had emigrated to Palestine.

An orthodox Jew, Bak had established a farm as well as a printing press on his arrival in Safed, and had begun to till his own soil. But both press and farm were destroyed: the press by the earthquake of 1837, the farm during the local unrest of 1838. Thus Bak moved to Jerusalem, where, in 1840, he established the first printing press in the Holy City. On this press he published the first Hebrew book to be printed in Jerusalem, a religious tract, by the Jerusalem-born scholar Hayyim Joseph David Azulai, who had died in Italy in 1806 after a lifetime as an emissary in Europe for the Jews of Jerusalem and Hebron.

Israel Bak remained in Jerusalem for the rest of his life, becoming a leader of the Jewish orthodox Hassidic community. His printing press flourished. By the time of his death thirty-five years later he had published more than 130 books, as well as innumerable religious tracts.

Also in 1840, in the Jewish quarter not far from Israel Bak's printing press, a Jewish religious school, the Etz Hayyim or 'Tree of Life', was established. The language of instruction was Yiddish. One of the first teachers at the school was Jacob Saphir, the young Russian-born Jew who had written the city's poem of welcome to Moses Montefiore in 1839.

Among the founders of the Tree of Life academy was Samuel Salant, the 25-year-old son-in-law of Rabbi Joseph Sundel, who had been sent to Jerusalem four years earlier as head of the community of Jews from Vilna. Samuel Salant had been born near Bialystok, and had studied in the famous Jewish religious academies of Vilna and Volozhin. On his way from Russia to Palestine, Salant had stopped for some while at Constantinople, where he met and befriended Sir Moses Montefiore.

As soon as Salant reached Jerusalem, Joseph Sundel vacated his rabbinical office in his son-in-law's favour. Salant was to serve the Ashkenazi Jews of Jerusalem for the next sixty-nine years, until his death, at the age of 93, in 1909. As rabbi of the 'Vilna' community, and later as Chief Rabbi of the

Above: Private houses on the edge of the Jewish quarter, 1876 (Sergeant J. MacDonald, Royal Engineers).
Below: The same houses, some years later, showing also the eastern edge of the Jewish quarter, and the poorer houses and ruins of the Muslim Arab Moghrabi quarter.

Ashkenazi Jews in the city, Salant was noted for his opposition to extreme orthodoxy, his search for the plain rather than the over-subtle meaning of religious doctrine, for his power of decision, and for decisions tending towards leniency and moderation.

Another of the Russian Jews who reached Jerusalem at this time was Moses Rivlin, from the small Ukrainian town of Shklov. Rivlin had been sent by the rabbis of Russia and Lithuania to be head of the Ashkenazi community in Jerusalem. It was a community which had grown considerably since the arrival of the first families from Vilna thirty-two years before, in 1809. Then they had numbered only twenty families: some seventy men, women and children. But now, as Rivlin arrived to be their communal chief, and Salant their most recent recruit as a rabbi, they were in their hundreds.

No single event was more to focus the mind of European Jewry on Jerusalem, and on the territorial future of Jewry, than the 'Damascus affair' of 1840. On 5 February 1840 a Christian monk, Friar Thomas from Italy, and his Muslim servant, Ibrahim Amara, disappeared from the streets of Damascus, and were never seen again. Suddenly, Christian and Muslim hostility towards the Jews joined forces. Seven Jews were accused of murdering Father Thomas and his servant, in order, so it was alleged, to use the two men's blood for Passover.

The seven Jews were held in prison in Damascus and tortured. Sixty-three Jewish children were then seized by order of the Governor-General of Damascus in order to force their mothers to reveal the 'hiding place of the blood of the two victims'.

The conscience of western Jewry was deeply stirred. Among those to protest was the Jerusalem printer Israel Bak who launched a massive petition. From England, Moses Montefiore, and from France the distinguished Jewish lawyer Adolphe Cremieux, were active in public protest. On 25 April 1840 the use of torture on those who had been seized was stopped. Four months later the surviving prisoners were released.

Among those who saw the Damascus affair as a turning point in the long epic of Jewish history was the 42-year-old Sarajevo-born sage, Judah Alkalai, the rabbi of the community of Semlin, on the Danube. Alkalai regarded the Damascus affair as the work of God, intended to shock all Jews – 'complacent dwellers in foreign lands' – into a greater awareness and concern for 'the remoteness of Jerusalem'.

Alkalai was to spend the remaining thirty-eight years of his life urging Jews to settle in Palestine, advocating large-scale acquisition of land, seeking international recognition for a Jewish 'Land of Israel', and arguing in favour of the establishment of a Jewish parliament of elders, a Jewish army, and the revival of spoken Hebrew as the language of everyday Jewish life in Palestine. In 1874, four years before his death, Alkalai himself returned to the city in which he had lived for a short while in the 1820s. In his published pamphlets, and in his articles in Hebrew newspapers, he argued that Jewish redemption would not come by miracles, but by the action of men themselves. It was this assertion of the element of free will and self-help which gave Alkalai's message its force, particularly for younger Jews.

It was not only Jews who understood the impact of the Damascus affair, and of a second blood libel accusation that same year in Rhodes, on Jewish aspirations, or who realized the appeal to persecuted Jewry of a territorial and spiritual centre. On 11 August 1840 Lord Palmerston, the British Foreign Secretary, wrote to the British Ambassador in Constantinople, seventeen days before the release of the surviving Jews in Damascus prison: 'there exists at present among the Jews dispersed over Europe a strong notion that the Time is approaching when their Nation is to return to Palestine; and consequently their wish to go thither has become more keen, and their thoughts have been bent more intently than before upon the means of realizing that wish. It is well known that the Jews of Europe possess greath wealth; and it is manifest that any country in which a considerable number of them might choose to settle, would derive great benefit from the Riches which they would bring into it.'

In September 1840 a young British architect, W.C. Hillier, reached Jerusalem with a commission to design the first Anglican church within the city walls. Hillier was 25 years old. On 9 August 1840, only a month after reaching Jerusalem, he died.

In the summer of 1840 an attempt was made on the lives of Queen Victoria and Prince Albert. As soon as news of the assassination attempt reached Jerusalem, eighteen British subjects in the city sent the Queen a humble address of loyalty. Dated 20 July 1840, it was signed by Vice-Consul Young and the Protestant missionary, John Nicolayson. Several other British missionaries also signed, as did the heads of several of the leading Jewish families. A second address to the Queen, written in Hebrew, was signed by the chief Ashkenazi and Sephardi rabbis. 'Her Majesty', Palmerston replied, 'has graciously received these tokens of loyalty of Her Majesty's subjects, and the respects of the native Jews.'

The tomb of Rachel, on the road between Jerusalem and Bethlehem, in the late 1870s (Bonfils).

Palmerston, had already sent his message to the Sultan at Constantinople, drawing attention to 'the strong notion' among the dispersed Jews of Europe 'that the Time is approaching when their Nation is to return to Palestine'. Three and a half months later, on 24 November 1840, Palmerston wrote again, for the Sultan's consideration, that 'very great benefit would accrue to the Turkish Government, if any considerable number of opulent Jews could be persuaded to come and settle in the Ottoman Dominion; because their wealth would afford employment to the People; and their Intelligence would give a useful direction to Industry; and the Resources of the State would thereby be considerably augmented.'

Not grandiose schemes, however, but small, piecemeal progress was to be the lot of Jerusalem's Jews, so many of them poor, so many of them refugees from persecution elsewhere. One such small change took place in 1841 as a result of Sir Moses Montefiore's visit two years earlier. On the road between Jerusalem and Bethlehem was a small stone building, originally built by the Crusaders, said to be the tomb of Rachel: here Rachel had died, after giving birth to Jacob's son Benjamin. 'And Jacob set a pillar on her grave: that is the pillar of Rachel's grave unto this day.'

Rachel's tomb had been a place of Jewish pilgrimage even before the Roman destruction of Jerusalem. For many centuries the tomb had been marked by a pyramid of twelve stones, each representing one of the tribes of Israel. Under the Ottomans, however, no Jew could visit it, and by 1841 the building over the tomb was in disrepair. Montefiore persuaded the Turks to hand over the key to the tomb for Jewish worshippers. He also paid for the building to be restored, and for a small courtyard to be added with a praying place for Muslims. For the next few decades, at times of famine, disease or drought, the Jews of Jerusalem would go to Rachel's tomb – more than an hour's walk from the Jewish quarter – to offer up prayers to 'Rachel our mother' to end their distress.

What Montefiore had done in repairing Rachel's tomb, as in so much of his work, was to give the Jews of Jerusalem a greater sense of belonging, and of security. Their lack of security was a source of comment by Europeans. On 24 May 1841 Vice-Consul Young reported to his superior, Colonel Hugh Rose, in Beirut, that complaints of 'bigotry and outrages' by Muslims against non-Muslims in Sidon, Tyre, Acre and Safed were confirmed 'by what is observed here in Jerusalem towards Christian and Jews'. The Turkish authorities in the city, Young added, were 'too feeble and indifferent to act effectively'.

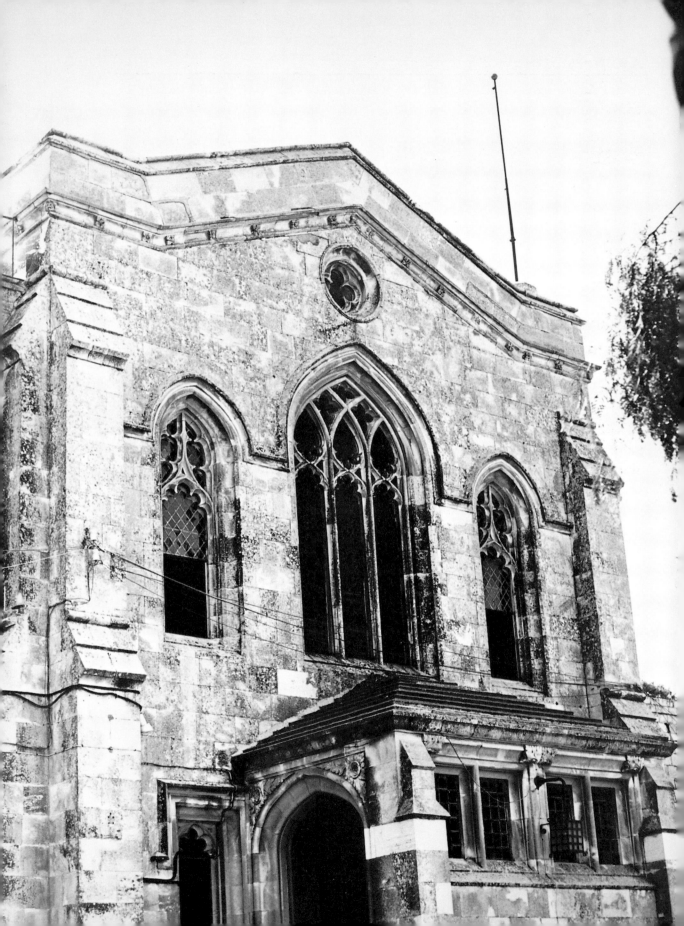

CHAPTER II

The 1840s: 'Conflicts and commotion'

On 25 February 1841 a party of British Royal Engineers, consisting of two Lieutenants and six other ranks, began, with the Sultan's approval, the first scientific survey of the walls of Jerusalem. The presence of a British fleet off the coast of Palestine was undoubtedly the chief factor in their being left unmolested.

The two British officers, Edward Aldrich and J. F. A. Symonds, worked for six weeks to map the city and its environs. Their instructions were clear: they were to evaluate the city in the light of the 'capability of defence or exposure to attack, or as accommodation for troops and depot for stores'. These military needs were their sole concern: no archaeological, historical or religious considerations were to impinge upon their mapping. But it was to be seventy-six years before British troops and stores were to be based – as conquerors – within the walls.

As soon as Aldrich and Symonds had completed their survey, the Officer Commanding the Royal Engineers in Syria, Colonel R. A. Alderson, journeyed specially to the city from the coast in order to take the final measurements himself: personally measuring the walls of the Citadel. Jerusalem had at last been surveyed.

Britain's growing influence in Jerusalem did not go unchallenged, however. In 1841 both the Russian and French Governments established consulates in the city. The British Government reacted by raising the vice-consular status of their representative to that of full consul. But an even more far reaching change in Britain's interest took place in July 1841, with the Prussian–British agreement, negotiated in Berlin by Baron Christian Bunsen, whereby an Anglican Bishop was to be the supreme Protestant religious authority in Jerusalem.

Christ Church, Jerusalem, built in 1842 (photographed in 1984).

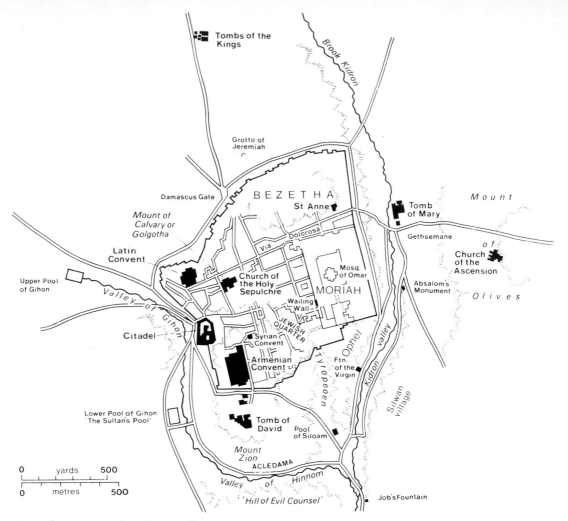

Jerusalem in 1843, based on William Bartlett's map of that year.

The man chosen for this task was Bishop Alexander, himself a Jewish convert to Christianity, who reached the city at the beginning of January 1842. Alexander's full title was 'Bishop of the United Church of England and Ireland', with 'spiritual jurisdiction' approved by both the British and Prussian Governments over all British Protestant congregations in Syria, Chaldaea, Egypt and Abyssinia 'as might be desirous of placing themselves under his authority'.

With Queen Victoria's personal approval, the new British Foreign Secretary, the Earl of Aberdeen, stressed to Consul Young that, while he should give Bishop Alexander British protection to the 'utmost' of his ability, he must 'carefully abstain' from identifying himself 'in any degree' with the Bishop's efforts to convert Jews to Christianity. 'You will clearly understand', Aberdeen warned, 'that Her Majesty's Government will not sanction, either in you or in any other servant of the Crown, any attempts, directly or indirectly, to interfere with the religious tenets of any class of the Sultan's Subjects.'

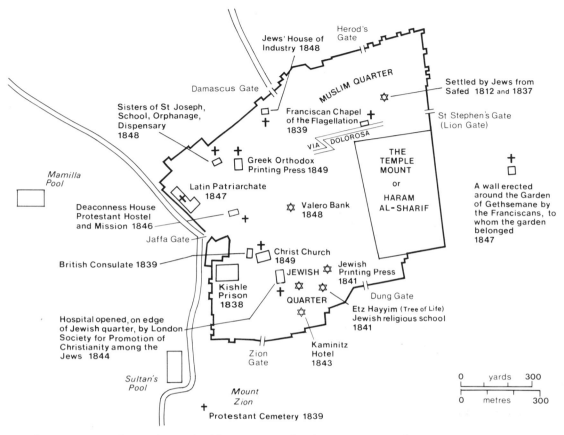

Jews' House of Industry 1848

Herod's Gate

Damascus Gate

MUSLIM QUARTER

Settled by Jews from Safed 1812 and 1837

Sisters of St Joseph, School, Orphanage, Dispensary 1848

Franciscan Chapel of the Flagellation 1839

St Stephen's Gate (Lion Gate)

VIA DOLOROSA

Greek Orthodox Printing Press 1849

THE TEMPLE MOUNT

or

HARAM AL-SHARIF

Mamilla Pool

Latin Patriarchate 1847

Valero Bank 1848

A wall erected around the Garden of Gethsemane by the Franciscans, to whom the garden belonged 1847

Deaconness House Protestant Hostel and Mission 1846

Jaffa Gate

Christ Church 1849

British Consulate 1839

JEWISH

Jewish Printing Press 1841

Kishle Prison 1838

QUARTER

Dung Gate

Etz Hayyim (Tree of Life) Jewish religious school 1841

Hospital opened, on edge of Jewish quarter, by London Society for Promotion of Christianity among the Jews 1844

Kaminitz Hotel 1843

Zion Gate

Sultan's Pool

Mount Zion

Protestant Cemetery 1839

0   yards   300

0   metres   300

Christian (✝) and Jewish (✡) building in Jerusalem between 1838 and 1849.

Lord Aberdeen's instruction was dated 3 May 1842. It arrived even as Bishop Alexander's church was in the process of construction, and when the hopes of the missionaries already in the city were much excited by their new episcopal status. Three months earlier, on 28 January 1842 the first stone had been laid of the English Church opposite the Citadel. The builders had dug to a depth of nearly forty feet before reaching solid rock. In the course of this digging they had discovered an immense water conduit, partly hewn out of the rock, partly built of masonry, and lined with cement an inch thick: visual evidence of the city's ancient past.

The English Church became the centre of the work of the London Society for Promoting Christianity amongst the Jews, known in the city as the London Jews Society. Its missionary activities, the conversion of the Jews of Jerusalem to Christianity, were headed by the Danish-born priest, John Nicolayson, who five years later was to become a British-protected person, and who was to

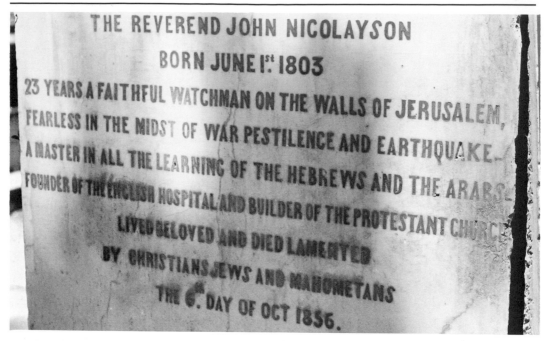

THE REVEREND JOHN NICOLAYSON
BORN JUNE 1ST 1803
23 YEARS A FAITHFUL WATCHMAN ON THE WALLS OF JERUSALEM,
FEARLESS IN THE MIDST OF WAR PESTILENCE AND EARTHQUAKE,
A MASTER IN ALL THE LEARNING OF THE HEBREWS AND THE ARABS,
FOUNDER OF THE ENGLISH HOSPITAL AND BUILDER OF THE PROTESTANT CHURCH
LIVED BELOVED AND DIED LAMENTED
BY CHRISTIANS JEWS AND MAHOMETANS
THE 6TH DAY OF OCT 1856.

Tombstone of John Nicolayson in the Protestant cemetery on Mount Zion (photographed in 1984).

remain an active missionary in Jerusalem until his death in 1856.

Bishop Alexander was soon confronted by some of the special problems of his episcopacy. One day, in order to bring a little colour to his drab house, he had the front gate painted green. That same night, Muslim Arabs scraped off the green paint: the Bishop's use of that sacred colour being an insult to their religious feelings.

In the summer of 1842 a British traveller, William Bartlett, reached Jerusalem, intent on writing 'a clear, connected and accurate view of the City'. He was also worried about the day when the land of Palestine 'becomes the prize of contending nations'. That summer, however, peace and solitude were the companions of his journey by horse from Jaffa to Jerusalem, the last stage across 'bleak and desolate hills'. As to the city itself, first seen at dawn, 'there was nothing grand or striking in the vision – a line of dull walls, a group of massive towers, a few dark olives, rising from a dead and sterile plain, were all that met the eye'.

Arriving at the Jaffa Gate early in the morning, Bartlett had to wait until the Turkish sentinel unbarred the great door. 'It swung slowly open', he wrote, 'and our horses' hoofs first sounded on the broken pavement, and we advanced among ruinous heaps and waste places.' After riding a few hundred yards

Bartlett reached the British Consulate. There, in the consul's absence, he was met by the new architect of the Church, J.W. Johns, then acting consul, and an old school friend. Night was spent in a 'cell' at the Latin convent: 'after late watches in open boats and elsewhere, a clean bed was no small luxury, though with sheets of penitentiary coarseness'.

The Latin convent, Bartlett noted, was, next to the Armenian convent, 'the best resting place in Jerusalem'. And so he began his explorations, and his reflections. It was probable, he wrote, in a reflection on the biblical era, 'that the sterile environs of Jerusalem were, at this period, converted by labour and irrigation into a scene of comparative fertility and beauty'.

'We need hardly say', Bartlett wrote of the City of David on the hill of Ophel, beneath which Smith and Robinson had wandered four years earlier, 'that there can be no remains of what was once the city of David. Monkish traditions, indeed, pretend to point out some, but they are wholly destitute of foundation; a vast accumulation of debris, from thirty to forty feet in depth, has buried every fragment of it.'

Bartlett was scathing about most of the site and scenes of Jerusalem. The only building in the whole city, he wrote, 'that presents any considerable appearance of comfort' is the Armenian convent; 'its compactly-built façade, the neatly-paved street in front, overshadowed by noble trees, and the portly and highly respectable looking monks about its doorway, are all redolent of ease, and wealth, and cleanliness – rare in the city of Jerusalem.'

Bartlett visited and described all the known sites of biblical and Roman Jerusalem. He also noted, in the Catholic cemetery on Mount Zion, 'the tomb of a young American, who, during his last illness in the convent, is said to have renounced the errors of Protestantism, and to have returned to the bosom of the true church'.

Nothing could more vividly portray the desolation of Jerusalem in 1842 than Bartlett's descriptions. Of the Jewish quarter he wrote: 'If the traveller have the courage to inhale the infected air of its close alleys, reeking with putrid filth, he will soon hasten out of them, with the deepest impression of the misery and social degradation of their unhappy occupants.'

Mount Zion left Bartlett equally unmoved. 'Its dull slopes', he wrote, 'once covered with towers and palaces, and thronged by a people whose bones are mingled with the soil, are now terraced and ploughed, and but sustain a poor crop of wheat and sprinkling of olive-trees. Broken paths descend into the valleys below; and a flock of goats, with a solitary shepherd, or at long intervals

Top: the entrance to the Armenian Church and Convent (Robert M. Bain, 1894).
Above: interior of the Armenian Church (Underwood and Underwood, 1898).

an Arab woman, slowly mounting the steep ascent, alone relieve the melancholy vacancy of a scene, which in general is silent as the grave.'

Bartlett's pen combined caustic comment with an appreciation of the deeper attractions of the city. Of the Church of the Holy Sepulchre he wrote: 'The centre of attraction to the devoted but ignorant multitude is, of course, the Church of the Sepulchre: and marshalled by their respective religious guides, they rush with frantic eagerness to its portal, and in this excited state visit the many stations invented or imagined in credulous ages. The whole scene of Christ's crucifixion and entombment are before the eye with such vividness, that even Protestants who come to scoff, have hardly been able to resist the contagious effect of sympathy.' But of those Christian chapels within the church, said to be on the site of Calvary, Bartlett wrote in more caustic tone. 'The ascent to the Mount of Calvary', he told his readers, 'is by a staircase cut in the rock: its form is almost entirely disfigured by marble and decorations; the holes of the crosses, evidently spurious, are beneath, and there is a fissure in the rock, said to have been produced by the earthquake. These contrivances tend both to produce disgust, and to weaken our faith in the locality.'

A final cry of despair from Bartlett's pen ends this selection of his vivid, but in the main disparaging comments. 'If the traveller can forget', he wrote, 'that he is treading on the grave of a people from whom his religion has sprung, on the dust of her kings, prophets, and holy men, there is certainly no city in the world that he will sooner wish to leave than Jerusalem. Nothing can be more void of interest than her gloomy, half-ruinous streets and poverty-stricken bazaars, which, except at the period of the pilgrimage at Easter, present no signs of life or study of character to the observer.'

Jews who came from outside the Ottoman Empire could secure the protection of the foreign consuls. But Jews born in the Ottoman Empire remained, as did all non-Muslim subjects, members of the 'dhimmi' community, assured of an inferior, if protected, status to Muslims. The location of the city's slaughterhouse at the edge of the Jewish quarter had been intended to emphasize that inferiority, as had the placing of a mosque overlooking the site of the Hurva synagogue, and of a minaret overlooking the square in front of the Church of the Holy Sepulchre. 'Dhimmis', whether Jewish or Christian, were spared the obligation to do military service. In its place, they had to pay a tax. Liable to suffer indignities on the street, they were nevertheless allowed to supervise their own religious courts in their respective communities.

To many of the Jews of Jerusalem, British Protection seemed the best security in times of upheaval or dispute. In 1843 this protection was granted to several Dutch-born Jews, there being no Dutch consul in the city. One of these was Nathan Coronel, who had lived in the city since 1834, and who, as a British-protected person, retained his status as a Dutch subject. Another Dutch Jew who received British protection in 1843 was Rabbi Israel Eliakim, who lived in Hebron, where the tombs of Abraham, Isaac and Jacob drew a small number of Jews to that overwhelmingly Muslim city.

Despite the increasingly crowded and uncomfortable life in Jerusalem, and the problems of being a Jew under Muslim rule, Jews continued to reach the city, and to settle there, from many lands. One witness to this was Frederick Ewald, a Bavarian Protestant, who had reached Jerusalem from Bavaria in 1842. Although a German, he was a Minister of the English Church, and had a passport from Lord Palmerston. Later, Ewald was to become a naturalized British subject. 'The influx of Jews has been very considerable of late,' he wrote in a missionary journal at the end of November 1843. 'A fortnight since, 150 Jews arrived here from Algiers. There is now a large number of Jews here from the coast of Africa, who are about to form themselves into a separate congregation.'

Another western observer of the city in 1843 was John Lothian, who wrote of the Jewish community at the end of the year: 'what a painful change has passed over the circumstances and condition of the poor Jew – that in his own city, and close by where his temple stood, he has to suffer oppression and persecution. In Jerusalem his case is a very hard one, for if he should have a little of this world's goods in his possession, he is oppressed and robbed by the Turks in a most unmerciful manner; in short, for him there is neither law nor justice!'

Bishop Alexander, and the London Jews Society, were soon effective not only in converting Jews, but in forcing the British Government to grant them some means of recognition as members of the Anglican community. Three of Alexander's earliest converts were two Russian Jews, Abraham Walphen and Elhaza Lorin, and an Austrian Jew, Benjamin Bynes. In October 1842, fearing 'personal violence in consequence of having declared their belief in Christianity', all three Jews had sought refuge in the home of Frederick Ewald. This led to an immediate protest from Isaiah Bordaki, a Jerusalem rabbi who was also honorary Russian and Austrian consul in the city. Rabbi Bordaki demanded the transfer of the three Jews to his own consular authority. Reluctantly,

Consul Young found himself explaining to Lord Aberdeen that if a Jew 'professes himself a Convert (as in the present case) his Government might prefer that he should unite himself to the Church recognized by his Government rather than to one in connection with a Foreign State'.

In defence of his action in obtaining shelter for the three – as yet unbaptized – Jews, Bishop Alexander informed Young that 'when three respectable learned Jews, being convinced of the truth of Christianity, on account of which they are exposed to fearful persecution on the part of the Rabbis, flee for refuge to any of our houses, we are bound as Christians to give them shelter, and not to do so, I should consider little short of cruelty, in exposing them to Chains and imprisonment'. The Bishop added: 'I very much mistake if the same view should not be taken by the Christian Government of England.'

Consul Young continued to uphold official British policy: not to give its political authority to conversion, nor to protect those who sought conversion. With the arrival in Jerusalem of the Russian Consul in Beirut, Constantin Basily, the three Jews were however able to negotiate an agreement, whereby their conversion could go ahead, under Bishop Alexander's spiritual guidance and authority. They were all three baptized on 21 May 1843, at the Anglican church, in a ceremony conducted in Hebrew. 'I was invited by the Bishop', Consul Young reported to Lord Aberdeen, 'to stand sponsor for these Converts – this I politely declined – but as the parties were to be publicly admitted members of the Church of England, I was present at this Ceremony, as I have been in the habit of being on similar occasions.'

At the beginning of 1843, news of the three would-be converts had reached Sir Moses Montefiore in England. He had for some time been aware that, for the poor Jews of Jerusalem, there was no qualified Jewish doctor. Sick Jews, if poor, had therefore to seek medical help from doctors attached to the English Christian mission. This made them vulnerable to the pressures of conversion. Montefiore decided to act, sending to Jerusalem at his own expense a young Jewish doctor, Simon Frankel, from Silesia. Montefiore also provided Frankel with the medical drugs and equipment needed to set up a dispensary of his own and with instructions to give medical assistance to the Jewish poor of the city.

A noted wit, Simon Frankel soon became one of the 'characters' of Jerusalem, as well as its only Jewish doctor. His delight was to spend time with the 'batlanim', the unpractical, unwordly loafers of the Jewish community: only their untidy and unhygenic manner of living stirred his rebuke.

The proselytizing activities of the London Jews Society continued to be both successful and provocative. In answer to Montefiore's despatch of Simon Frankel to Jerusalem, the Society decided to open a hospital on the very edge of the Jewish quarter, and did so within six months of Dr Frankel's arrival. But the Society did not always get its way. On 10 June 1844 Consul Young reported to the Foreign Office in London the case of three Jewish children who were 'received by agents' of the Society and, after some time, baptized. Their father, a Jew, sought to reclaim them. The eldest boy refused to return, 'and was allowed to please himself'. The two youngest children were restored to the father by the Turkish authorities. In another case, the wife of a Jew who had converted to Christianity refused to let him have his two children, and was supported in her refusal by the Rabbi. The converted Jew being an Austrian subject, Consul Young declined to 'interfere'.

Young was also able to avoid direct involvement in several cases where Jewish converts to Christianity went, as he reported to Lord Aberdeen, to the Jewish cemetery on the Mount of Olives 'and desecrated the Tombs, by displacing some, and inscribing crosses and their names as Believers in Christianity on others, to the great annoyance of the Jewish community'. Fortunately, as one of those who had complained was a Russian subject, the other a Prussian by nationality, the complaint would be dealt with by the Russian Consul in Beirut, Constantin Basily, and the Prussian Consul in Jerusalem, Dr Schultz.

For travellers to Jerusalem, accommodation inside Jerusalem could be found only in the monasteries and convents. But in 1843 a Russian Jew, Menachem Mendel of Kaminitz, opened the first modern commercial hotel in Jerusalem. Mendel had come to Palestine in 1833, settling in Safed; from 1838 to 1842 he had travelled through Europe seeking funds for the Jews of Safed and Jerusalem. The aim of his hotel was to provide lodgings for new Jewish arrivals. His wife, Miriam Mendel, quickly became known as an accomplished baker.

During 1844 an American from Philadelphia, Warder Cresson, a Christian, set himself up as 'United States Consul in Jerusalem'. He had no such appointment. The nearest representative of the United States was in Beirut. But for two years Cresson maintained the fiction, for himself, and for dozens of gullible citizens, that he was indeed the representative of Washington. Frequently 'exposed', in 1846 he enabled the State Department to breathe more freely by voluntarily 'resigning' his post. He was later to become a convert to Judaism.

In the pre-photographic age, Jerusalem had frequently been depicted by painters, most of whom had never seen the Holy City. Throughout the eighteenth century artists had copied the panorama of a Dutch artist, Cornelius de Bruin, who had visited the city in 1682 and sketched it from the Mount of Olives. De Bruin's view, which had taken him three days to complete, under the hostile gaze of the Turkish authorities, was often embellished and 'improved' by those who had never stood within a thousand miles of its viewpoint. In 1844 a painter from Munich, Ulrich Halbreiter, visited Jerusalem to paint a new panorama. For his vantage point he chose the Tower of the Church of the Ascension, then the highest building on the Mount of Olives. His painting, 5.4 metres high and 30 metres long, was eventually presented to the Vatican.

In 1844 a book was published in London which was to have a considerable impact upon the holiest Christian site in Jerusalem, the Church of the Holy Sepulchre. Its author was a British Member of Parliament, Robert Curzon, who had visited the city ten years earlier, in search of early Christian manuscripts. Now, in a book entitled *Visits to Monasteries in the Levant*, he described in unambiguous language the state of disrepair of the Christendom's holiest shrine. Christians throughout Europe were shocked by what Curzon wrote, and the idea began rapidly to gain ground of some direct European control over the holy places.

In his book, Robert Curzon noted that in Jerusalem the Arabic language was 'generally spoken', although Turkish 'is much used among the better class'. He added that inhabitants of the city 'are composed of people of different nations and different religions, who inwardly despise one another on account of their varying opinions'. The Muslims, he wrote, 'ridicule the Christians' who visit and revere the Holy Sepulchre. The Jews, 'the children of the kingdom', had come 'from the East and the West to occupy their place in the desolate land promised to their fathers'.

While Curzon was in Jerusalem, he was the guest of one of the rabbis for Passover. 'The outside of the house', he wrote, 'and the court-yard indicated nothing but poverty and neglect; but on entering I was surprised at the magnificence of the furniture. One room had a silver chandelier, and a great quantity of embossed plate was displayed on the top of the polished cupboards. Some of the windows were filled with painted glass; and the members of the family, covered with gold and jewels, were seated on divans of Damascus brocade. The Rabbi's little son was so covered with charms in gold cases to keep off the evil eye, that he jingled like a chime of bells when he walked along; and a still younger boy, whom I had never seen before, was on this day

An orthodox Jew leaving the Damascus Gate.

exalted to the dignity of wearing trousers, which were of red stuff, embroidered with gold, and were brought in by his nurse and a number of other women in procession, and borne on high before him. . . .'

Reflecting on the Jews whom he saw and befriended, Curzon wrote: 'It is remarkable that the Jews who are born in Jerusalem are of a totally different caste from those we see in Europe. Here they are a fair race, very lightly made, and particularly effeminate in manner; the young men wear a lock of long hair on each side of the face, which, with their flowing silk robes, gives them the appearance of women. The Jews of both sexes are exceedingly fond of dress; and, although they assume a dirty and squalid appearance when they walk abroad, in their own houses they are to be seen clothed in costly furs and the richest silks of Damascus. The women are covered with gold, and dressed in brocades stiff with embroidery. Some of them are beautiful; and a girl of about twelve years old, who was betrothed to the son of a rich old rabbi, was the prettiest little creature I ever saw; her skin was whiter than ivory, and her hair, which was as black as jet, and was plaited with strings of sequins, fell in tresses nearly to the ground. She was of a Spanish family, and the language usually spoken by the Jews among themselves is Spanish.'

A Jewish family on Mount Zion, a print of 1844.

Also in 1844, and also in London, another book, *A Survey of the Holy Land*, was published by J.T. Bannister. He himself had never visited Jerusalem. In his book he praised the London Society for Promoting Christianity amongst the Jews for sending 'a host of veterans into the field' in order to remove 'the veil of unbelief' from the Jews. The need for conversion had become urgent. The 'pangs and throes' which were 'tearing at the heart' of the Ottoman Empire 'announce that its dissolution is near at hand'. Once Ottoman power were overthrown, 'a series of events' would ensure 'conflicts and commotion among the nations of the earth', ending in the downfall of Antichrist, the emancipation of Judaea from a foreign yoke, and the dawn of 'a brighter and more glorious epoch' in the Holy Land.

According to Bannister, the return of the Jews to Judaea, and the subsequent fulfilment of biblical prophecies, was made easier because 'the exiled Jews' had, as he wrote, 'no country to call their own – no home – no local attachments'. They had no landed property in the lands of their dispersion, 'nor do they intermarry with other nations, so as to be hindered by family alliances and attachments from returning to the land of their fathers'. Ottoman power was 'almost the only other hindrance now remaining' for the return of the

Jews to Jerusalem. After the restoration of the Jews to Judaea would follow their conversion to Christianity; and then 'the triumphant reign of the Messiah in majesty and great glory'.

These ideas were echoed, in New York, by Judge Noah, who wrote on 29 November 1844, in the *Voice of Jacob*: 'Every attempt to colonize the Jews in other countries has failed – their eye has steadily rested on their beloved Jerusalem.'

For the leading Arab families of Jerusalem, whose authority had been destroyed by the Turks forty years before, all changes in the city seemed galling and unnecessary, a western intrusion which they had neither invited nor welcomed. Those who remembered the earlier times would tell their children of the old days, when the caravans would be forced to remain outside the city walls once darkness had fallen. They would tell of the caravans, not with nostalgia, but with a certain shame that their own people, their own fathers, had fallen so low, had become the footstool on which other peoples, other faiths, other ways of life, archaeology, commerce, Christianity, Judaism, Christian missionary zeal, had put their imprint. How well I recall a distinguished Jerusalem Arab showing me one of David Roberts' prints on his drawing-room wall. Here was an idyllic scene, of peaceful antiquity. But for my host, it was a source of anguish, a pointer to bad times, when pride and spirit had been crushed and the city's true guardians humiliated.

'Not very complimentary to us,' was his comment, grieved as he was, not by the pastoral portrayal, but by what the drawing said of the low state into which Arab aspirations had fallen. For my host, too, the causes of this sad decline were clear: Turkish dominance, neglect and greed, and the arrival of westerners with different outlooks on life, different traditions, different aims. To transform the old city within its walls into something modern, something larger, something filled with new aspirations, was quite in order for the newcomers, he accepted that; but for the Muslim Arabs it was quite out of tune with what they might wish to do, and how they might wish to live.

In 1845 the Prussian Consul, Dr Schultz, sent to Berlin his estimate of Jerusalem's population in that year. There were, he reported, 7,120 Jews, 5,000 Muslim Arabs and 3,390 Christian Arabs in the city: some 800 Turkish soldiers, and 100 Europeans.

Of the people whom these statistics enumerated, and the state of their city, a French visitor that year, Alphonse de Lamartine, has left an account. 'Outside the gates of Jerusalem', he wrote, 'we saw indeed no living object, heard no living sound, we found the same void, the same silence ... as we should have expected before the entombed gates of Pompeii or Herculaneum.' As for inside the city, 'a complete eternal silence reigns in the town, on the highways, in the country ... the tomb of a whole people'.

A similar trans-Atlantic view was expressed by Judge Noah, writing in the *Voice of Jacob* on 11 April 1845. 'The distress to which these poor people are reduced', the Judge declared, 'it is painful to contemplate; they possess few opportunities of self-maintenance, they are subjected to many oppressive exactions, and moreover, such is the lawless state of the district, that sometimes they dare not stir beyond the walls even to fetch water.'

It was at such a dismal time that conflict between the Christian missionaries and the Jews reached a climax.

The mission hospital established by the London Jews Society took in sick Jews, as well as converts, and provided these Jews with meat and chicken slaughtered according to Jewish practice. The hospital also employed a number of Jews to help with the day-to-day work. This roused the anger of both the Sephardi and Ashkenazi rabbis, who united in protest. In a proclamation read in all Jerusalem synagogues on 25 January 1845, 'notice and warning' was given by the Sephardi rabbinate 'that no child of Israel, whether a man or a woman, is permitted to be employed in the service of the said hospital, and if anyone transgress these our words, then shall his sons not receive the rite of circumcision, and no lawful meat shall be given to him - not into his hands nor into the hands of any other, not even a lawful fowl'. Indeed, the rabbis declared, if someone were to take lawfully slaughtered meat or fowl to one of the Jews in the mission hospital, 'we shall pronounce it unlawful, and so it shall be as if he would eat carrion and unlawful meats'.

The Ashkenazi rabbinate added, in its proclamation, that anyone entering the London Jews Hospital as a patient 'will not be purified, after his disease, by Jews, nor buried in their burial ground'.

Jewish hostility to the mission hospital led in 1846 to what its chief physician, Edward MacGowan, described, in a complaint to the British Consulate, as 'a very unpleasant difficulty'. The case arose with the refusal of the Sephardi Chief Rabbi, Mercado Gagguin, to allow the burial, in Jewish consecrated ground, of a Jewess, Esther Arruas, who had died in the mission hospital, even though she was not a convert, but a practising Jewess.

In order to bury Esther Arruas, Bishop Alexander authorized the purchase of a small piece of ground from a Muslim Arab, Mohammed Ghoul, of the

Inside the Old City, the first mission house of the London Society for Promoting Christianity amongst the Jews (photographed in 1984).

village of Silwan. The purchase was carried out on behalf of the hospital by David Rachman, a Jew who was an Ottoman subject.

On the day after Esther Arruas' burial in the new plot, both Ghoul and Rachman were arrested, by order of the Turkish Governor of the city, Mohammed Pasha. Both men were thrown into prison, and, as Dr MacGowan reported, 'severely bastinadoed' – beaten with rods on the soles of their feet.

The alliance between the Turkish Governor and Chief Rabbi Gagguin made British consular intervention virtually impossible, especially as Consul Young had just left the city, and his successor had not yet arrived. British interests were upheld by the acting consul, Henry Newbolt: but his reports showed a worsening situation for the mission and its interests. On 5 March 1846 Newbolt informed Lord Aberdeen that since the punishment inflicted on Ghoul and Rachman 'there have been a series of disturbances amongst the Jews, the butcher who kills the meat for the hospital, a French subject, has been robbed, and severely beaten, and the hospital has been daily surrounded by a number of Jews sent by the Rabbis to prevent patients and even servants access to it'. Newbolt added that Dr MacGowan had received 'secret information' of a sum, offered by the rabbis, to murder him, 'and had been advised not to enter the Jewish quarter alone'.

In 1846 two men reached Jerusalem who were to have a considerable impact on the city: Consul Finn and Bishop Gobat. Finn was to serve as British Consul and Gobat as Anglican Bishop. The two men were to quarrel without respite. Finn believed, in contrast to his predecessor, Consul Young, that Christian missionary work in Jerusalem was the will of God, and that the prime task of all such missionary work in Jerusalem was to convert Jews to Christianity. Gobat, on the other hand, stressed the need to convert the Arab Christians to Anglicanism, to persuade them to forgo the 'errors' of Greek Orthodoxy.

Finn's missionary zeal was shared by his wife, Elizabeth Anne, who was to welcome several other British missionary women to Jerusalem in the coming years, and to encourage them in their work for the conversion of the Jews.

Also in 1846, a Swiss Protestant, Conrad Schick, reached the city. His first appointment was to the Bruderhaus, or Swiss-German Brotherhood, a Protestant missionary hostel, set up just inside the city walls, which trained Muslim Arab boys in 'useful trades'. Later, Schick moved to the London Jews Society Mission, as head of its House of Industry. There, most of the boys were Jewish converts to Christianity, or potential converts.

One of the founders of the Brotherhood was Ludwig Schneller, who was already in Jerusalem at the time of Schick's arrival: both men were to make their mark on the city's development in the coming decades, Schick as an archaeologist and a missionary, Schneller as an educator.

Among the Russian Jews who reached Jerusalem in 1846 was Isaiah Poresh, a prosperous watchmaker. Three years later he was to acquire British protection, one of the first Russian Jews to seek under the authority of the Union Jack a means of defence against Ottoman, or Muslim, antagonism.

In 1847 a British visitor, Dr John Kitto, described the sorry state of the city, as seen by someone used to the ever-advancing prosperity of Europe. 'A large number of houses in Jerusalem', he wrote, 'are in a dilapidated and ruinous state. Nobody seems to make repairs so long as his dwelling does not absolutely refuse him shelter and safety. If one room tumbles about his ears, he removes into another, and permits rubbish and vermin to accumulate as they will in the deserted halls.' Dr Kitto also commented on the inhabitants. 'Although', he wrote, 'we are much in the habit of regarding Jerusalem as a Moslem city, the Moslems do not actually constitute more than one-third of the entire population.'

That year, it was Christian building that predominated; and not building alone, for the Latin Patriarchate, in abeyance since 1291, was, with the Sultan's permission, restored, and the Patriarch took up residence. Henceforth this representative of Roman Catholicism was to lead the 'Latins' of the city, encourage the building up of the Christian quarter, and serve as the Vatican's principal instrument of biblical exploration and preservation, marked that same year by the first building outside the city: a stone wall, erected by the Franciscans around their olive trees in the Garden of Gethsemane.

From its foundation five years earlier, the work of the London Mission, now supported by Consul Finn, had been limited to converting Jews who were not Ottoman subjects: principally Russian, French, Prussian or British-protected subjects. The conversion of 'Rayah', or Ottoman Jews, was believed to be strictly prohibited by Constantinople. In 1847, however, Finn reported an incident which opened up the Mission's work to the thousands of Jews who were Ottoman subjects. As he reported to Lord Palmerston on 11 March 1847:

'A youth named Myer Maruka of Jewish parents desired to become a Christian. In the absence of his father the Rabbis interfered, declaring him to be under age. On this proving inaccurate, they declared him to be a Rayah subject,

The Mount of Olives with, on the right, the wall around the Garden of Gethsemane. This photograph was taken by Francis Bedford on 2 March 1862.

and therefore as a subject of the Sultan, his conversion was illegal. The Pasha referred the question to Constantinople.'

The youth was kept under the guardianship of the Pasha, 'sequestered', Finn reported, 'from both relatives and missionaries, and sheltered from the measures of cruelty to which Rabbis are accustomed to resort whenever any inquiry respecting Christianity is detected among their people'. Finn added: 'A letter arrived (the contents of which were not divulged) and the youth was set at liberty. He attends the Church of England services, and is said to be about to be baptized.'

At Easter 1847 the streets of Jerusalem resounded to the worst of all possible religious accusations: a ritual murder charge against the Jews. As in Damascus and Rhodes seven years earlier, Jews were accused of murdering a Christian child, in order to use his blood in the baking of Passover bread.

The accusation began with a seemingly trivial incident. On 8 March 1847 a Christian Arab boy had attacked a Jewish boy in the street. The Jewish boy managed to run off, hiding in a nearby house. Then, believing himself unobserved, he left his hiding place, only to find the Arab boy lying in wait for him. The Jewish boy then threw a stone at the Arab boy, cutting the Arab boy's foot.

Within hours, the Greek Orthodox community 'raised a tumult', as Consul Finn reported to Palmerston. The Jewish boy, it was alleged, had 'stabbed an innocent Christian with a knife'. When the case was brought before the Governor he refused even to examine 'so childish a quarrel', and dismissed the complaints. The Greeks, however, were not to be silenced or placated.

On 11 March 1847, three days after the incident, the Greeks, and several other Christian denominations – but not the Anglicans or the Protestants – succeeded, by their clamour, in forcing the Turkish authorities to hold a 'legal' investigation. Deputations were called for, from the Greek Patriarchate, the Chief Rabbinate, and the Muslim religious authorities, 'to argue', as Consul Finn reported, 'the reality or otherwise of the horrible crimes so often imputed to the Jews'.

In the debate that followed, the Greek Orthodox deputation 'pleaded that their most venerated theologians in all ages had uniformly asserted this accusation'. In support of this Christian assertion, the Mufti, the Cadi, and other Muslim leaders 'asserted that their Sacred book declared the source indirectly and by implication'.

As in the Middle Ages, the Jewish religious leaders found themselves on trial, not only for their own young lad's alleged 'crime', but for the long historical imputation of blood sacrifice: the 'blood libel' for which, in every century since the crucifixion, Jews had been accused, abused and murdered.

Now, for the first time, it was the Jews of Jerusalem who had to answer the age-old calumny. They did so, at the meeting of Deputation, by appealing to the Bible and its interpretations, to prove that 'not only is such practice not enjoined, but that the principles universally pervading those writings are diametrically opposed to it'. The rabbis also referred to an official document which they had received from the Sultan in 1841, immediately after the Damascus and Rhodes 'blood libels'. This document stated, with the full authority of the Sultan, that search had been made 'into all the Jewish writings' and that no trace of such a practice was to be found there.

Among those who sought to defend the Jews of Jerusalem against the 'blood libel' of 1847 were two of the Christian missionaries in the city, one of them a converted Jew, the other a clergyman in the Church of England. Both men went to the Chief Rabbi to offer their support 'in demonstrating that the charge is but a wicked fabrication'. But, as Consul Finn reported, there was a 'good deal of fanaticism' at that time 'ripening in Jerusalem'. Greek Orthodox pilgrims were known, he wrote, 'to lay hold of Jews in the streets and use menacing languages'. On one occasion a group of Greek Orthodox women called out to a British-born Jew in the street: 'Ah! Jew, have you got the knives ready?'

In October 1847 a British Protestant, Lucy Harding, reached Jerusalem in search of missionary work. She at once opened a school, in which for three years she taught Jewish children and their parents. In May 1851, after what Consul Finn described as an 'unpleasant business', otherwise unexplained, she left the city and returned to England.

Among those employed by the Anglican Mission was James Elijah Shufammi, a Sephardi Jew who had reached Jerusalem in 1848, converted to Christianity, and whose job was to distribute Anglican religious tracts to the Jews. A year after Shufammi's arrival, a former Prussian subject, David Daniel, reached Jerusalem. He too was a Jew by birth, who had both converted to Christianity and become nationalized as a British subject. Once in Jerusalem, Daniel and his wife worked as missionaries, seeking to persuade other Jews to follow their own path of conversion.

A third converted Jew who was repeatedly to rouse the anger of the Jewish quarter was Simeon Rosenthal, an Austrian whom Consul Finn had not only converted to Anglicanism but employed as dragoman in all consular relations with the Ashkenazi Jews. The sight of an apostate holding authority, and obliged to be in frequent contact with them, was galling to the Ashkenazi Jews, and hardly a tactful appointment by the increasingly imperious consul.

Another new visitor to the city in 1847 was a British woman, Caroline Cooper, who came to Jerusalem intent upon the conversion of the Jews to Anglican Christianity. The daughter of a physician, she was financially independent, and worked also independently of the London Jews Society, her own hostels becoming known as 'Miss Cooper's Institutions'. As with other British ladies who arrived from time to time with the same aim, Miss Cooper was quickly befriended, and helped, by Consul Finn and his wife, strong supporters of the Anglican Mission. She also worked closely with Lucy Harding.

The hazards of imprudent action could affect Christian and Jew alike. In 1848 Dr MacGowan, having attended a sick person in one of the leading Muslim Arab families of the city in the Muslim's house next to the Haram enclosure, was taken, in gratitude by his patient, a few steps inside one of the Haram gates. The patient had only in mind enabling Dr MacGowan a closer view of the Dome of the Rock and its surroundings. Both MacGowan and his patient were immediately attacked with clubs by the Sudanese guardians of the Haram, and knocked to the ground. Had not the Hereditary Guardian of the Sanctuary intervened at that moment, both would undoubtedly have been killed.

Shortly after this incident, at Easter, a Jew was recognized by Christian pilgrims inside the Church of the Holy Sepulchre. He was at once attacked, and was being severely beaten, when some of the Governor's guards tried to come to his rescue. They too were then rushed by the mob, and one of the guards, seeking to protect the Jew with his own body, was also beaten. The Governor's guard managed to get the Jew out of the church. But the crowd, rushing out after them, continued its attack. At that moment the Governor himself came, and, drawing his sword, drove the pilgrims back into the church.

The Jew was protected that night in the Governor's own quarters. Then, being an Austrian subject, he was handed over for safety to the Prussian Consulate. His excuse, that he was the brother of a converted Jew living in Jerusalem as a missionary, and that he was visiting the church with a converted Jew, did not seem adequate reason for what Consul Finn considered 'imprudence'.

The beating of the Jew was defended by the Greek Patriarch on the grounds that an official document existed, from the Sultan, allowing Christians to beat Jews if found within the Church of the Holy Sepulchre, 'or even if passing along the street in front of it'. Even if a Jew were killed in such a beating, this document asserted, the 'price' of his blood was only ten piastres – three farthings, or a cent.

In reply to this document, however, the Governor produced a Public Order signed by his predecessor, forbidding Christians themselves 'to beat the aggressors', and commanding that they be brought to the Governor himself for punishment.

Russian Christians continued to reach Jerusalem each year in their thousands, as Easter pilgrims. As soon as their pilgrimage was over, they returned to

Russia. But Russian Jews had other ideas. On 20 November 1848 the British Consul-General in Beirut, Colonel Rose, reported the belief of his Russian opposite number, Constantin Basily, 'that from hence forward every year some two or three hundred Jews a year will leave Russia for ever for Palestine'. Rose added: 'Mr Basily thinks and hopes that the whole Jewish population in Russia will eventually do the same.'

Although it was the pilgrimage to Mecca to which all Muslim pilgrims aspired, most of those who came to the Near East from a great distance also wished to visit Jerusalem. Thus in 1849 an Indian Muslim, Abdul Waheb, sought, and received, a certificate from the British Consul 'that he had been in Jerusalem'.

One further complexity in the religious counter-currents of Jerusalem: during 1848 a Jew reached the city who had been converted to Islam. This had happened in the town of Aleppo, in northern Syria. In Jerusalem, this 'Muslim' had practised Judaism in order to protect himself from Jewish anger. Then, in January 1849, he was recognized in the street by a Turkish visitor from Aleppo, and greeted as a Muslim. 'He has in terror concealed himself', reported Consul Finn to Constantinople, 'and applied to me for protection.' Three weeks later Finn reported that the Turk had left the city, and that the Jew, coming out of hiding, 'is attending to his affairs without molestation'.

In 1847, in Washington, the United States Secretary of the Navy had agreed to sponsor an expedition to the Dead Sea, under the command of one of his officers, Lieutenant W. F. Lynch. On 25 March 1848, Lynch's expedition landed at Acre, from where it proceeded overland, with its own boats, to the Sea of Galilee. Thence, sailing down the River Jordan, Lynch and his colleagues surveyed the river from the Sea of Galilee to the Dead Sea, before exploring the Dead Sea itself, and surveying the deep ravines on either side of it.

His work done, Lieutenant Lynch then rode up to Jerusalem through the gorges of the Judaean desert, and on 16 May 1848, as he ascended the deep cleft of the Kidron valley, first saw the city, as few travellers did, from below. 'Mellowed by time, and yet further softened by the intervening distance,' he wrote, 'the massive walls, with their towers and bastions, looked beautiful yet imposing in the golden sunlight; and above them, the only thing within their compass visible from that point, rose the glittering dome of the Mosque of Omar. . . .'

Lynch arrived too late in the evening to be allowed to enter the city. He and

Jerusalem from the south, the domes of Omar and Al-Aksa on the left; Silwan village on the right (1880s).

his men slept, instead, in the meadow above the Sultan's Pool. 'The dew was heavy', he wrote, 'and we suffered from the cold, although the thermometer did not range below 52 degrees in the night. The grain, already cut, laid in heaps in the valley below, exposed to the depredation of the spoiler, for none dared remain to guard it. Of all that solitude, we were the only tenants.'

Lynch awoke at four in the morning of 17 May 1848. Walking further away from the city, beyond the Jaffa Gate to the higher ground north-west of the walls, Lynch passed 'many Jewish women and children, clothed all in white, under the olive trees in the valley'. These, he wrote, were families from the city, 'who thus came to spend the day beneath the shade, away from the stifling air of the Jews' quarter'.

One of Lieutenant Lynch's men kept a diary. In it he described their entry into the city and approach to the Church of the Holy Sepulchre. 'Scattered about the court', he wrote, 'were motley groups of Jew pedlars, Turks, beggars, and Christian pilgrims. The appearance of a poor cripple excited my compassion, and I gave him a piastre; but the consequences were fearful. The war-cry of the Syrian pauper, "backshish! backshish!", instantly resounded from all quarters, and we were hemmed in, pressed, and swayed to and fro by the rabble. Our cicerone plied his stick vigorously in our defence, and it truly seemed to be gifted with miraculous powers, for the blind saw, and the lame walked, and amid their imprecations upon our Christian heads we entered the church.'

Jerusalem, Lynch himself commented, 'is, geographically, better known to the educated classes in the United States, than Boston, New York, or Philadelphia, to those who do not reside in them and have not visited them'. But one of his own descriptions of the human scenes was a striking one, not hitherto penned. 'North of the city', he wrote, 'on the margin of the Damascus road, was a picturesque scene – hundreds of Jews, enjoying the fresh air, seated under enormous olive-trees – the women all in white shrouds, the men in various costumes – some with broad-brimmed black hats, and many with fur caps. There were also many Turks and Christians abroad. The Jewesses, while they enveloped their figures in loose and uncomely robes, allowed their faces to be seen; and the Christian and the Turkish female exhibited, the one, perhaps, too much, the other, nothing whatever of her person and attire. There was also a marriage-procession, which was more funeral than festive. The women, as usual, clothed all in white, like so many spectres, chaunted unintelligibly, in a low, monotonous, wailing tone; while some, apparently the most antique, for they tottered most, closed each bar with a scream like a diapason. The least natural and the most pompous feature of the scene, was the foreign consuls, promenading with their families, preceded by Janissaries, with silver-mounted batons, stalking solemnly along, like so many drum-majors of a marching regiment. As the sun sank behind the western hills, the pedestrians walked faster, and the sitters gathered themselves up and hastened within the walls.'

Within those same walls, 1848, the year of revolutions in Europe, saw an economic revolution in Jerusalem: the establishment of the first European bank, the Valero bank. Also in 1848, the London Jews Society set up a 'House of Industry' for young men, providing work in various crafts, and the temptation of conversion. For Muslim Arabs, the Roman Catholic Sisters of St Joseph established a school and an orphanage: again offering not only education and care, but Christianity.

A Jerusalem porter (American Colony photograph, 1900s).

Poor Muslims, like poor Jews, could not always resist the blandishments, however unintentional, of the nineteenth-century church militant. The Jewish response was still to search for charity among European Jewry: in 1848 Rabbi Samuel Salant set off for Europe in search of further funds for the Jewish religious schools in the city. His mission, although successful, took three years. Meanwhile, the poverty worsened.

In 1849 the power of Britain in Jerusalem was enhanced by the decision of the Tsar to end Russian protection to Russian Jews who remained more than six months in the city. The leaders of the Russian Jews in the city at once approached Consul Finn, who informed them that, unless the Russian authorities opposed their being received by him as British-protected persons, 'I was at liberty to do so.' As Finn explained to Palmerston on 23 March 1849: 'It has hitherto been the policy of the Russian Empire to detain its Jewish subjects as much as possible within its own confines – and when passports have been granted to Jews for leaving the Empire, they have been granted for as short a time as possible, seldom exceeding a year, and that term of time was stated in the passport.'

But Jews coming to Palestine, Finn explained, 'never intend to return to Russia – they come here from an impulse of religious feeling, and are contented to drag out a life of extreme poverty, and to die here rather than return to Russia – especially as the military conscription involving duties so hostile to their religious observances of dress, food, and Sabbath or other festivals, excites their utmost dread'.

Within two months of sending this letter, Consul Finn was instructed by the British Consul-General in Beirut, with the approval of the Russian Consul-General, 'to receive under British Protection all Russian Jews who may apply to you'.

Russian Jews began at once to seek British protection. But complaint was soon made that these Jews, once under British protection, would be converted to Christianity. Consul Finn vehemently denied the charge, which could only have been made, he wrote to the Consul-General in Beirut, by Jews 'ignorant of English character, and so absorbed in bigotry and ignorance that they live apart by themselves, and know nothing of Europeans, but by the hardships they may have met with on their travels from Slavonic peasants and venal postmasters'. Such Jews, Finn added, and there were 'undoubtedly many in the Jewish quarter', spoke 'but few words of any language but corrupt Hebrew, and have all nations and centuries (as Edomites with Italians, the second century with the nineteenth) confounded in their minds'.

Consul Finn did his utmost to educate, and to convert, the Jews. He was supported by Edward Rogers, who had reached Jerusalem in 1848, and was Chancellor of the consulate. A bachelor, in 1855 Rogers brought his sister to Jerusalem to keep house for him.

The consulate's dragoman for Jewish matters was Raphael Minhas, grandson of a former Sephardi Chief Rabbi. The senior dragoman was a Christian Arab, Moosa Tanoos, a Protestant who, although an Ottoman subject, had received British protection on entering the consulate's service in 1848. An extra interpreter was needed at the end of 1849, to deal with the large number of Russian Jews now seeking British protection. These Russian Jews were all

Ashkenazi, Finn explained to Palmerston on 3 December 1849. The Sephardi Jews, for whom he already had Minhas as interpreter, 'disdain to speak, or read, or write in that particular language': Yiddish.

British consular business involved all the communities of the city. In his diary for September 1849 Finn recorded how he took deposition at the bedside of one Abram of Vilna, 'assaulted by the Liefshutz family'. Within two weeks, Edward Rogers had brought against a Muslim Arab 'a charge of stealing fowls from Miriam Mendel' – the wife of Menachem Mendel, the hotel keeper. There was an official complaint to Taib Aga, the Commander of the Turkish troops in Jerusalem, when his men failed to salute a British officer in uniform, Colonel John Gawler, an evangelical Protestant and former Governor of South Australia, who wished to help the Jews to engage in agricultural settlement in Palestine. There was also a complaint to the newly arrived Governor of Jerusalem, Adhem Pasha, for not allowing Finn to enter the Jaffa Gate after nightfall, when the gate was habitually closed.

Miriam Mendel was to be involved in another consular protest that year, when, on the Muslim feast day of Corban Beiram – the Feast of the Sacrifice – a donkey was accidentally shot during a salute by the Citadel guns. On the day after the feast Edward Rogers, in his Chancellor's uniform, visited the Governor to demand measures to prevent a repetition of the incident. Roger's protest did not arise out of concern for the donkey alone. The Consul's wife, Elizabeth Anne Finn, was a friend of Miriam Mendel, who provided kosher bread for the Consul's Jewish employees. Miriam had been on her way towards the Citadel when the salute began. At that moment, a train of donkeys pushed by her, forcing her to the wall. The shot that killed the donkey could well have killed Miriam Mendel, had she not been pushed aside only seconds before.

An uneasy truce existed between Jews like Miriam Mendel and the consulate. There was also the problem of the other Christian consuls, whose subjects too were seen by Finn as potential converts. Indeed, one of his first converts to Anglicanism was an Austrian-born Jew, Mendel Deniss.

Two European diplomats, the Russian Consul-General in Beirut, Constantin Basily, and the Austrian Consul in Jerusalem, Count Pizzamano, immediately protested about the British Consul's missionary success. But although Pizzamano eventually secured proof that Mendel Deniss was an Austrian subject, and thus under the protection of the Austrian Consulate, Deniss converted nevertheless. Later he was employed by another Anglican missionary, Dr Barclay, as his interpreter.

New minaret, built in 1858, overlooking the forecourt and damaged cupolas of the Church of the Holy Sepulchre (Robertson and Beato, 1865).

Local Jewish antagonism to the new convert was considerable. On 28 August 1849, Finn reported to Palmerston 'that numerous Jews had climbed over the neighbouring terraces and roofs, uttering violent menaces'.

In the Christian quarter, progress was marked in 1849 by the establishment of a printing press by the Greek Orthodox: a further stage in the competition, as well of the conflict, between the 'Greeks' and the 'Latins', whose rivalry had become as shocking to the outside Christian visitor as the rivalry of the Ashkenazi and Sephardi Jew appeared to the visiting Jew. Only the Muslims, and especially the leading Muslim families, looked with detached surprise at these Christian and Jewish quarrels, and held aloof from the process, painful to them, of Jerusalem's march forward to the century's mid-point.

CHAPTER III

The 1850s: 'More bustle, and more business'

Throughout 1850 James Finn continued to assert his authority as British Consul. On New Year's Day he received a deputation of Russian Jews, overjoyed at Britain's willingness to act as their protectors, but asking him to delete the words 'Russian subjects' which had been inserted by mistake in some of their documents. They wished, Finn noted in his diary, 'to obliterate all recollection of having ever belonged to Russia', and, on having their request granted, asked 'to have Her Majesty's name in Hebrew', in order to insert it in their prayers.

Six weeks later, a Russian Jew under British protection was passing in the street in front of the Church of the Holy Sepulchre when, as Finn noted, he was 'beaten by a mob of pilgrims rushing on him'. Finn complained to the Governor, insisting 'upon the right of the Jew as well as other people, passing along any street they pleased'. The matter was not satisfactorily resolved, however, 'as it was impossible to bring to justice a whole mob of strangers'. Instead, Finn gave the Jew some money, 'which he could with difficulty be induced to accept'.

That same month there was a second assault in which Finn was involved: the attack by Sheikh Attallah of Silwan and about sixty of his followers on a Jewish funeral procession as it emerged from the Lion Gate. Following Finn's protest, and the Governor's enquiry, it emerged that the men of Silwan had hoped to extort money from the Jewish mourners on their way across the Kidron to the Mount of Olives. The Sheikh having gone down to the river Jordan with a visiting European Princess, Marianna of Holland, 'a horseman was sent to bring him back'.

Sheikh Attallah's compliance arose because Finn, as British Consul, was in the habit of signing formal, and lucrative, contracts with the Arab village

Façade of the Church of the Holy Sepulchre (1880s).

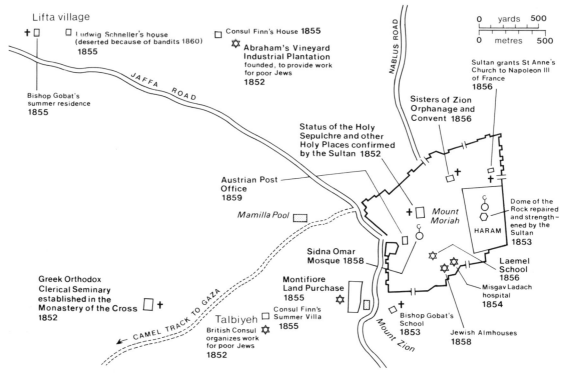

New Muslim ($\substack{g \\ 0}$), Christian (✝) and Jewish (✡) building in Jerusalem in the 1850s.

sheikhs, to act as guides to British pilgrims passing through their areas. To lose such a contract could be a serious financial blow: hence the ability to bring back Attallah with a single emissary. His punishment was a warning: a threat of 'fearful consequences by the Pasha, if he should continue to extort money from the Jews'.

One more such punishment was meted out that spring by Taib Aga, Commander of the Jerusalem garrison, following the stabbing by two Turkish soldiers of Rabbi Joseph Lander more than a year before. Lander was a British Jew who had been living in Jerusalem since 1838. To expedite justice, when delay mounted, Sir Stratford Canning, the British Ambassador at Constantinople, had already protested to the highest military authorities of the Ottoman Empire. Now the two accused, one a private and one a corporal, were paraded outside the Citadel, and marched to Lander's house. There, Finn noted in his diary, the two soldiers 'begged pardon of the family – the private even embraced Lander! Most wonderful! a Turkish solder kissing a Jew while begging his pardon.' Finn noted that this kind of punishment was 'far more efficient for preventing future excesses than imprisonment', especially in view of the general 'good conduct' of Turkish soldiers in the city in the past year.

This 'good conduct' was regarded by Finn as a direct result of Taib Aga's personal efforts. Since Taib Aga had taken 'sole command' of the garrison a year earlier, Finn reported to the British Ambassador at Constantinople on 11 April 1850, 'the soldiers have been remarkable for civil and quiet conduct, so much so as to draw forth frequent expressions of satisfaction from the European residents'.

Consul Finn's authority, like that of the Jerusalem Governor and Military Commander, also extended to Hebron, seven hours south of the city by horseback. There, in August 1850, he had ordered a Muslim to be bastinadoed – beaten on the soles of his bare feet – 'for pulling a Jew's beard and reviling the Consul'. The beating was stopped, however, at the third stroke, 'in consideration of the fanaticism of the place'. Twenty-six years later, Baedeker's guidebook was to write of the Muslims of Hebron that they 'are notorious for their fanaticism, and the traveller should therefore avoid coming into collision with them'.

In November 1850 there was inter-Arab violence both near Hebron and in the Galilee. Near Hebron, the eldest son of the principal local sheikh, Abderrahhman el Amer, had been 'cut to morsels'. The culprit was a rival sheikh, Abd-in Nebi. In response to the killing, Taib Aga at once despatched troops from Jerusalem, explaining to Finn that he had in all 700 infantry and 200 irregular troops under his command. Within two months, Abd-in Nebi had been captured, and was brought to Jerusalem as a prisoner.

While troops from Jerusalem were being used to settle distant Arab feuds, Consul Finn purchased a large plot of land on the low hill just under a mile to the west of Mount Zion: the Talbiyeh estate. Here he was to build a fine house, and to employ a number of Jews in agricultural work. When local Turkish officials protested at his having been allowed to buy this land, Finn sought, and obtained, a letter from the Grand Vizier at Constantinople, giving the Sultan's consent to the purchase of land for a 'summer residence'. At the same time, he encouraged the foundation of a Jerusalem Literary Society, of which he became President.

Finn was in confident mood as 1850 came to an end. Not only were a growing number of Russian Jews turning to him for protection, he had also gained the right, on behalf of Britain, to represent the Abyssinian, Coptic and

Armenian priests.

Armenian churches in all political matters. As the Armenians had previously looked to Russia for protection, this was an important increase in British influence in Jerusalem.

On 29 November 1850 yet another British woman, Matilda Creasy, reached Jerusalem. A teacher and a missionary, she was active, together with Caroline Cooper, in the foundation of the Sarah Society, intended to encourage the conversion of Sephardi Jewesses to Anglican Christianity. Miss Creasy's particular interest lay in teaching the women needlework, and then selling their handicrafts, both to pay them a wage, and to support the expenses of the Society.

Many visitors to Jerusalem remained only a few days, some even less. One such 'brief' visitor was Colonel Hugh Rose, the former Consul-General in Beirut, who was on his way to India to take up a military command. Rose remained in the city for less than twenty-four hours, arriving in the evening of 10 March 1851 and leaving on the following day. But he greatly impressed all those whom he met by the fact that, despite a severe bout of malarial fever, he visited all the senior Turkish officials, played chess with the Military Comman-

One of the streets of Jerusalem (late 1870s).

der, Taib Aga, and 'delighted' Adhem Pasha, the Governor, with a piano recital.

Rose then went on his way: later he was to become Commander-in-Chief of the British Forces in India, and a peer.

Another visitor, H. B. Whitaker Churton, an English vicar, returning on 8 April 1850 for his second visit in three years, and staying for six days, reflected that Jerusalem 'looked more fresh, more cheerful, and less ominous, than when I was here three years since'. But Churton added: 'The streets of poor Jerusalem were still filthy, almost beyond description, mud and deep dirt being added to the usual heaps of human ordure, dung of dogs, sweepings of various filth and dust, that one sees at every angle and corner of frequented as well as unfrequented streets. In the midst of some streets were gutters of filth and offscourings: this is especially the case just below the Holy Sepulchre. Here the stench of raw hides and public privies, &c., are combined.' Nowhere else on his travels, Churton averred, had he seen streets 'abounding in the worst kinds of filth, as the streets and winding lanes of Jerusalem'.

At the English church, on April 14, Churton attended two baptisms, one of a convert's family. A few weeks later, the first Jerusalem-born, as opposed to foreign-born, Jew sought conversion to Christianity, and, in preparation for it, sent his two children to the Protestant school for their education. The Jew's name was Daood Rahhmon, also known as David Rachman. On 19 June 1851 Rachman 'presented himself crying' at the house of the Protestant missionary, John Nicolayson. The story he told was as follows: that Saturday afternoon while walking in the Jewish quarter he had been given a message to go to the Chief Rabbi. On arrival at the Chief Rabbi's house 'he found an assembly of Jews', who immediately shut him in a room until the end of the Sabbath and then brought him before the Chief Rabbi. 'All the Assembly then rose up against him and beat him with sticks, also pipe sticks, without enquiring anything of him.'

Rachman was then taken to the Governor's palace, and imprisoned. On release on the following day he was again taken to the Chief Rabbi's house, and again beaten – '327 blows' – before being imprisoned again. At this second beating, the beaters were not Jews but Turkish soldiers of the Governor's guard.

Consul Finn took up Rachman's case, warning Adhem Pasha 'against allowing your power and influence to be made use of by persons who believe violence and falsehood to be lawful', and who violate 'by means of beating' the benevolent intentions of the Sultan 'in matters of religion'.

Rachman was held in the Governor's prison for three months. The Jewish community offered him release on condition that he renounced all intention to convert to Christianity. Rachman refused. Consul Finn continued to champion the would-be convert's cause, and did so successfully: Rachman was released, and then baptized. Later, Finn fought a long battle with the rabbinical authorities to allow Rachman's wife and children to live with him: they, for some years, were forcibly prevented from joining him. But eventually Finn was successful.

On 7 November 1851 a Jew, Abram ben Gershon, disappeared. Rewards were offered, but after four weeks there was still no sign, or news, of him. Searches began, including one in the hostel for Indian Muslim pilgrims in the north-east of the Muslim quarter. The search then turned to the quarter of the Moghrabi, between the Jewish quarter and the Wailing Wall. A Jew named Mercado had suggested that the searchers look at a house there, belonging to a Muslim, Mohammed Damiati. Consul Finn, who led the search, recorded in his diary: 'after ransacking every corner and even ripping open cushions in search of small items of property belonging to Gershon – but in vain – the Consul left the party to prosecute the search through every house in that quarter while he returned to finish letters for the Post'. Before this letter-writing was finished a consular servant came to announce that the corpse of Abram Gershon had been found in a well, fully clothed.

As soon as he had finished his correspondence, Finn went down to the well, 'which is in the plantations of prickly pears between the Temple Wall and the Jewish quarter'. A great crowd, he wrote, 'was assembled, and the roof of the Jewish houses on Zion were crowded. The corpse was brought up and found to have been wounded in several places near the ribs – the heart and throat were stabbed – the body not discoloured though somewhat swollen, and the stench truly horrible.'

Damiati was duly tried by the new Turkish Governor, Hafiz Ahmed Pasha, but was released, 'the Pasha being unable', Finn recorded, 'to detain him any longer on mere suspicion of murder'.

Each year, at Easter, the friction between the local Arab Christians and the Christian pilgrims could explode into physical violence. Each year, therefore, the European consuls, who were responsible for the safety of the pilgrims, would ask for Turkish soldiers to keep the local Christians at bay while the principal pilgrim churches were holding their services. On the eve of the festivities in 1852, Consul Finn noted in his diary a visit to the Governor to discuss among other matters 'the military force for Good Friday in the Church'.

To enhance the work of converting Jerusalem's Jews to Christianity, an Englishwoman, Miss Cook of Cheltenham, had donated the enormous sum of ten thousand pounds for the endowment of a 'House of Industry' outside the city. This sum was the value of a thousand camels, or two thousand oxen fit for ploughing.

Four separate projects were developed with Miss Cook's money: a farm at Artas, south of Bethlehem, under the control of John Meshullam, the English Sephardic Jew who had converted to Christianity and settled in Palestine in 1842; Consul Finn's estate at Talbiyeh where Jews were trained to cut stone; the house inside the Old City where, under Miss Cooper and Miss Creasy, 150 Jewish women were taught needlework; and Abraham's Vineyard, a farm a mile north-west of the Jaffa Gate, turned into an 'industrial plantation', and employing by 1855 more than 600 Jews in various agricultural pursuits.

Also under Anglican auspices, a hospital inside the city walls provided for

Jewish stonemasons at Abraham's Vineyard (1906).

all sick Jews, whether potential converts or not, and gave those who wished it kosher meat and bread. The rabbis had, however, 'forbidden' observant Jews to have anything to do with Finn, Meshullam, Miss Cooper or Miss Creasy, so that only those Jews who were at the extreme of poverty or destitution accepted their hospital beds, or agreed to work in their institutions.

The thousand or so Jews working at Abraham's Vineyard, the Talbiyeh estate, Artas, or the needlework school were considered by the rabbis, and by most other Jews in the city, to have already deserted their religion. Treated as pariahs, they were frequently assaulted in the streets. Although Finn himself denied that any attempt was made to convert those working in the four institutions, he did mix already converted Jews with the newcomers, in the hope that the newcomers might be taught to accept Christianity.

Five random entries in Finn's diary for 1852 give a flavour of the year:

March 15: 'Settled in an amicable manner a quarrel between an English Jew and a Turkish subject who struck each other in the Street.'

March 23: 'A Mossulman appeared in the office and complained of an English Jew – who had hired his donkey to Rachel's tomb and returned without it. A few hours afterwards the donkey was found ...'.

April 10: 'Some skirmishing between Greeks and Armenians at the Holy Fire. It is said some persons were trampled and stifled.'

April 23: 'Quarrel in the Abyssinian Convent of a few days ago attended to.'

May 15: 'The little Jewish tailor from Warsaw imprisoned for refusing to support his wife or restore her clothes.' Four days later the tailor was released on agreeing to return his wife's property to her.

In 1852 an American physician, Dr James Barclay, reached Jerusalem, not as a missionary or as a tourist, but as a guest of the Turkish authorities. He had been invited to Jerusalem to make suggestions for the repair of Muslim religious buildings in the city. In the course of his examination of the buildings to be repaired, Barclay made several archaeological discoveries. The most important of these was his identification of a huge lintel stone at the women's section of the Wailing Wall as the top of what had once been a gate leading to the Temple courtyard. This stone became known, and is still known today, as Barclay's Gate.

On 28 April 1852, another American, Edward Robinson, entered Jerusalem, the city in which he had first set foot fourteen years earlier. Just outside the Jaffa Gate, he noted, 'a long narrow structure had been erected against the wall, in which were coffee-houses'. This small change was symptomatic of far larger ones, the reason for which, Robinson noted, was the 'powerful foreign influence' brought in since the establishment of the Anglo-Prussian bishopric, and he went on to explain how: 'The erection of the Protestant cathedral on Mount Zion, as part and parcel of the English consulate; the opening of the Jewish hospital also on Zion, under the auspices of the English mission; and likewise of the Prussian hospital under the care of the German "deaconesses" so called; the establishment of schools and the introduction of agricultural labour in connection with them; all had served to increase the circulation of money, and to stimulate the native mind to like efforts. The convents had erected several large buildings, and established schools; and there was a process going on in Jerusalem, of tearing down old dwellings and replacing them by new ones, which reminded me somewhat of New York. There were at this time more houses undergoing this transformation in the Holy City, than I had seen the year before in six of the principal cities of Holland. As a natural result, there was more activity in the streets; there were more people in motion, more bustle, and more business.'

The buttress of Robinson's Arch, curving out from the Herodian masonry of the Temple Mount, a photograph taken in 1984. In 1852 the arch was at ground level.

Robinson stayed in Jerusalem for twelve days, visiting each day several biblical and archaeological sites. Like Barclay before him, he also identified an arch, then at ground level, as one of the ancient bridges linking the Temple Mount with the western slope of the Tyropaean valley: the arch known today as 'Robinson's Arch'.

While in Jerusalem, Robinson lodged in the Bruderhaus, the missionary residence established in 1846 by Swiss Protestants. In his diary for April 29 he noted: 'The general idea was, that, living here together unmarried, and teaching native youths mechanical arts and trades in connection with religious instruction, they might gain the confidence of the people and exert an influence as Christians, both by precept and example. But their hopes had not been fulfilled; and three of the brethren had already left and gone into other employments, where they might labour more effectively, and without the restraint of celibacy. One of them was now connected with the English schools, and another with the English farm. The one who remained, Mr Muller, our host, was from the Schwarzwald; and had the simple piety of southern Germany, as well as the mechanical skill of his native region. He had two or three Arab boys in his

Russian pilgrims at the Monastery of the Cross (before 1914).

workshop below; while the large upper rooms were hired out. He too seemed to have the conviction, that he could probably labour to more purpose in some other sphere.'

Notwithstanding the 'appearance of change', Robinson concluded, 'Jerusalem is still in all its features an oriental city; in its closeness and filth, in its stagnation and moral darkness.'

Stern words: but for those who had to live in the city there was much being done, unspectacular but part of the slow process of spiritual as well as physical growth. In 1852 the Greek Orthodox Church established a seminary for priests in the venerable Monastery of the Cross, a mile and a half to the west of the Jaffa Gate, deep in an undulating valley.

In search of biblical sites and echoes, Arthur Stanley, a distinguished churchman and geographer, reached Jerusalem in the early months of 1852, travelling from the Sinai desert. The old city itself, he wrote '– and I felt a constant satisfaction in the thought – lies buried twenty, thirty, forty feet below these wretched shops and receptacles for Anglo-Oriental conveniences'. From whatever vantage point one looked at the city, Stanley added, one was struck 'by the grey ruinous masses of which it is made up; it is the ruin, in fact, of the old Jerusalem on which you look, – the stones, the columns – the very soil on which you tread is the accumulation of nearly three thousand years'.

Stanley was equally impressed, as Lieutenant Lynch had been, by the view over the city from the Mount of Olives. Looking down on the Mosque of Omar and the Haram he felt 'almost disposed to console myself for the exclusion by the additional interest which the sight derives from the knowledge that no European foot, except by stealth or favour, had ever trodden within these precincts since the Crusaders were driven out, and that their deep seclusion was as real as it appeared. It needed no sight of the daggers of the black Dervishes who stand at the gates, to tell you that the Mosque was undisturbed and inviolably sacred.'

In 1856, as Canon of Christ Church, Stanley published the most popular of all the British books on the lands of the Bible, *Sinai and Palestine in connection with their history*, which was to be re-issued almost every year for more than fifty years. In it, his description of the visual aspect of Jerusalem in 1852 was of 'a city of ruins'. Stanley went on to describe how 'Here and there a regular street, or a well-built European house emerges from the general crush, but the general appearance is that of a city which has been burnt down in some great conflagration; and this impression is increased to the highest degree when, on penetrating below the surface, the very soil on which the city stands is found to be composed of ruins of houses, aqueducts, and pillars, reaching to a depth of thirty or forty feet below the foundations of the present houses. This circumstance is important, not only as imparting to the city its remarkable form and colour, but also as telling the story of its eventful course.' The 'old Jerusalem', Stanley added, 'is buried in the overthrow of her seventeen captures'.

Long after this description had ceased to be an accurate reflection of the city's appearance, it was the most widely read and most frequently recalled, fixing in the public mind an exaggerated scene of desolation.

In February 1852 the Ottoman Government issued two decrees in Constantinople, one of which guaranteed the rights of the Latin Church in Jerusalem, the other guaranteeing the privileges of the Greek Church, concerning their respective access to, and control over, the Holy Places. Trapped in their own rivalries, neither Latins nor Greeks were satisfied by these decrees, so much so that the French Ambassador in Constantinople had to obtain a third decree, declaring that neither Church had any 'exclusive right' to the Holy Places, but that the Latins were to have 'custody' of the key of the Church of the Nativity at Bethlehem.

The Greek Orthodox Church protested. The Russian Government, declaring the Tsar to be the protector of Orthodox Christianity, took up their protest. Early in the New Year of 1853, two Russian army corps were sent to the Turkish frontier, and the Russian Government announced its claim for a Russian 'protectorate' over the Greek Orthodox Christians in the Ottoman Empire. Rejecting this demand, the Sultan appealed to Britain and France for protection against Russia. Negotiations began, then broke down. The issues and conflicts widened, European rivalries intensified, and in March 1853 Russia invaded Turkey. The British and French fleets, now in alliance with Turkey, entered the Black Sea, and landed troops on Russian soil: on the Crimean peninsula. The Crimean War had begun. It ended with the Anglo-French capture of the Crimean port of Sebastopol, and the destruction of the Russian fleet.

Russian claims for a protectorate over the Holy Places in Jerusalem were abandoned. Instead, the Ottoman authorities, 'victors' in the war, agreed to allocate specific sites to specific denominations, with the most important sites, including the Holy Sepulchre, to be used by all denominations in common, each with its own chapel, or portion of a tomb or relic. Turkish guardians were to maintain order, and to see that one Church did not 'encroach' on the sites or chapels of another.

In the summer of 1853 the environs of Jerusalem echoed with gunfire. This was no Russian army about to win a spectacular victory in the Crimean War, but rival Arab tribes in contention for disputed lands. East of the city, the Sheikh of Abu Ghosh was challenging Osman Lehham over the ownership of the village of Ain Karem – the supposed birthplace of John the Baptist. Some of Osman Lehham's men entered the Talbiyeh estate of Consul Finn, in order to fire at their rivals from behind the consular wall.

West of the city, the Sheikh of Silwan was fighting with one of his rivals. 'Shouts of summons over the hills among the peasantry,' Finn recorded in his diary on 19 July 1853, and six days later he complained to the Hafiz Ahmed Pasha about the anarchic state of affairs so near to the city. On August 4 the Sheikh of Abu Ghosh called on Finn to tell him that the quarrel was resolved: 'a truce of three months had been made', Hafiz Ahmed Pasha 'had made Osman and him kiss each other' and agree that the fought-over village was to be 'put in repair', and 'all was likely', so the Sheikh declared, 'to end well'.

Silwan village and the Kidron valley (Francis Bedford, 2 March 1862). Lower left, the tomb-stones of the Jewish cemetery.

In 1853 the painter William Bartlett returned to Jerusalem, to work on a second book, *Jerusalem Revisited*. His book completed, and having been sent to the printer, on 20 June 1853 he left Jerusalem for the last time, and was on board ship between Malta and Marseilles when he died. Bartlett was buried at sea. His new book was published posthumously in 1855.

For Jerusalem, one unfortunate repercussion of the war between Russia and Turkey continued to be the increased courage of the Bedouin, once regular troops had been sent to the Russian frontier of the Ottoman Empire. On 12 September 1853 Consul Finn reported to the Earl of Clarendon in London that, two weeks earlier, on 31 August, the Tiyaha Bedouin had felt sufficiently free to pass by 'the very walls of Jerusalem'.

Nor was this a mere innocent passage on their way from the Negev to their grazing lands east of the Jordan river. For several days the Tiyaha had 'subsisted by violence' in the villages around Jerusalem. Three hundred tribesmen had 'slept and fed' in Bethlehem, eighty in Beit Jala, seventy in Beit Sahhur, and some in Abu Ghosh, on the road to Jaffa. Fifty of these Bedouin, Finn had noted in his diary on September 1, 'came into Jerusalem yesterday to have their horses shod'.

In his diary, Finn was in the habit of referring to the Bedouin as 'the wild Arabs'. During the disturbances Elizabeth Finn saw women among the warrior bands. On asking Hhamdan, the Sheikh of the Taamri Bedouin, if the presence of women would not lessen the ferocity of the fighting, the Sheikh replied: 'On the contrary, the women do not go unless it is to be a bad fight, to encourage the fighters and carry ammunition.' It being 'wrong to hurt a woman', Hhamdan added, 'the men will get behind their wives and rest their gun on her shoulder when they fire'.

Two years earlier, Finn had signed a formal contract with Hhamdan for the safe conduct of travellers on the way from Jerusalem to Petra. This contract had been honoured, and travellers on this remote and difficult journey went unmolested. When, earlier in 1853, the Arabs of Abu Dis and Silwan had proved unreliable as escorts between Jerusalem and the river Jordan, Finn appointed Hhamdan as 'guide to Jordan'.

On 9 December 1853 a Scottish missionary, James Graham, reached Jerusalem as Lay Superintendent of the Jewish Mission. Graham was yet another of those who believed that the work to be done in Jerusalem was, as Consul Finn believed, the conversion of the Jews, as opposed to the anglicanization of Arab Christians, as urged by Bishop Gobat. As well as being a missionary, Graham was an amateur photographer and astronomer, and would often spend the night atop a tower on the Mount of Olives.

Graham remained in Jerusalem for four years. On this return home, he published a stern attack on the inefficiency, and indeed immoral conduct, of Bishop Gobat's school, established in 1853 on the western slope of Mount Zion.

To help him at the Anglican bishopric, Bishop Gobat had appointed as his 'attaché' Joseph Dupuis, formerly British Vice-Consul in Tripoli and Tunis. Dupuis spent two years in the city, and on his return to England, published two volumes of recollections. Not only to 'its dispersed children', he wrote, but to all who saw 'modern Jerusalem', there was nothing to do but to mourn 'what scarcely can be considered a shadow of the sacred city and temple, or but the shadow of a shade, as compared with the magnificence of the original metropolis of Judaea during the reign of Solomon ...'. But although Jerusalem, added Dupuis, 'is now shorn of its vitality, its halo can never be extinguished'.

Dupuis, like Bartlett five years before him, was depressed by what he saw.

Top left: the Hinnom valley, walls of Jerusalem, and Bishop Gobat's school (Captain Wilson, 1865). *Top right:* Bishop Gobat's school (1984). *Above left:* entrance to Bishop Gobat's school (1984). *Above right:* inside Bishop Gobat's school, the doorway window (1984).

'If there is beauty in Jerusalem or in the hills immediately surrounding the city,' he wrote, 'this beauty can only be conjured into life by the force of imagination, amidst silence and decay within, and a scanty growth of vegetation on the hills more or less barren and rocky, and always dreary, without the walls.'

Under the 'supine sway' of Muslim government, Dupuis commented, everything is allowed to fall into ruin 'for want of timely reparation'. The Governor and his chief officials, 'considering themselves but birds of passage, as it were, from one command to another, and their emoluments being but small, concern themselves with little besides the temporary arrangement and superficial embellishments of those portions of the public buildings which their families may require during the term of their jurisdiction in the country' – about three years.

'Of the Muslims of Jerusalem, Dupuis noted that they were made up almost equally of 'Ottoman Turks, Arabians, Syrians, Egyptians, and other Africans': the Christians of Greeks, Latins, and Armenians. The Armenians, although second to the Greeks in number, 'far exceed them in wealth and influence'. The Muslims were 'unquestionably the most numerous class', except at Christmas and Easter, when Christians 'outnumber for a time the lords of the soil' and turn Jerusalem, 'this metropolis of many rival faiths' into 'a crowded fair'. As for the Jews, 'Jerusalem', wrote Dupuis, 'is the centre around which the Jew builds in airy dreams the mansions of his future greatness. Thither he returns from Spain, Portugal, Germany, Bombay etc, after all his toilings and all his struggles up the steps of life, to walk the streets of his own happy Zion.'

Dupuis noted how, in Jerusalem, all Jews adopted 'the costume of the country' with one exception, 'the Polish Jew, who adheres with nervous pertinacity to his fur-mounted cap of the snowy region'. Dupuis also saw Jews at work in Abraham's Vineyard, Consul Finn's newly established farm to the north of the city. 'On one occasion', Dupuis wrote, 'I witnessed about forty Jews engaged in clearing a field, which had been purchased, or leased, by some society at home, and these Jews were employed to work the land by the English Consul, in order to afford some relief, however partial, to their exigencies. They appeared very thankful, and willing to work for the trifling wages given them. A more interesting sight, among sights in Palestine, could not have been witnessed, than once more to behold these people working and tilling that land which ratified the covenant between God and man: this was a revival of field labour after the lapse of so many ages marked by destruction, dispersion, and desolation of every kind.'

Joseph Dupuis, an Anglican, had been impressed by the sight of working Jews at Abraham's Vineyard. He had been less impressed by the 'intolerance' of the Greek and Roman Catholic Churches towards the Jews: in these two Churches, he wrote, one could not find 'a single spark of genial feeling'.

In the Anglican Mission, the work of conversion continued calmly and methodically: on 22 September 1853 Consul Finn was able to report to London that the congregation at Christ Church, Jerusalem, included thirty-two adult Jewish converts, and twenty-seven converted children.

On 17 December 1853 the Governor of Jerusalem, Hafiz Ahmed Pasha, left Jerusalem to return to Constantinople. Old and sick, he was carried from the city in a palanquin. To mark his departure, a sixteen-gun salute was fired at the Citadel. One of the guns misfired, blowing off the arm of a Turkish artilleryman. The outgoing Governor reached Jaffa, but went no further, dying in the port on 14 January 1854. Jerusalem, yet again, awaited a new Governor.

In 1854 the first photographs were taken in Jerusalem by Auguste Salzmann, working for an archaeologist friend, Louis Félicien de Saulcy, who wanted photographic evidence to use in helping him date stone walls and ancient buildings. That same year, John Murray of London published the first 'handbook for travellers' in the Holy Land. But it was in New York that the most outspoken description of life in Jerusalem was published that year, by Karl Marx, in an article in the *New York Daily Tribune* on 15 April 1854. 'Nothing', wrote Marx, 'equals the misery and the sufferings of the Jews at Jerusalem, inhabiting the most filthy quarter of the town, called hareth-el-yahoud, in the quarter of dirt, between the Zion and the Moriah, where their synagogues are situated – the constant object of Mussulman oppression and intolerance, in-sulted by the Greeks, persecuted by the Latins, and living only upon the scanty alms transmitted by their European brethren.'

Marx also gave his readers an account of the distribution of people in the city. 'The sedentary population of Jerusalem', he told his readers, 'numbers about 15,500 souls, of whom 4,000 are Mussulmans and 8,000 Jews. The Mussulmans forming about a fourth part of the whole, and consisting of Turks, Arabs and Moors, are, of course, the masters in every respect.'

A growing number of Jews had received British protection. On 23 March 1854 Consul Finn reported to London that there were 190 British-protected families in Jerusalem, thirty-three in Safed, nineteen in Hebron, and sixteen in Tiberias: the majority being Russian-born Jews, a few, Jews from Algiers. But despite the efforts of the missionaries, most Jews clung tenaciously to their

The Ecce Homo arch (Auguste Salzmann, 1854).

faith. As Edward MacGowan wrote in his missionary letter for 1854, 'the traditional feeling which draws the Jews of Jerusalem, affecting though it be as a national feature of their character, has been allowed to operate, unchecked, to a lamentable extent, and hundreds of the poor descendants of Jacob, annually make their way to the Holy Land, where nothing but misery and starvation awaits them'.

As well as continued Jewish immigration, the year 1854 saw an enhancement of the authority of Jerusalem, when the provincial authority for the Gaza district was transferred from the Turkish Governor of the coastal town of Sidon to the Governor of Jerusalem. This administrative change, decided upon at Constantinople, extended Jerusalem's control over the Bedouin tribes of the Negev desert, then at the end of a long period of bitter and at times bloody rivalry. For the previous ten years, this rivalry had made the overland journey from Jerusalem to the desert and monasteries of Sinai a virtual impossibility for European pilgrims and travellers.

On 16 March 1854 Hafiz Ahmed Pasha's successor as Governor entered the city. He was a leading Turkish nobleman, Yakoob Pasha, bearing the right to fly an ensign of three horses' tails, and as such, the equal of the usually more senior Governor of Beirut. This augured well for Jerusalem. But Yakoob Pasha was eighty-four years old, ailing, and with a passion for bribery unusual even by Ottoman standards.

One of the new Governor's first acts was to purchase a house from some Jewish owners, in order to fit up the extra premises for his coming harem, and also for the prison cells which he set up below his living quarters.

Yakoob Pasha's authority extended to the weekly, Wednesday, despatch of the Turkish post. To the surprise of many citizens, and the annoyance of some, one Wednesday he summarily dismissed the postal clerks, and forbade any further postal work to be done. He had, he explained, consulted astrologers, as was his habit, and they had informed him that that particular Wednesday was 'unlucky'. Shortly before another such 'unlucky' Wednesday, Yakoob Pasha sent the post off a day early, to the even greater inconvenience of those commercial and consular users dependent upon a regular weekly service.

Consul Finn's diary for 1854 records the daily incidents of Jerusalem life: a consular guard – a Muslim – sent to Hebron 'to stop ill-treatment of the Jews'; a Jew, Hhaiim Faivitch Rubinstein, 'complaining against a Greek for 60 piastres' – the cost of a sheep; a Muslim imprisoned 'for beating some Abyssinians'; and a Jewish convert to Christianity, Simon Betman, appearing in the

The Citadel, David's tower, and Turkish troops of the Jerusalem garrison (before 1914).

consulate, 'his face covered with blood', having been beaten by an observant Jew, Ruben Grunstein.

In April 1854 Finn recorded the 'great uproar' when a British visitor, Colonel West, was assaulted by a Turkish soldier, after West had complained that two other soldiers had jostled his wife. West, in protest, struck the soldier with his cane, and then followed him to the barracks, accompanied by 'numerous English travellers'. The soldier who assaulted West was sentenced to fifteen days in prison. The two other soldiers were sentenced to a week each. 'All our people satisfied,' Finn noted in his diary on April 9, and on April 10: 'Colonel West consented to mitigate the punishment of the soldiers.'

In June, Finn had to arbitrate between the two main Jewish groups in the city. As he explained in his diary: 'A deputation of the Sephardim came to complain that the Ashkenazim were not willing to divide the money sent by Montefiore in the manner he directed.' Both sides agreed to obey Finn's decision. Montefiore, himself a Sephardi, was married to an Ashkenazi, and had always been emphatic, in all his charitable donations in Jerusalem, that both communities should benefit equally.

Even while the question of how to divide Montefiore's charities was being brought to Christian arbitration, evil times fell upon Jerusalem's Jews: at least those of Russian birth. For since the outbreak of the Crimean War in March 1854, and the beginning of Turkish hostilities with Russia, all links with their Russian brethren, and with the Russian Jewish charities on which they were so dependent, had been cut.

To alleviate the distress in Jerusalem, Jacob Covo, the Sephardi Chief Rabbi since 1848, decided, despite a grave illness, to go personally to western Europe to appeal for funds. No Chief Rabbi had ever before travelled in search of charity. But the hour seemed desperate. Hardly had he reached Alexandria, however, than Rabbi Covo died. The Jews now turned, for the first time, to Consul Finn, and in their poverty, accepted food from the hated missionaries.

After Rabbi Covo's death, other Jews set off for western Europe, and for the United States, in search of far greater aid than the missionaries could provide. This western quest was to have an immediate impact on the nature of Jewish life: for whereas Russian Jews tended to send money to support religious institutions, and a life of prayer and study, western Jews were more concerned with the setting up of hospitals, and schools for the education of children in 'useful' trades and professions.

This transformation began within four months of the start of the Crimean

War, and can be dated with precision: the arrival in Jerusalem on 11 July 1854 of an Austrian Jew, Albert Cohn, then a member of the Jewish Consistoral Committee in Paris. Cohn came, as Consul Finn noted in his diary that day, 'to distribute relief, establish institutions for the distressed Jews'.

Albert Cohn brought with him to Jerusalem funds provided by the French Rothschild family. His plans included an industrial school for boys, a school for girls, a special low-interest lending fund on pledges, a means of poor-relief for women, and the distribution of bread to the poor twice a week.

Within fifteen days of Cohn's arrival in Jerusalem, the most ambitious of all his schemes was ready to be launched: the inauguration on 26 July 1854 of a Jewish hospital in the Jewish quarter. Known at first as the Rothschild, and later as the Misgav Ladach, hospital, its foundation marked a major step on the road to modernity for the Jews of Jerusalem. Henceforth, they were not to be, as hitherto, dependent on Christian hospitals, Christian doctors, and the inevitable missionary hopes which these represented.

The Jewish hospital, inaugurated in 1854.

A second result of the Crimean War was the British Government's willingness to use its increased influence at Constantinople, as Turkey's military ally, to insist upon the issuing of the necessary decree for the rebuilding of the Ashkenazi synagogue in Jerusalem: the ruined Hurva.

Not only the British-protected Jews but the remaining Ashkenazi Jews of Jerusalem were able to turn for support to the British consulate. On 13 July 1854, two days after Albert Cohn's arrival in Jerusalem with Jewish funds for

Jewish institutions, Consul Finn wrote to the British Ambassador in Constantinople: 'I have the honour to present a Petition from the Ashkenazim Jews in Jerusalem, with whose affairs I am well informed, and beg to recommend their request for a favourable issue.' Finn added: 'It is a sad circumstance that these numerous people, above 2,000 souls, have not even one synagogue in Jerusalem – for although the Sephardim Jews (being mostly Orientals and Turkish Subjects) have synagogues, they have their ritual books and their pronunciation of Hebrew different from these: besides that there is always a considerable amount of bickering existing between the two Sects. – And the Sephardim have no more space in their Synagogues than they require for themselves.'

The petitioners, Finn explained, 'are almost exclusively natives of Europe; but it is to be observed that even among the Sephardim, many are foreigners likewise, from Africa, Italy, Persia, &c. Yet these have their Synagogues.'

In recommendation of the petition, Finn wrote, 'I may remark that a considerable number of the Community in whose name the Rabbis have signed, are Russians, retaining a keen sense of the cruelties they have endured in that country, and who are happy to find here not only their religious centre, but the liberty which the Turkish government affords in these days. They would of course feel a great increase of gratitude if their synagogues be allowed – and this gratitude would tell upon their relations still detained in Russia.'

It also seemed 'very probable' to Finn that on the Turkish recovery of their lost Danubian provinces, 'as the Allied army approaches the Russian frontier many more Jews will escape from that territory to Palestine'. As for the need for an Ashkenazi synagogue, Finn commented, 'the experience of the past shews that if exclusively Turkish formalities be required in this business, they will amount to a denial of the Petition'.

The funds for the new synagogue, the Ashkenazi Jews explained to Finn, had been collected by Sir Moses Montefiore twelve years before. At the same time, a 150-year-old decree, signed by the Sultan, had been found, authorizing the Ashkenazi Jews to repair their ruined synagogue. This was sent to Constantinople as proof of the petitioners' rights. In Constantinople, Sir Moses Montefiore added his personal plea for permission to rebuild.

In June 1854 the British painter, Holman Hunt, set off from Cairo to Jerusalem, entering Jerusalem, he wrote, 'to the sound of savage music and shouting'. Exhausted, he and his friend goaded their mules through the tumult to the monastery recommended by the Consul in Cairo. On the Consul's advice,

Hunt had already invested in a second pistol and a double-barrelled gun, hoping to look 'mature and forbidding'.

'I walked about the walls and up the Mount of Olives,' Hunt wrote. 'The view was wild, barren, and diaphanous, like a vision of the surface of the moon.'

Despite the indolence of his servants, Hunt was entranced by Jerusalem. On 3 June 1854 he wrote to a friend in London: 'I can't at all understand what is said of the unhealthiness of this city. The air is the most delicious I ever breathed. Timid precautions such as the avoidance of fruit and the like are laughed at.' Hunt added: 'When the absurd notion of the danger of this climate is corrected many English people will immigrate here instead of to bleak un-interesting places such as Australia. When I turn farmer I shall bring my mother and father and sisters here, and keep a flock of camels, and grow artichokes and palm trees.'

One of those who had seen Hunt at work in Jerusalem was the Reverend J. L. Porter, who later wrote of Hunt's painting, the 'Finding of Christ in the Temple': 'The conclave of Jewish rabbis, sitting there in mute astonishment before the Divine Boy, are all of them life portraits, painted on the spot. In one of them I easily recognized my Jewish guide, who took me through many a line and with many a horse among his people on Mount Zion.'

In Jerusalem, in August 1854, a Turkish gunner on the Citadel turned one of his guns round and, firing as if a routine salute, broke the windows in the Anglican church, and struck the Consul's residence. Finn, his wife and their young daughter were at their Talbiyeh house, fortunately so, for their daughter's crib was struck in the shooting. By order of the Major in charge of the Citadel, the culprit was punished.

In October 1854 it was the turn of the orthodox Jews to be distressed, when some Europeans in the city opened up the entrance to a rock tomb among the ancient tombs in the Kidron valley. Finn recorded in his diary the 'great distress' of those Jews who objected to any digging, even for archaeological purposes, at a tomb or cemetery.

Early in the New Year of 1855 there was an incident at Rachel's tomb, on the road to Bethlehem, when Sheikh Hhamdan of the Taamri Bedouin, with sword drawn, extorted money from Jews visiting the site.

The events of 1855 followed the usual pattern: on February 14 an Ashkenazi Jew accused a Turkish irregular soldier of breaking his watch and pulling his beard: the soldier was sent to his officer to be punished. On the following day

Above: the Dome of the Rock, or Mosque of Omar, and part of the Temple Mount, or Holy Sanctuary, with, far right, the Jewish quarter (two photographs taken by Francis Bedford on 6 April 1862). *Right:* a print captioned: 'Telescopic peep at the Haram' (1855).

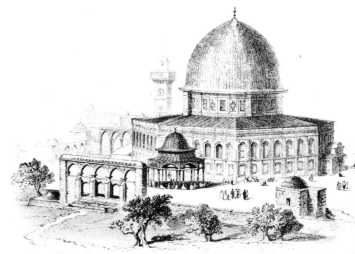

the new Governor arrived, the third in four years. He was Kiamil Pasha, a liberal Turk in his early twenties, pro-British, and in later years, at Constantinople, four times Grand Vizier of the Empire.

In March Kiamil Pasha welcomed the Duke and Duchess of Brabant to Jerusalem. They had come for a nine-day visit. The Duke, the eldest son of King Leopold of the Belgians, succeeded his father as King in 1865, and, as Leopold II, reigned until 1909. The Duchess being a Habsburg, the details of the ducal visit were handled by the Austrian Consul, Count Pizzamano, who arranged for them to enter the 'mosque' of Omar, or Dome of the Rock, and the Al-Aksa mosque: the first time that the Muslim authorities had allowed non-Muslims to enter the Haram.

Permission for this break with precedent had come direct from the Sultan. To ensure that Islamic fervour did not prevent the Duke and Duchess from entry at the last moment, Kiamal Pasha placed the Muslim guards of the Dome under temporary arrest.

The Duke and Duchess did not enter the Haram alone. Using to the full the Sultan's authority for non-Muslims to see the Dome, the royal couple were accompanied by all the European consuls in the city, and by many European travellers who happened to be visiting on that day, among them a Scottish peer, Lord Napier of Ettrick, and his wife.

On the last day of June 1855 Jerusalem received its noblest Christian visitor since the time of the Crusades, Archduke Ferdinand Maximilian of Austria. The Archduke stayed for three days, and, armed as the Duke and Duchess of Brabant had been with the Sultan's permission, entered the Haram on July 1. The Archduke was only 23 years old, but was at the time of his visit the heir presumptive to the Habsburg throne. A Vice-Admiral in the Austrian navy, he had come to Jerusalem with the officers of his flag-ship. Later, he was to be elected Emperor of Mexico, and to die at the hand of an assassin.

In July 1855, a Muslim Arab from Silwan stabbed a Jewish woman in the face. He was caught, put in irons and imprisoned for eighteen days. A week later Sir Moses Montefiore arrived: it was his fourth visit to the city since 1827. Now aged 70, he came with a document from the Sultan, authorizing the rebuilding of the Hurva synagogue, and with two letters from the Grand Vizier, one to permit the Jews of Jerusalem to engage, as Jews, in agricultural pursuits, the other to build a Jewish hospital. The design for the hospital had been prepared by the British architects Papworth and Alison, in mock-Gothic style, then much in favour.

Design for a new Jewish hospital (1855).

Once more, Montefiore camped outside the city, his tents being pitched just beyond the north-east corner of the walls, his arrival being greeted by the populace 'by continually firing off guns and pistols as a sort of *feu de joie*'.

As well as the Sultan's permission to help his fellow Jews, Montefiore had also obtained authorization for a personal visit to the Haram: the third such authorization from the Sultan within three months of something hitherto not only forbidden, but dangerous in the extreme.

Carried in a Sedan chair, Montefiore was taken up to the Haram on 26 July 1855. Orthodox Jews were outraged, since by tradition no Jew should set foot on the site of the former Holy of Holies. But Montefiore did not enter the Dome itself, nor, as he remained throughout in his sedan chair, did he actually 'set foot' on the Temple Mount. As a mark of piety, on being carried up the steps to the Mount, Montefiore recited Psalm 121: 'I will lift up mine eyes unto the hills, from whence cometh my help.'

The Muslim guards showed no hostility to this extraordinary act by a Jew. Perhaps, as Elizabeth Finn believed, the recent visits by the Duke of Brabant and Archduke Maximilian had dulled their sense of outrage. But on the Jewish cemetery on the Mount of Olives, while Montefiore was still in the city, Muslim Arabs from the village of Silwan opened fifteen graves, and took the tomb-stones for building a new house in their village. Kiamil Pasha ordered an immediate enquiry.

Montefiore brought with him on this visit of 1855 the largest charitable funds yet provided for the Jews for Jerusalem, as well as for agricultural villages near Tiberias, Safed and Jaffa: a total of eleven thousand pounds. The money had been raised in England by the Ashkenazi Chief Rabbi of Great Britain, Nathan Marcus Adler, who in the same year established the London Jews' College, a joint Ashkenazi–Sephardi venture to train English-speaking rabbis in Jewish secular subjects, and to educate Jewish boys in a Jewish secondary school.

Adler and Montefiore both saw education, whether in London or Jerusalem, as the cornerstone for a future Jewish life in the modern world. Unfortunately for them, there were greater prejudices in Jerusalem than in London. In Jerusalem, many of the Eastern European and Russian Jews opposed Montefiore's plan for the establishment of schools for two reasons: because girls would be admitted, and because non-religious subjects would be taught. Only the Sephardi Chief Rabbinate showed itself sympathetic to these proposals.

So hostile could some Ashkenazi Jews be towards Montefiore's charities that one Russian Jew was imprisoned during Montefiore's visit for 'insult and violence' to Sir Moses himself. Only Montefiore's personal intervention secured the man's release from prison on the day after his arrest.

Montefiore's visit of 1855 gave rise to extravagant rumours. Many of the poorer Jews believed that his wealth was sufficient to solve all their problems for all time. The main achievement of the visit was the permission which he had been given by the Sultan to purchase land. Only Consul Finn, among Europeans, had hitherto received permission to own land in Jerusalem.

The land chosen by Montefiore was on the shore facing Mount Zion, several hundred yards nearer to the city than Finn's Talbiyeh property. On this land, Finn reported to the British Ambassador in Constantinople on 30 August 1855, Montefiore had received permission 'for erection of a hospital, and employment of poor Jews in gardening'.

The year 1855 ended with an incident at John the Baptist's village of Ain Karim, west of the city, where the French Consul removed a Cross which had been put up by the Spanish Consul. The dispute was resolved by Kiamil Pasha in person, but was typical of the recurring and often petty disputes for control of the religious shrines in and out of the city.

The dispute at Ain Karim showed two Roman Catholic powers at logger-heads. The more usual friction was between the Latin Churches on the one side – Roman Catholic and Anglican – and the Greek and Russian Orthodox Churches on the other. At Easter 1856, on Holy Fire Day, Consul Finn noted laconically: 'Greeks and Armenians fighting there – many wounded – but no lives lost.' The disorder was serious enough, however, to lead Kiamil Pasha to order all Christians to leave the city, in order to restore calm. A month later it was the Abyssinians who complained 'in great distress', at the small quantity and 'poisonous quality' of the food supplied to them by the Armenian Convent. They even brought some of the food with them in a pot, to prove their point.

In 1855 an American citizen reached the city. His name was Robarts, and he was followed by boxes of books sent after him from Constantinople to Jaffa. A zealous Christian, Robarts would stand outside the Jaffa Gate with Bibles in several languages, accosting passers-by until he found a person able to read one of the languages. He would then persuade his hapless victim to read aloud several chapters to the customary throng.

Robarts' eccentric activities posed no threat to Consul Finn and the mission-aries of the London Jews Society. But the British Protestants did have a rival in their missionary work, the Church Missionary Society. This latter Society, however, took no part in the conversion of the Jews but limited its activities to converting Arab Christians of the various eastern Churches to Protestantism.

The secretary of the Church Missionary Society was Charles Sandreczki, a Polish Roman Catholic who had himself converted to Protestantism before taking up missionary work.

In 1854 the Church Missionary Society had successfully converted a Roman Catholic Arab, Tannoos Kerm, to Protestantism, but not his wife. The issue of their children's education then became a subject of claims and counter claims. On the death of Kerm early in 1855, the French Consul, Pierre Emile Botta, successfully contested with Consul Finn that, Kerm 'having died a Catholic, the children could not be taken from the mother in such early age', whereupon the Protestant Sandreczki 'agreed to renounce all claims on the children'.

Consul Finn now built his house at Talbiyeh, outside the city walls, and other residents soon followed. In 1855 Bishop Gobat set up the Anglican bishopric's summer residence in the Muslim Arab village of Lifta, on a steep but cool slope some miles outside the city on the Jaffa road. That same year the Protestant missionary, Ludwig Schneller, who had arrived in the city ten years before as part of the 'Brotherhood Centre', likewise built a house just to the east of Lifta. Schneller's aim was to influence the Muslim Arabs to convert to Christianity. Repeated attacks on his house forced Schneller to abandon it, and to return to the Brotherhood lodgings inside the Jaffa Gate.

The reports of the Christian missionaries give a further glimpse of the Jerusalem of 1855. 'The London Society', wrote one, 'established and at a vast annual outlay supports at Jerusalem an hospital, an experienced physician and an eminent surgeon, with all the requisite stores and appliances, and thus wisely and piously exhibits practically before the eyes of unbelieving Israelites the mercy and charity of their Divine Master.'

Of the hundreds, indeed thousands, of poor Jews in the city, the missionaries reported: 'They live in miserable holes, unventilated and filthy, subject to low fevers, opthalmia etc. etc; they have no occupation; Jerusalem does not afford that opportunity of precarious petty traffic which supports so many of their brethren in the great cities of Europe.'

Surrounded by distress, Christian good works flourished, never so much as during the Crimean War, when no Jewish charitable donations could reach Jerusalem from Russia, nor any of the Russian Orthodox Easter pilgrims, whose presence revivified Christian Jerusalem. 'There was such a lack of money', noted the missionary report for 1855, 'that even the Muslim population suffered hunger. The poor Jews starved. A few kind Christian people, chiefly ladies, at Jerusalem, gave relief as they could, and wrote home for help. The distribution immediately commenced, partly by means of an association of Christian ladies of various nations called the "Sarah Society", who visit the poor Jewesses at their homes.'

Britain was not the sole power to gain greater influence in Jerusalem as a result of the alliance with Turkey against Russia. France also sought advantage, and obtained it. During 1856 the Sultan granted the Emperor Napoleon III the Church of St Anne, the most magnificent surviving crusader church in the city. That same year, on 1 April, the French Consulate gave a public dinner to celebrate the birth of the Prince Imperial, Napoleon III's only child. Twenty-two years later, with his father in exile in England, the Prince was to be killed while fighting in the British army against the Zulus.

Among those present at the celebration of the Prince Imperial's birth was Father Alphonse Ratisbonne, a French Jew who, together with his brother Theodore, had been converted to Roman Catholicism. In 1843 Theodore and Alphonse had founded in Paris the Congregation of Notre Dame de Sion – the Sisters of Zion – for Roman Catholic women. Nine years later they had founded the Fathers of Zion for men. Both 'Ratisbonne' societies had as their aim a better understanding between Jews and Christians, and the conversion of Jews to Roman Catholicism.

Alphonse Ratisbonne had been ordained priest in 1848. Seven years later he had come to Jerusalem, and in 1856, within a year of his arrival, he established in the Via Dolorosa the Ecce Homo convent for the Sisters of Zion, one of the first 'modern' religious buildings in that hitherto decrepit street.

A similar rebuilding was soon to be in progress in the Jewish quarter, thanks to the Sultan's decree and Sir Moses Montefiore's munificence: on the ruins of the Hurva synagogue a noble edifice was planned. On 14 May 1856 the European consuls attended the synagogue's rededication, Rabbi Samuel Salant being among those present.

One beneficial effect of the Crimean War was consular pressure to remove two 'insults' long before established by Muslim fanatics of an earlier century on the edge of both the Christian and Jewish quarters. One, a stench-ridden tannery, had been built close to the Church of the Holy Sepulchre. Another, the equally foul-smelling slaughterhouse, had been placed at the southern entrance to the Jewish quarter.

Using the new-found power and alliance of Britain and France, Edward

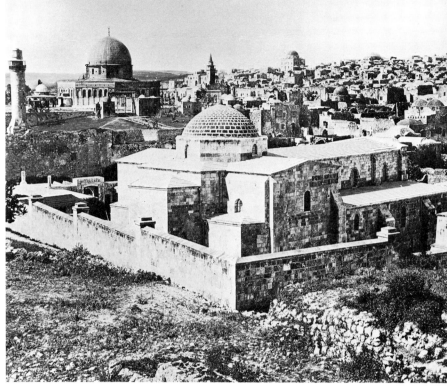

Top left: the crusader façade of St Anne's Church (1984). *Top right:* St Anne's Church (foreground), the Mosque of Omar and the new Jewish synagogue (on the horizon above St Anne's, with dome). (Bonfils, 1880s). *Above left:* Alphonse and Theodore Ratisbonne (1880). *Above right:* at work in the carpenters' shop in the Ratisbonne monastery (1880s).

MacGowan, the physician, and his two assistants at that time, Dr Sims and Dr Atkinson – the only European doctors then living in the city – persuaded the Governor to re-locate both the tannery and the slaughterhouse. Kiamil Pasha, in a gesture of friendship to the British, had attended religious services at the Anglican Church in 1856. That same year, Christians had been allowed to visit the Haram, among them Colonel Walpole, commander of the Turkish Land Transport Corps, and his wife, in January; the officers of the French frigate *Mercure* in June; and in October several naval officers from HMS *Stromboli*, together with General Chesney and Sir John MacNeill, two leading British engineers who had just surveyed the Euphrates river valley for a possible railway line.

The earlier hostility of the guards of the Haram had almost entirely disappeared. Colonel Walpole, like Sir Moses Montefiore before him, had also been careful to distribute a handsome baksheesh to the Sudanese soldiers who guarded the mosques: Elizabeth Finn described these black stalwarts as 'suddenly quite tame and friendly'.

There was a proud moment for Roman Catholic missionary work in August 1856, when the Latin Patriarch held an examination of the Arab boys at the Roman Catholic College. These boys were all former Muslims who had been converted to Catholicism. Elizabeth Finn was struck by the high academic level of the boys, and reflected that, looking at them in their smart uniforms, 'one would not have recognized them as the peasant boys they once had been'.

Kiamil Pasha's pro-British sentiments were made clear at the end of 1856, when he personally supervised the preparation of a present for Queen Victoria. This was a specially built model of the Church of the Holy Sepulchre, which was first displayed at the British Consulate, and then packed, under Kiamil's own gaze, for despatch to London. Many years later, in London, Elizabeth Finn was surprised to come across the model when visiting the Victoria and Albert Museum in South Kensington.

Among the visitors to Jerusalem in 1856 was Ludwig August Frankl, the secretary and archivist of the Vienna Jewish community. A man of considerable learning, and a poet of both patriotic and Jewish verses, Frankl had been one of the first Jews to attend a non-Jewish secondary school in Bohemia. In 1836, at the age of 26, he had received a prize from the Emperor Francis for his first collection of ballads. Twelve years later he had taken an active part in the revolution of 1848. To Frankl, visiting Jerusalem for the first time at the age of 46, the city appeared as 'a pilgrim, grey with age, who has come here and

'Types at Jews' Wailing Place' (American Colony photograph, Eric Matson, 1910).

sunk down to die; his pain has turned into stone like that of the mother whose children had been throttled by the wrath of God'.

Through Frankl's eyes, Jewish life within the city walls was a curiosity, seen as if from afar: something which he could in no way relate to his own experiences as an emancipated Jew from western Europe. The Sephardim, he admitted somewhat patronizingly, were 'colourful and attractive', but because they could not afford even a single religious school they were, in his view, more wretched than the poorest and smallest European Jewish community: for in Europe, however poor and however small, a Jewish community 'would be ashamed' not to have such a school.

The Ashkenazim, Frankl wrote, were 'unpleasant'. Their unpleasantness arose, in his opinion, from their 'well-known ugly Polish costume and the dirt clinging to it'. Dirt and appearance were accompanied by equally unpleasant 'grimacing' and by 'superciliousness in conversation'.

Frankl's disapproval centred upon the refusal of these Polish Jews to improve their situation by learning useful crafts, and by their reliance upon European charity. Himself a man of means, Frankl went so far as to propose a trade school. On his return to Vienna he found a philanthropist willing to finance it.

Once again, the shock of the plight of Jerusalem's Jews had led to action: and to effective action. For as a result of Frankl's visit, and of his criticisms, a new school was founded which offered the Jewish children of the city a secular as well as a religious education, and which, to the intense anger of the more orthodox Ashkenazi rabbis, admitted female students.

Known as the 'Laemel school', and opened in the presence of the British and several other consuls on 27 June 1856, the new school's teaching constituted the first educational intrusion by modern, European Jewry. The Laemel after whom it was named, Simon Laemel, was one of the most influential Jews of the Habsburg monarchy, a leading negotiator on behalf of Jewish emancipation, and a friend of Goethe. Ennobled as Simon von Laemel, he had died in 1845; it was his daughter Eliza who had sent Frankl to Jerusalem to find some means whereby her father's memory could be perpetuated.

Frankl returned to Vienna, leaving behind him, in embryo, the revolutionary experiment of secular Jewish education. Like many of the European visitors to Jerusalem, his influence persisted in his absence. Jerusalem was to be reformed, but from afar. The Laemel School survives to this day.

One result of the increased reliance of Turkey upon Britain during the Crimean War was the decision, taken in Constantinople, to use British expertise to improve the Ottoman postal services. The man chosen for this task was E.J. Smith, who had served as Field Postmaster during the Crimean War. As a result of Smith's enquiries, a weekly postal service was established between Jerusalem and Beirut, leaving each city on Wednesday, and enabling collection and delivery at the five coastal towns of Jaffa, Haifa, Acre, Tyre and Sidon. No daily postal service was to be available from Jerusalem for another thirty-six years, until the opening of the railway in 1892.

Discoveries in Jerusalem were not always of ancient remains. In 1856 an explorer in the Hinnom valley, examining the rock tombs of Roman time, found to his surprise that the inner chamber of one of the tombs, far from being deserted, was a veritable Aladdin's cave of rolls of cloth and calico, saddles and riding harnesses, copper utensils: the loot of some local Ali Baba and his robber gang. Nor were all these tombs deserted: as late as 1908 two of them were still in use as dwellings by Muslims from the village of Silwan.

Above the Hinnom valley, on Mount Zion, all religions were represented. The hereditary privilege of guarding the tomb of King David being held by a Muslim, Mohammed Darweesh Effendi, a member of one of Jerusalem's oldest and most noble Arab families.

The Tomb of David, and more recent tombs, on Mount Zion (1880s).

In the first week of February 1857 Jerusalemites of all faiths and nationalities were startled by a remarkable downpour of yellow mud, 'plastering the houses from top to bottom'. All the exposed southern and south-eastern faces of the outer walls, and of many of the buildings, were stained a dull ochre, 'the traces of which', a visitor in 1926 noted, 'the rains of seventy winters have not yet washed away'. Particularly in soft limestone, the tell-tale stains survived.

Among those visitors to the city during the yellow deluge was a distinguished naturalist, Professor Roth of Munich. He examined the yellow mud, and found that it consisted in part of minute shells known only in the Sinai desert.

In the summer of 1857 a Jew, Ephraim Sopher, was badly beaten by a peasant near the monastery of Mar Elias, on the Bethlehem road. The punishment: the peasant was forced to kiss hands, pay ten piastres – the cost of a pair of Muslim's red shoes, or a donkey's load of wood – and have his sword confiscated for several days. Further south, at Artas, John Meshullam's gardens, trees, and property walls were swept away when someone opened the sluice-gate of the lowest of the three Pools of Solomon. Elizabeth Finn was of the opinion that those responsible had been put up to it by the Greek Orthodox Church, or even by the Roman Catholic clergy, jealous of the growth of

Anglicanism in Palestine. But, as one of his last decisions before giving up the governorship of the city, Kiamil Pasha refused to set up an effective commission to investigate the crime, afraid to disturb the delicate balance of interests in the area: Muslims, peasants, Christian Arabs, Anglicans and Bedouin.

On 24 March 1857 the first United States Consul to Jerusalem reached the city. His name was John Warren Gorham, and almost his first task, that July, was to fly the Stars and Stripes on Independence Day. Kiamil Pasha's successor as Governor, Suraya Pasha, being then in the north, at Nablus, Gorham had to negotiate with the Garrison commander for a twenty-one gun salute. This, the Turkish officer refused, arguing that as the United States was governed by a 'mere' President, it did not deserve the same courtesies as a country ruled by a King.

Throughout the night of July 3, Gorham was busy exchanging notes with the Commander, who at one point argued that he could not possibly agree to the salute without the permission of the municipal council. Gorham, near to defeat, then told the Commander that he would complain directly to Constantinople if the Stars and Stripes did not receive the salute due to it. The Commander capitulated. Promptly at ten in the morning of 4 July 1857 the United States flag was raised over Jerusalem, and twenty-one Turkish guns barked out their reluctant acclaim.

Suraya Pasha was to remain Governor for twelve years. In an unguarded moment he confined to Elizabeth Finn that 'he had been sent to Jerusalem to break the power of the English Consulate and to destroy British influence in Palestine'. But British influence also came through western Jews, and when Sir Moses Montefiore returned to the city in June 1857 his presence was once more the occasion of great enthusiasm among the Jews, especially the poor. Montefiore had built a house in Talbiyeh, near to Finn's, and now he also brought with him English ironwork for a new hospital, and for a windmill which he was building on the slope above the hospital; the aim of the enterprise being that Jews, being offered work, would give up their reliance upon charity.

Montefiore was particularly anxious, on this particular visit, to raise money for the building of a railway from Jaffa to Jerusalem. He brought with him from Jaffa a leading British railway engineer, Mr Galloway, who had already laid the basis for the Egyptian railway system. A railway could be built, Galloway declared after he and Montefiore had traversed its possible route, 'but from the peculiar nature of the ground he believed it would be unusually expensive'.

Montefiore proposed a railway loan with a seven percent return guaranteed by the Ottoman Government. This the Ottoman authorities refused, arguing that in commerce Jerusalem 'can produce nothing for itself', and that Ottoman funds would therefore be given solely 'for the advantages of a few pilgrims'.

While he was in Jerusalem, Montefiore learnt that the Russian Tsar had sent £50 to those poor Jews in the city who were members of the Warsaw congregation, while at the same time he had given permission to his Jewish subjects in Poland 'to send money to the Holy Land'. Montefiore and his wife 'were much pleased with this gratifying news'.

Another visitor in 1857 was a British missionary, the Reverend W. M. Thomson. After visiting Mount Zion, Thomson noted in his diary, on 11 May 1857: 'I was taken to see the village or quarter assigned to the lepers, lying along the wall directly east of Zion Gate. I was unprepared for the visit, and was made positively sick by the loathsome spectacle.'

This was not Thomson's first sight of the lepers. 'Sauntering down the Jaffa road, on my approach to the city', he later wrote, 'in a kind of dreary maze, with, as I remember, scarcely one distinct idea in my head, I was startled out

Lepers above the Tomb of the Virgin (American Colony photograph).

of my reverie by the sudden apparition of a crowd of beggars "sans eyes, sans nose, sans hair, sans everything". They held up toward me their handless arms, unearthly sounds gurgled through throats without palates – in a word, I was horrified.' It appeared, Thomson added, 'that these unfortunate beings have been perpetuated about Jerusalem from the remotest antiquity'.

Also in 1857 the British painter and writer, Edward Lear, was commissioned by the Prince of Wales – later Edward VII – to make a painting of Jerusalem. He took his commission seriously, spending some months in the city: 'that vile place!', he described it in a letter to a friend, 'For let me tell you, physically Jerusalem is the foulest and odiousest place on earth.'

Lear's painting was of a different city, mystical, serene and holy. He could not avoid, however, the realities of Jerusalem life, and having decided to make a journey to Petra – the 'rose-red city half as old as time' – and needing loyal Bedouin guides, he ended up in litigation with the Jehalin tribe, as to the amount he had agreed to pay. Lear himself was not to blame: it was the seizure of Petra by a Bedouin 'interloper' that had forced travellers, and indeed the experienced Consul Finn himself, to negotiate new contracts with new guides, and to buy protection, not only from Bedouin new to the area, but from a Hebron sheikh who decided to act as 'agent' for the Bedouin chief.

In 1857 the American writer Herman Melville also visited Jerusalem. The Jews of the city, he wrote, were 'like flies who have taken up their abode in a skull'. But by the efforts of these 'flies', during 1857, the ruins of the Hurva synagogue began at last to be turned into a new house of worship. The new building, Consul Finn reported to London on 1 January 1858, 'will be one of the remarkable edifices of the city: under the designs and superintendence of the Sultan's architect, Assaad Effendi'. This Constantinople worthy was both the Sultan's protégé, and a Muslim. He was working on the synagogue, Finn expained, 'during the time that he remains unemployed on the Church of the Holy Sepulchre'.

For Jerusalem's Jews, the construction of the new synagogue represented both a triumph and a challenge. The triumph consisted in the realization of the aspirations of several generations, as well as in the wording of the Sultan's decree, which stated: 'It is self-evident that justice and generosity alike enjoin that complete peace be assured to members of all faiths and religions dwelling in My sublime kingdom...'. The challenge was financial: the money needed to create a noble edifice was far beyond the capacity of the perpetually impoverished community.

The Tiferet Israel Synagogue, 'one of the remarkable edifices of the city'. Destroyed in 1948.

The search for funds took place throughout the Jewish Diaspora. The largest single gift came from the 'Rothschilds of the East', the Reubens of Baghdad, who gave 100,000 of the million piastres required. This donation, made by Yehezkel Reuben, was later augmented by his son, Rabbi Menasse, and his daughter, Lady Sassoon. The combined 'Reuben' donations eventually covered more than half the cost, a point testified to by an inscription on the completed building, and marking an important step in the unity of the Sephardi and Ashkenazi Jewish relations in the city.

In Prussia, King Friedrich Wilhelm IV gave permission for donations to be collected from his Jewish subjects. Throughout western Europe emissaries sought donations with the slogan 'Gain Eternal Life with one Stone'.

One donation, of 4,000 piastres, from Rabbi Schmuel of Rogola, was for a hostel in the synagogue compound, in which guests were to be entitled to an unlimited period of lodging, as well as three days free board.

One of the most handsome of the donations to the new synagogue came from Pinchas Rosenberg, the Imperial Court tailor of St Petersburg, who set out in writing the details of his benefactions in the diary of the emissary who had gone to the Russian capital in search of rubles. As Rosenberg wrote:

'I give thanks to the Lord for his mercy with which he has moved my heart to donate to the holy building 100 Rubles and two big bronze candelabras, each with thirty-six branches to light the lamps thereof, at the cost of 80 Rubles. And I also donate a Hanuka candlestick 42 pounds in weight and three ells in height with eight branches, for which I spent 1,750 Rubles on silver work and 125 Rubles on transportation to Jerusalem through our dear emissary Rabbi Chaim Halevi, and this candlestick arrived miraculously on the 1st Tevet precisely in time to light the last eight Hanuka candles, whereupon I donated another 50 Rubles for candles and oil and a further 100 Rubles for cantors, beadles and Torah scribes and another 25 Rubles to have an iron door made under the Holy Ark for safe-keeping of the candlestick, and another 200 Rubles for the return of the above emissary and as a present to him. Altogether, with God's help, I spent on the above candlestick 2,150 Rubles and another 28 Rubles on candles and oil for the two bronze candelabras. And now I offer my thanks to God who has enlightened my spirit to embellish the above house of worship by building an artistically wrought iron fence round the roof under the upper windows so that there be a veranda on which may stand all our brethren who go up in pilgrimage to behold our desolate Temple, and also a partition for the womenfolk on the Feast of Tabernacles and Simchat Torah.'

Another gift from Tsarist Russia was the Holy Ark itself. Surrounded by four Corinthian columns and decorated with baroque carvings, this ark had for several years been the pride of the Nikolaijewsky synagogue in the Black Sea port of Kherson. The Nikolaijewsky synagogue had been the House of Prayer for those unfortunate Russian Jews who had been forced to spend twenty-five years as conscripts in the Tsarist army. Not only the ark of the synagogue, but also its gates, were brought to Jerusalem for the new building.

Among the emissaries who searched for funds for the new synagogue was Jacob Saphir, the Russian-born Jerusalemite who, as a 17-year-old boy, had written the poem in honour of Moses Montefiore's visit in 1839. In 1857 Saphir hoped to travel as far as India, to obtain contributions from the Jewish communities there.

On the first stage of his journey, while only in Egypt, Saphir was robbed of most of his money. Realizing that he must follow a less ambitious course, he gave up his immediate plans to reach India, and made instead for the Yemen. There, in 1858, he visited, amid conditions of considerable hardship and indeed danger, the Jewish communities scattered throughout the virtually unexplored and rugged interior. The way of life of the Jews of Yemen, and their devotion to Judaism, greatly impressed him. They, for their part, learned from their unexpected visitor something about the real Jerusalem: their first news of its 'modern' as opposed to spiritual existence.

Leaving the Yemen for Aden, Saphir was eventually able to continue his travels; indeed he went much further than he had originally intended, sailing not only to India, but eastward to Java, Australia and New Zealand, and visiting, on his return journey, Ceylon.

In May 1863 Saphir returned to Jerusalem, four years and ten months after he had left on his mission. With him he brought back substantial funds for the new synagogue, as well as material for a two-volume work, which he published in 1866 and 1874, describing the lives and customs of the Jews of the East. Saphir was the first Jew to publish Yemenite poems. Twenty-four years after his epic journey, and only three years before his death, he was to welcome the first Yemenite Jewish settlers to the city.

In his report of 1 January 1858, Consul Finn had commented on the 'present state of Rabbinical despotism' in Jerusalem. Dr Frankl's school, set up in 1856, had been boycotted entirely by the Ashkenazi rabbis, 'under penalty of excommunication': Ashkenazi Jews were forbidden 'from even passing along the street of the new school to this day'.

Finn's report ended: 'It is a matter of serious concern to observe the increase of Jews in Jerusalem, and the busy throng filling their streets, without a proportionate increase of means of livelihood. Prices of every kind in food, lodging and fuel, are greatly enhanced: but not only is there no sufficient remunerative employment for mechanical or other labourers; but it is said that the collections from Russia and other countries are failing. On the ground of extravagant reports of funds being supplied by Montefiore, Rothschild, Cohn, etc. the poor also of those countries leave their homes to come and share in their imagined riches: of course they are disappointed.'

One remedy alone, Finn believed, would be effective, 'namely agricultural or other manual employment to be afforded to the Jews by others than their own people – for were even these means of livelihood provided by their own ecclesiastical oppressors, the fetters of their slavery would only be fastened the more; coupled with the contempt which the Rabbis incessantly express for agriculturalists and mechanics'.

In February 1858, the Russian Government and Russian Orthodox Church made every effort to establish an even stronger influence on the city than before, spurred on by Russia's defeat at the hands of Britain, France and Turkey during the Crimean War. For the first time, a Bishop was appointed to head the Russian Orthodox Church in Palestine, thus ending the old subordination, in rank at least, to the Greek Orthodox Patriarch. The Bishop chosen was Cyril Naumov, the former Inspector of the St Petersburg Ecclesiastical Academy, and a scholar of note. He reached Jerusalem on the night of 13 February 1858.

To the surprise of many observers, Bishop Naumov arrived in Jerusalem with a Russian-born Jew who had converted to Russian Orthodoxy, and whose mission was to convert the Jews of the city to the Russian Orthodox faith.

Within a week of Bishop Naumov's arrival, scandal had broken out in a rival church and among rival missionaries. Simeon Rosenthal, a Jewish convert to Anglicanism, joined with other parents of children who were at Bishop Gobat's school, to complain that their sons – all the sons of former Jews – had been subjected to perverted sexual practices by the older, Arab boys.

Gobat's school, and Gobat himself, were defended by the new Prussian Consul, Dr Georg Rosen. Pamphlets and accusations were issued. Consul Finn joined the dispute by accusing Gobat of being anti-British, and also of exceeding his authority as Anglican Bishop of Jerusalem in his efforts to convert Greek Orthodox Christian Arab boys in Nablus to Anglicanism. At one point in the quarrel, in an attempt to humiliate Finn, Rosen put Rosenthal in prison, keeping him for some while in solitary confinement. After more than a month of mutual vilification, Rosen released Rosenthal, and passions slowly but uneasily subsided.

On 4 September 1858 the British missionary, Matilda Creasy, disappeared. At first she had not been missed. Accustomed to lead a solitary life, she frequently slept in a tower on the Mount of Olives. But three days later, when she could be found neither on the Mount of Olives, nor at the Finn's Talbiyeh residence, she was posted missing. Searches were at once made in the city itself, and around the consular and Montefiore properties in Talbiyeh. Parties of soldiers combed the nearby villages. A reward was posted: 'Twenty pounds for her being found' – the value of at least forty sheep. The Consulate cisterns were searched. Then, on September 9, Miss Creasy's body was found in a field; she had been stoned to death while walking near the Monastery of the Cross, a mile to the west of the Talbiyeh estate.

The main suspects were Bedouin of the Taamri tribe, and on September 24 twelve Turkish irregular troops, the locally recruited Bashi Bezuks, left Jerusalem for Bethlehem, where they seized three Taamri tribesmen, hoping to force them to reveal the murderers.

Five of the Bashi Bezuks then escorted two of the tribesmen back towards Jerusalem. But on reaching the monastery of Mar Elias – from which the Citadel and Jaffa Gate could be seen in the far distance – more than fifty Taamri rode up, as Consul Finn noted in his diary, 'with spears and guns to the rescue', and attacked the Bashi Bezuks. The leader of the Taamri party, Saf ez Zeer, was warned repeatedly to desist: but he charged again and again, his keffiye headcloth 'thrown back for battle'.

According to Gorham, the United States Consul, who reported on the incident to Washington, four of the five Bashi Bezuks were killed, including the Captain, who was 'cut into small pieces' by the Bedouin swordsmen. The sole Bashi Bezuk survivor was then sent to Mar Elias with the boastful message from Saf ez Zeer to the Governor of Jerusalem: 'Go, tell your Pasha that, if he wishes our men, let him come himself; and we will serve him, and the Sultan himself, as we have served their Captain.'

Such was the weakness of the Jerusalem authority over the area only a few miles to the south of the city, that neither the murderers of the four Bashi Bezuks, nor those of Matilda Creasy, were ever brought to trial.

In 1859 Sir Moses Montefiore's architect and builder, J.W. Smith, arrived to begin construction of a hospital on Montefiore's land outside the city walls, next to the windmill which he had already built on the same site. The new Turkish Governor sought to prevent any further building so near to the walls, for reasons of 'military security', and ordered the building to be constructed a mile and a half away. Montefiore's cause was taken up, successfully, by Consul Finn. But instead of a hospital, Montefiore decided to build 'some Alms-houses for poor Jewish families'.

At first, all did not go well for this new enterprise. As Consul Finn reported to the Foreign Office in London: 'I have the honour to report that on the nights of the 3rd and 4th instant, the grounds and premises of Sir Moses Montefiore's charitable establishment, outside the city, were robbed, by persons as yet unknown.'

On the first of these nights, Finn reported, 'the door of the house was broken open, and twenty-three bags stolen, besides a medicine chest and several other

Montefiore's cottages and windmill (1860).

articles. On the next, a much more extensive burglary was effected, and injuries inflicted on one of the African watchmen as reported in the enclosed Minutes of depositions made before me.' There was also, Finn noted, 'an assault made upon an Englishman, foreman of the works there, while on the high road, near that ground, and proceeding to his labour'.

On learning of these attacks, Finn immediately sent the case to the Pasha, 'and a Commission was appointed for the discovery of the offenders'. Shortly afterwards, 'the peasant Salekk was imprisoned, as it was considered that strong suspicions lie against him'.

Consul Finn continued to protest to the Governor of Jerusalem on Montefiore's behalf, at 'the injustice shown to England'. The building work continued: and the 'Montefiore cottages', henceforth a Jerusalem landmark, came into being. The Jews who had to live in them, Ashkenazi and Sephardi paupers, were so afraid of robbers, however, that for many months they would slip out of their houses at night, cross the upper slopes of the Gihon valley, and seek the security of their former crowded hovels within the walls.

It was an American philanthropist from New Orleans, Judah Touro, who in 1860 provided most of the money needed for the 'Montefiore cottages'. A

The Austrian Hospice of 1862 (1984).

wealthy recluse, Touro had been severely wounded when fighting in 1812 at the Battle of Orleans, as a volunteer in the American army against the British. He had died in 1854, at the age of 79, leaving vast sums to charity, including 60,000 dollars 'for the relief of the poor' in Palestine. This sum, Touro stated, was to be used at the discretion of Sir Moses Montefiore.

At Montefiore's suggestion, half of the new houses were to be for Sephardi Jews, half for Ashkenazi. Despite Touro's patronage, the house became known locally as 'Sir Moses Montefiore's Jewish Hospice' or, colloquially, the 'Montefiore cottages'. Their official name was 'Mishkenot Sha'ananim', 'dwellings of delight'.

Montefiore was not alone in bringing modernity to Jerusalem: in 1859 the Austrian Government opened the city's first Post Office, eight years before the Ottoman Government was to open one. It issued its own Levant stamps, and its own 'Jerusalem' cancellation, now a philatelic rarity. Four years later, a further Austrian inroad was the Austrian Hospice, built on the Via Dolorosa where it crossed one of the main bazaar streets, offering Christian and European medicine to the local inhabitants, and beds for pilgrims.

CHAPTER IV

The 1860s: 'Jerusalem to perfection'

In 1860, in an attempt to lessen the dangers of robbery on the journey from Jaffa to Jerusalem, the Turkish authorities began the construction of a series of stone watchmen's houses – squat, square and at intervals of between one and a half and two miles – along the whole length of the route. In all, eighteen such guard houses were built: a welcome re-assurance, especially for those who were familiar with the stories of the highway robbers of Abu Ghosh. But it was to be nine years before the construction of the first metalled road.

In 1860 the Governor of Jerusalem, Suraya Pasha, forbad the Jews to slaughter sheep according to the requirements of rabbinic law. This gave the British Consul the opportunity he sought to defend the rights of his 'British' Jews. Finn argued that on humanitarian grounds the Jews needed meat to maintain their health, and, in a letter to Suraya Pasha drafted on 20 March 1860, he showed his copious knowledge and understanding of the religious and cultural implications of the Jewish dietary laws. Finn's protest was successful.

Changing times were also noted by Consul Finn in 1860. Eighteen years earlier 'fanatical Muslims' had scraped off the green paint on Bishop Alexander's door: 'now a Jew boy may, as I have often seen, wear a dress entirely of the peculiarly sacred shade of green colour in the most public places'.

There was a further indication of changing times in 1860, when David Yellin, a Russian-born Jew, bought a plot of land near the Arab village of Kaloniya, five miles west of the city, on the road to Jaffa: a road which was, at last, being guarded by watchtowers and Turkish soldiers. Yellin, a man of means, had left Russia for Palestine in 1834. Unusual for an Ashkenazi, his son Joshua married a Sephardi Jewess, Sarah, the daughter of Shelomo Yehezkel, a wealthy Jew

Absalom's Tomb, also known as Absalom's monument (1880s).

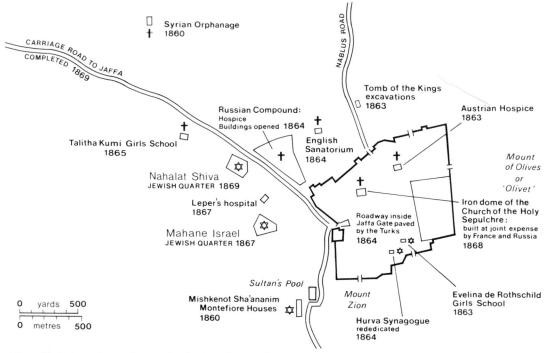

New Christian (✝) and Jewish (✡) buildings of the 1860s.

who had come from Baghdad in 1856. After his marriage, Joshua Yellin learned Arabic, his wife's native tongue, and lived for two years with his Sephardi in-laws in order to understand the 'customs, language and dress' of Sephardi Jewry.

Events in Beirut in 1860 were also to have their impact on Jerusalem. As soon as news reached Jerusalem of the widespread massacre of Christian Arabs by Muslim Arabs throughout the Lebanon, Ludwig Schneller, the Protestant missionary of the Swiss-German Brotherhood, travelled from Jerusalem to Beirut, where, despite the suspicion of the local Christian Arabs, he collected nine orphan boys, and brought them back to the city.

Schneller housed his orphans in a new building, set in the fields a mile and a half north-west of the Jaffa Gate. Known as the Syrian Orphanage, later as the German or Schneller Orphanage, it quickly grew in size and scope, with classrooms, dormitories, a chapel, a kitchen, and a dining hall grouped around a central courtyard. Within twelve months, Schneller had forty-one orphans in his care. His aim was to turn them, the destitute of a distant civil war and of local poverty, into productive Protestant craftsmen, capable in due course of supporting both themselves and a family.

The Syrian Orphanage to the north-west of the city (before 1914).

Among the trades taught by Schneller and his fellow Protestant teachers in a number of red-roofed brick outbuildings were printing, bookbinding, carpentry and shoe-making. Within the grounds, fruits and vegetables were grown in a series of agricultural experiments. The symbols of the orphanage, engraved on the four-storey Gothic entrance tower, were eaves of corn, a biblical lamb and acorns.

Visitors to Jerusalem hardly noticed these 'modern' buildings and enterprises. Their concern was with the distant past. A Christian traveller of 1861, a member of the Religious Tract Society of London, noted, after a visit to the mosque on Mount Zion, site of the Last Supper, that, for nearly four hundred years, Christians, Jews and Muslims had agreed in regarding it 'as the spot beneath which lie the royal sepulchres of Judah's kings', among them David and Solomon. The traveller added that Jews 'may often be seen gazing sadly upon the ancient building within whose walls they may not enter, and which probably for near fifteen centuries has covered the royal psalmist's dust'.

There were other legends, too, which the traveller noted of the crypt upon Mount Zion. Here, some believed, the Virgin Mary had died, and here also, according to others, St Stephen had been martyred. This accumulation of legends, typical of so many of the city's sites, gave pilgrimage an added fervour. The most sacred of all, the Via Dolorosa, met with caustic comment from this devout visitor from London. 'Now it is childish', he wrote, 'to suppose that this narrow street, with its sharp turns and twists, precisely follows the course of one of the great thoroughfares of the ancient city, after its almost total destruction, and the lapse of many centuries.' The identification of the various Stations of the Cross was clearly 'an absurdity'. But the belief of pilgrims was strong, so much so that 'a small knot of strangers, devout and believing, may often be seen gazing reverently on the spots hallowed by such associations'.

Not only the alleged Stations of the Cross, but even the name 'Via Dolorosa', were, the London traveller surmised, 'inventions of ecclesiastics'. As to the Garden of Gethsemane, the Latin ecclesiastics had not long before 'got exclusive possession' of it, and built a wall around it, not, he added, 'for the sake of protecting the trees, but to enable them to levy toll upon all those strangers and pilgrims who would naturally visit the sacred garden'.

The anonymous London visitor did not limit his criticism to religious claims. 'Of late years', he commented, 'antiquarians and archaeologists have made Jerusalem and its neighbourhood one wide battle-field.' 'Learned and pious men', he added, 'whose minds are stored with history, and whose hearts earnestly desire truth, view the localities of the city in their present state, and continually face the same facts, arrive at conclusions strangely dissimilar'.

One puzzle which intrigued this visitor of 1861, as it had intrigued many visitors, was the source of the water which had been stored in ancient times in the 'cisterns of marvellous capacity' under the Temple platform. At present, however, 'Moslem bigotry is a bar to all investigations'.

In 1862 Ermete Pierotti, an Italian who had spent eight years in Jerusalem, prepared an account of the city in which he combined his own architectural and topographical expertise with observations of the human aspects of the city. Few European writers on the city had spent such a long time in it. 'All the native population', Pierotti wrote, 'unfortunately hold the opinion that to injure a Jew is a work well pleasing in the sight of God. On going out of my house in Jerusalem, I saw a very respectable Jew running at full speed, pursued by some Arabs.' Pierotti added: 'The Jews in the East, as I have had proof over and over again, seek not to destroy the life of others but to preserve their own, enduring with meekness, constancy and patience, the insults and injuries which they receive from Christians and Mohammedans alike.'

Pierotti's observations, published two years after he left the city, give an insight into its moods, and perils. 'The poorer Jews', he wrote, 'when going on or returning from pilgrimages between Jerusalem and Hebron, avoid passing through Bethlehem to escape the insults which the "good Christians" of that place, excited by their monks, always inflict upon them'. As to Europeans like himself, 'when a European is walking through Jerusalem by night, he is always followed by a number of canine attendants, and greeted at every step with growls and howls'.

Despite his sympathy for the Jewish victims of Christian and Muslim attack, Pierotti was scathing about the Jewish quarter, describing it as 'the dirtiest, most fetid and wretched' of all the quarters of Jerusalem, nor was this 'on account of its topographical positioning', he added, 'but entirely from the habits of the people, who pay no attention to cleanliness, either in their houses or in their dress; they wallow in the mire, so to speak, and carry it on their persons as though fearing to be robbed of it'.

The Jews, Pierotti added, 'dwell in small houses huddled together in great numbers, like moving heaps of filth, and seem only to use their reason for the purpose of lounging more deeply into the dirt. I have repeatedly entered their habitations, and observe that in the courts masses of filth were accumulated year by year and producing various physical evils, simply because the occupants would not spend the few piastres necessary for its removal.'

Ever mindful of the biblical curse 'that hangs over the children of Israel', Pierotti found it impossible, while visiting the Jewish quarter, to forget the biblical verse 'understand, therefore, that the Lord thy God giveth thee not this good land to possess it for thy righteousness for thou art a stiff-necked people'.

In the year in which Pierotti was preparing his account of Jerusalem, the city was visited by Queen Victoria's eldest son, the 20-year-old Albert Edward, Prince of Wales – who thirty-nine years later was to become King, as Edward VII. The Prince had left London on 6 February 1862 for a comprehensive journey through the lands of the Bible. Travelling across Europe by train to Trieste, and then by sea, he reached Alexandria, 'our first sea port in the East', on 1 March. There, as he noted in his journal, he was joined by Dr Arthur Stanley, Canon of Christ Church, Regius Professor of Ecclesiastical History at Oxford, and one of the great Victorian experts on biblical history. He was also accompanied by one of the leading photographers of the time, Francis Bedford.

The Prince of Wales remained in Egypt until the end of March, making an excursion by steamer down the Gulf of Suez to Moses' Wells, at which place, he noted in his journal, 'are natural salt springs and it is supposed that the Israelites stopped there on leaving Egypt'.

On 28 March the Prince left Alexandria by sea for Jaffa, 'a curious looking small town', from which he was escorted by Turkish cavalry across the plain to the foothills of Judaea. 'We shall live in tents during our whole tour,' the Prince noted that evening when, at the foot of the Judaean hills, he was joined in his dining tent by Consul and Mrs Finn.

On the morning of March 31, escorted by a hundred Turkish cavalrymen, the Prince, Canon Stanley and their party, accompanied by fifty servants, proceeded on horseback towards Jerusalem. As they reached the first high ground, the Prince noted that 'we had a splendid view, and saw Valley of Ajalon, famous for Joshua's battle, and the place where Richard Coeur de Lion's army was encamped'. Then, passing 'the so-called tomb of Samuel!', the Prince and his escort rode on to Jerusalem, which they reached some six and a half hours after having set off from the edge of the plain. 'The Pasha had met us on the way,' the Prince noted. 'We had luncheon, in a small house belonging to Mr Finn outside the town.'

From Finn's house, the Prince rode to his encampment on the high ground outside the Damascus Gate. 'After having rested a little', he noted, 'we walked to the Damascus Gate, being piloted by Dr Stanley, and walked along the walls of the town to the Gate of St Stephen having an excellent view of all the points of interest inside and outside the town.'

On the morning of April 1, the Prince entered the city through St Stephen's gate and, accompanied by Dr Rosen, the Prussian Consul, visited the Dome of the Rock. 'The Mosque is very fine', the Prince noted, 'but not so fine as the one at Cairo.' From the Dome of the Rock, Rosen took the Prince through the large subterranean vaults underneath the Temple Mount, explaining that these had been used by the Crusaders as stables. From the vaults, and the adjacent reservoir, the Prince then visited the Al-Aksa mosque, being shown 'the supposed footprint of Our Lord' as well as 'some fine glass windows'. The Prince was also shown a small subterranean mosque, called the Mosque of the Cradle, 'where the Lord as child is supposed to have lived'.

While still on the Haram, the Prince was taken to see the Pillar of Mahomet, 'where the Mahomedans fancy He will come and judge the world', and the Golden Gate, 'which is very handsome'. The Prince was then taken to the top of the minaret belonging to Suraya Pasha's house 'and had a splendid view from the top'.

Top: the Prince of Wales' tented encampment (Francis Bedford, April 1862). *Above:* subterranean vaults underneath the Temple Mount, a print made in 1864 by Pierotti, from one of his own photographs.

Lunch on 1 April was at Consul Finn's house, where the Prince met one of the Jewish converts to Christianity, John Meshullam, 'who belongs to the English Consulate'. After lunch, the Prince visited the Church of the Holy Sepulchre and was shown over it 'by Greek, Roman Catholic and Armenian priests (to whom it all belongs) also to Copts and Syrians'.

From the Church of the Holy Sepulchre, the Prince proceeded to the Prussian and English hospitals, 'which are admirably conducted' and where he met Bishop Gobat, 'who seems a nice person'. He then 'looked into' the Armenian convent and visited the Tower of Hippicus, 'the only remaining one which Titus did not destroy when he destroyed Jerusalem'. Having looked over the city from the top of the tower, the Prince left through the Jaffa Gate and walked back to his encampment. That evening, the Prince noted, Dr Rosen, 'who had so ably acted as our cicerone all the day, dined with us'. After dinner, the Prince was tattooed on the arm 'by a Native', the tattoo consisting of the five crosses and three crowns of Crusader Jerusalem.

On April 2, once more accompanied by the Prussian Consul, 'we again went sightseeing', the Prince noted in his journal. Their first visit was to 'the so-called Wailing Place of the Jews and close to it the remains of an arch of the bridge between the Temple and Palace of King David'. From there, accompanied by Consul and Mrs Finn, the Prince went to the Jewish quarter where he visited 'a Spanish synagogue, and a very good one of its sort, also a new German synagogue': this was the Tiferet Israel, whose high dome had just become a feature of the city's skyline. The Prince and the Consul then looked briefly into the Jewish hospital founded by Baron Rothschild, a hospital which the Prince found 'very well kept'.

Proceeding from the Jewish quarter to Mount Zion, the Prince was shown Bishop Gobat's school and the Protestant cemetery, noting the 'very fine view' from the top of the terrace belonging to the cemetery. From the cemetery he went up Mount Zion to see 'the so-called Tomb of David, in a subterranean Mosque', noting in his journal: 'we were very anxious to have a door opened to see what is really supposed to be David's tomb. But the keepers all had objected, as in their eyes it was too Holy for others to see it, and after some consultation with the Pasha who arrived there, we had to leave the place in disgust, and give up seeing it which annoyed us very much.'

Returning to his encampment, the Prince lunched with Dr Rosen and then rode to the Garden of Gethsemane, 'in which there are eight olive trees, and a very nicely kept garden'. He then descended into the Tomb of the Virgin,

Top: Jews at the Wailing Wall (Bonfils, 1880).
Above: the Rothschild Hospital (1905).

The Garden of Gethsemane, with the walls of Jerusalem beyond, photographed by Francis Bedford on 2 March 1862.

'which belongs chiefly to the Greeks' and where, as he noted with his customary scepticism, 'the so-called tomb was shown to us'. From there he continued on horseback to the summit of the Mount of Olives, noting that the olive trees 'are very scanty just now but fresh ones are being planted', and from the top of the minaret of the Mount of the Ascension 'saw Jerusalem to perfection, also the Dead Sea and the mountain ranges to perfection'. In the mosque 'they showed us the footprint of Our Lord on the rock', after which the Prince rode back down the Mount of Olives to his encampment.

On the morning of 3 April the Prince set off on horseback to Bethlehem, stopping briefly at Rachel's tomb and noting with approval that 'it has been ascertained for certain that the tomb is on the site of the real one'. From Bethlehem, he and his party rode through the Judaean desert down towards the Monastery of Mar Saba. On their way, 'a quantity of Arabs with guns came over the hills' but were frightened off by the Prince's large escort. The Arabs, the Prince noted, 'had lately had a scrimmage with the Turks, but we assured them that our intentions were not hostile'.

From Mar Saba the Prince rode down to the Dead Sea, bathing at its

Top: the Mount of Olives and the Mosque of the Ascension (1880s). *Above left:* the site of the Ascension (1880s). *Above right:* the footprint of Jesus at the site of the Ascension (1880s).

northern end. 'It was not quite as disagreeable as I expected', he wrote, 'but my eyes and nose smarted a good deal and the taste was horrible.' Riding on to the River Jordan, the Prince and his party bathed in the fresh water, 'and I was very glad to get the salt out of my skin'. The river, he noted, was 'rapid and very muddy'.

From the Jordan, the Prince rode to Jericho, 'now a small, dirty village', passing on the way 'a large encampment of pilgrims of different Christian nations who had returned from bathing in the Jordan, which is a custom at this time of year'. That evening some twenty or thirty Arab women 'danced before our tents in a wild fantastic way, as a welcome, which we rewarded by giving them some "backshish"'.

On April 5 the Prince rode back from Jericho to Jerusalem, stopping briefly at the Inn of the Good Samaritan. Entering Jerusalem along the Jericho road, 'from what is considered the best point of view, we saw the spot where it is said Our Lord wept over the city'. The Prince then descended into the Kidron valley to visit the pool of Siloam, 'passing Absalom's and Zachariah's tombs'. He then returned to his 'old camping ground' outside the Damascus Gate.

On the morning of Sunday, April 6, the Prince attended Divine Service at the Protestant church. 'The day being intensely hot', he noted, 'we remained in our tents the greater part of the day, and I wrote letters and journals.' That evening, Bishop Gobat, Consul Finn and Dr Rosen came to dine.

On April 7 the Prince again left Jerusalem, riding south to Bethlehem and Solomon's Pools, where he walked about 'with my gun and shot at some birds, but was not successful at getting any'. He then proceeded to Hebron, where he was escorted personally by Suraya Pasha into the mosque which covered the site of the tombs of Abraham, Isaac and Jacob. Canon Stanley, on a previous visit to Hebron, had failed to obtain permission to see the tombs of the Patriarchs. 'Well', the Prince chided him, 'you see, exalted rank has some advantages, after all!'

Returning on April 9 to Jerusalem, the Prince again stopped at Solomon's Pools, where he had 'a delightful bathe', swimming across the middle pool and back again with the diplomat Noel Temple Moore.

Approaching Jerusalem from the south-west, the Prince visited the Monastery of the Cross, and then, at noon, entered Jerusalem 'for the third time', adding in his journal: 'we rested and wrote letters during the rest of the day', leaving the encampment late that afternoon to walk 'right round the city outside the walls in 45 minutes'.

Solomon's Pools (1880s).

The Prince spent his last morning in Jerusalem on April 10. 'We wrote some more letters', he noted, 'and packed up,' before lunching in Suraya Pasha's house. 'He gave us an excellent luncheon, or rather dinner, and 62 dishes were handed round! including dessert.' The lunch over, at 4 o'clock that afternoon 'we took our final leave of Jerusalem'.

The Prince continued his journey northwards, spending Good Friday at Nazareth and Easter at Tiberias, before proceeding to the ancient hill town of Safed, the Banias spring, Damascus, Baalbek and Beirut. From Beirut, he left the scenes of his biblical journeyings, to sail by sea to Constantinople, where he was received in audience by Sultan Abdul Aziz. Returning to London, he reached the capital on June 14, eighteen weeks after having set out.

During his visit to Jerusalem, the Prince had found himself briefly at the centre of a controversy surrounding Consul Finn. Shortly before the Prince's visit, the Ashkenazi rabbis had appealed direct to Queen Victoria not to recall the Consul. 'Year by year', they told the Queen, the 'dread' of Finn had so increased among the Muslims, 'the dwellers in this land', that they had been unable 'to do their pleasure for doing evil' to the Jews 'Thy servants'. Were

Finn to leave, the rabbis added, 'and until the coming Consul shall subdue the men of this land, we fear for our lives, lest the inhabitants should swallow us up with wrong doing'.

Many of the signatories were not British-protected Jews, but Jews who, as Finn explained in a covering note, 'have Consuls of their own'. But they looked to Britain to defend them against the Muslim Arabs. A reply from the Foreign Office on 21 January 1863 stated that the Queen 'has learned with much pleasure that the interest which she has ever taken in the welfare of the Jewish community is duly appreciated'.

Support for Finn remaining in Jerusalem was not universal among those who accompanied the Prince of Wales to Jerusalem. Among the Prince's retinue was a British diplomat, Noel Temple Moore, who, during his stay in the city, had seen many petitions handed to the Prince, urging Finn's removal on the grounds of his quarrelsome nature. Nine months later, Moore himself was appointed to replace Finn. Shortly after he did so, the Supreme Consular Court of the Levant, sitting in Jerusalem under a British judge, Sir Edmund Hornby, examined charges brought against Finn, of considerable indebtedness, mostly to Jewish bankers and creditors.

The case against Finn opened on 8 June 1863. It soon became clear that Finn had borrowed far more heavily than he could possibly have repaid, in order to provide for the maintenance of his various properties. Giving judgement on July 6, the court ordered Finn to repay debts totalling £2,348, and to do so by selling his Talbiyeh house and estate, the land and houses at Abraham's Vineyard, and several other properties, including land at Artas. In giving judgement against Finn, Sir Edmund Hornby nevertheless blamed the case upon the Jewish creditors' demand for 'their pound of flesh', and commented, of Elizabeth Finn: 'The Jews repaid the philanthropy manifested for their race by the wife of the British Consul by purchasing her husband's bills at a discount of 50 to 60 percent.' The image of Shylock had been given legal expression in the Holy City.

Since 1841 Israel Bak had been the sole printer of Hebrew books and pamphlets in Jerusalem. But a second printing press was established in 1862. Its founder, Joel Moses Salomon, had been born in Jerusalem in 1838, went to Europe as a young man to study at the Jewish religious academy in Kovno, and, on his way back to Palestine, had spent three months in Germany, studying lithography.

The Salomon Printing Company was yet another step towards the secularization of Jewish life in Jerusalem. Its only competitor was the press of Israel Bak, an orthodox Hassidic Jew whose work was not satisfactory to the non-Hassidic Perushim. Within a year of its establishment, the Salomon Company embarked upon a competitive venture with its rival. Both decided to publish a Hebrew-language newspaper. No such newspaper had been published before in Palestine. Now there were to be two. Both were to be published monthly.

Joel Salomon's newspaper was the first to appear. It was called *Ha-Levanon*, 'The Lebanon', and issue number one was published in March 1863. Its editor was a 27-year-old Russian-born Jew, Jehiel Brill, who had for some years been working in Jerusalem sending reports on Jewish life in the city to Hebrew newspapers in Eastern Europe. Brill was married to the daughter of the Jerusalem emissary, Jacob Saphir. Indeed, in May 1863, only two months after Brill began his editorship of *Ha-Levanon*, Saphir returned from his epic five-year journey to the Antipodes.

As editor of *Ha-Levanon*, Jehiel Brill argued that the Jews of Jerusalem should establish suburbs outside the city walls. He also insisted that those Jews who depended upon the charity of their European co-religionists should take to productive occupations, especially farming, in order to escape from the humiliation of the charity system.

On 13 July 1863, only four months after the first issue of *Ha-Levanon*, Israel Bak issued the first number of the rival *Havatzelet*, named after a flower of the Judaean hills. The two newspapers were in instant conflict, as well as competition, their editorial columns trumpeting their disputes throughout the city.

The Turkish authorities were not amused by this literary conflict, and within a year both newspapers had been closed down. Only *Havatzelet* was to rise again in Jerusalem. Brill, disillusioned by Jewish life in the city, moved to Paris, where he revived *Ha-Levanon* as a weekly. Later he moved to the German city of Mainz, where it again appeared. After a second brief and equally unsuccessful attempt to settle in Palestine, Brill moved to London; it was there, shortly before his death in 1886, that he issued the final eleven issues of his newspaper.

It was also in 1863 that a new group of Jews reached Jerusalem, from a distant province of the Russian Empire. A few families only, they came from the towns and villages of Georgia, on the eastern shore of the Black Sea and the southern slopes of the Caucasus: a region in which the settlement of European Jews had been forbidden by Tsarist decree of 1835. These Jews of Georgia were an ancient community: they themselves believed that they were one of the ten 'lost' tribes of Israel dispersed by the Assyrians in 700 BC. Passing through the Georgian city of Tbilisi in 1272, Marco Polo had seen them. Their language was that of the local population: Georgian. By the mid-nineteenth century they numbered some 12,000, mostly living in the town of Kutaisi. Now they too, with their strange Georgian tongue, became a part of the medley of tongues and characters in the Jewish quarter.

In 1863 the process of modernization in Jerusalem was further advanced by Sir Moses Montefiore, with the establishment of a school for Jewish girls. Four years later it received further funds from Baroness Lionel de Rothschild, in memory of her daughter Evelina, who had died in 1866, and after whom the school was then named. In 1894 the school was transferred to the Anglo-Jewish Association, becoming the principal focus of the Association's philanthropic work in Jerusalem, the funds being raised by British Jewry.

Schools for the young and excavations for the scholar: such were the twin educational achievement of 1863. For in that year the French archaeologist, Ferdinand de Saulcy, began his excavations at the Tombs of the Kings, just outside the city walls, to the north of the Damascus Gate: a site dating back to the time of the Jewish Kingdom, subsequently destroyed by the power of Rome.

The Montefiore cottages outside the walls, and the Austrian Hospice inside, represented the Jewish and European efforts to deal with the growth of population, and of pilgrims. But both were to seem inoffensive examples of modernity when contrasted with the buildings that were completed in 1864 to the north-west of the city: the Russian Hospice.

Dominated by the bright green cupolas of a Russian Orthodox church, the stern stone buildings of the hospice were now the first buildings to be seen by those who reached Jerusalem from Jaffa. Capable of housing more than a thousand pilgrims, mostly on its straw-strewn floors, and including a hospital, the Russian Hospice was to provoke contradictory reactions. 'This immense establishment', wrote Besant and Palmer in 1871, 'is furnished with dormitories, refectories, chapel, reading-rooms, hospitals etc., and for cleanliness and good management would compare favourably with any institution of the kind in Europe.' But Thomas Cook, the visitors' guide, was censorious: 'The traveller', he wrote five years later, 'will be vexed to see a mass of ugly buildings erected by the Russians, principally for the benefit of pilgrims.'

No survey had been made of the city since the Royal Engineers' map of

Top: the Russian Orthodox Church, built in 1864 (1984). *Above:* the Russian Orthodox Church, and Russian Hospice, with the city walls beyond (photographed from the north-west of the city, 1864).

1841, a map which had been published in 1849 with the places and inscriptions of religious interest added on it by two theologians, George Williams and Robert Willis. By 1864 the need for a new survey had become urgent, and once again it was the Royal Engineers of the British Army who undertook the task. This time their funds came, not from the War Office in London, but from a benefactress who wished to improve Jerusalem's water supply.

The survey of 1864 was led by a Captain in the Royal Engineers, Charles William Wilson. The result of his work, known as the 'Ordinance Survey of Jerusalem', was published in Britain in 1865, in three parts. The first part was a map of the city and its surroundings, scale 1:1,000. The second was a plan of Jerusalem with streets, buildings and contour lines, scale 1:2,500. The third was a plan of the Haram, showing cisterns, vaults and contours.

Wilson and his fellow Engineers completed their survey in 1865. It at once became the standard reference work for all subsequent maps and plans of the city until the First World War.

In writing about his discoveries, Wilson praised the achievement of those who brought Jerusalem's water to the city in Roman times: 'works which', he wrote, 'for boldness in design and skill in execution, rival even the most approved system of modern engineers, and which might, under a more enlightened government, be again brought into use'.

Wilson also commented on the problems of archaeological exploration. 'Outside the city', he wrote, 'there was no trouble, the fellaheen being glad to have the opportunity of gaining a few piastres, but inside there was some hard bargaining, especially with the family of Abn Saud, for permission to dig.' These bargainings, Wilson added, 'would be rather amusing if they did not cause such a waste of time, as there is no bringing an Arab to the point under a couple of hours' smoking and coffee drinking. It was found, at last, best to commence digging without any one's leave, allowing the proprietors to find out what was being done, and to come and claim compensation.'

As he explored the city's by-ways, Wilson could not avoid daily contact with the insanitary conditions. 'Of the drainage of the city', he commented, 'it is sufficient to say, that there is none in our acceptance of the word, for there are no drains of any kind from the city, and the accumulation of filth of every description in the streets is most disgraceful to the authorities.'

In 1864 the opening of a telegraph cable from Jaffa to Constantinople had linked Palestine with Europe by telegraph. A year later, the establishment of the overland telegraph from Jaffa to Jerusalem provided visual proof of modernity. An Arab who defiantly struck the wires with his spear, and who damaged one of the telegraph posts, was caught, brought to trial, found guilty of damaging Ottoman property, and hanged – upon the very post that he had damaged.

On 12 May 1865 a group of distinguished British scholars, churchmen and public figures gathered in London in the 'Jerusalem Chamber' of Westminster Abbey. Their aim was to set up a society to study every aspect of modern Palestine: its archaeology, geography, geology and natural history. The society, which was under the patronage of Queen Victoria, was to be called the Palestine Exploration Fund. Its guidelines were threefold: all projects were to be carried out on scientific principles, the Fund as a body was to 'abstain from controversy', and it was not to conduct its affairs as a religious body.

It was at this inaugural meeting that Captain Charles Wilson, who had just returned from Jerusalem, on the completion of his Ordinance Survey, set out for the assembled enthusiasts what he considered to be the immediate need: to send out an expedition, made up of men of the Royal Engineers, to explore and map the whole of Palestine, with a view to a systematic survey. With Wilson as the leader, and Lieutenant Anderson as his assistant, the expedition travelled from Mount Lebanon southward, reaching Jerusalem in April 1866. As a result of its findings, the Palestine Exploration Fund decided to give Jerusalem priority for all future work.

In Jerusalem, the Swiss Protestant missionary, Conrad Schick, undertook on behalf of the Fund to supervise all building activities and excavations. His own house, Thabor, on the Street of the Consuls, had been built to his design, and many other new buildings outside the walls were to bear the impress of his architectural interests. Thabor survives to this day.

Jerusalem was becoming the focal point of many European initiatives. The success of Ludwig Schneller's orphanage, established outside the city wall in 1860, led in 1865 to the building of a school for orphan girls. This too was built outside the walls, in fields just south of the Jaffa road. The founders were deaconesses from Rhineland-Westphalia, and they called their institution Talitha Kumi, after the New Testament story of the 'ruler of the synagogue' who was told that his daughter was dead. Jesus, hearing this, had gone at once

Conrad Schick's house, Thabor (photographed in 1984).

to see the dead girl: 'And he took the damsel by the hand, and said unto her, Talitha Kumi; which is, being interpreted, Damsel, I say unto thee, arise. And straightway the damsel arose and walked.'

Within ten years, a hundred Arab girls were being educated at Talitha Kumi, in the care of seven deaconesses and a Lady Superintendent, after whom the orphanage had become known as the Charlotte School.

These European achievements went unnoticed by many European visitors, who spent only a few days, seldom a week or more, in the city, searching for antiquity and finding, so it often seemed, only dirt and filth. Among the visitors to Jerusalem in 1866 was William Hepworth Dixon. 'No gas, no oil, no torch, no wax lights up the streets and archways of Jerusalem by night,' he wrote; 'half an hour after gun-fire the bazaar is cleared, the shops and baths are closed, the camels stalled, the narrow ways deserted.' As for the Jewish quarter, 'which a man may smell afar off', its alleys and courts were 'unspeakably offensive to eye and nostril, the Polish synagogue a new and tawdry work, the ancient synagogue, a vault half buried in the soil'.

There was, Dixon noted, a Jewish infirmary for the sick, 'of whom there is abundant supply', while around the buildings of the Jewish quarter 'reek and starve about four thousand Israelites, many of them living in a state of filth as unlike the condition of their clean, bright ancestors as the life of an English gentleman under Victoria is unlike that of a Britain serf under Boadicea'.

The smells were in many ways deceptive. Within the courtyards and the religious schools not only daily life according to the sanitary precepts of Judaism, but scholarship and literature, flourished. Dixon's visit co-incided with the publication in the Old City of the religious writings of Shalom Sharabi, a Jew who had been born in the Yemen in 1720, and spent all his adult life in Jerusalem, dying in the city in 1777. Sharabi, a man of outstanding piety, and an exponent of the mysticism of the Kabbala, was revered after his death as a saint and miracle worker. His works had first been published in Salonica in 1806; their republication in Jerusalem in 1866 helped to preserve the traditions of early mysticism and religious meditation.

The religious diversity of Jerusalem included, in 1866, fifteen 'Jewish Protestants', some with families, who that August petitioned Consul Moore for British protection. These Jews had all been born in Russia. In their petition, they explained that 'it is well known that Russia has the largest number of Jews in her dominions, because she has the largest share of Poland, so it is but natural that the greatest number of European Jews in Palestine are from Russia. We, your petitioners came here at different times with our parents, relatives or friends who are now estranged from us. Now according to the rule of the Russian Government the Jews are dismissed from protection when their passports which have only one year's duration terminate, and Russia does not renew passports if their owners do not return to their native country.'

British protection was duly extended to these Jewish converts to Protestantism. Four years later, Moore noted that there were in all 726 British-protected persons, all 'Polish Jews, ex-Russian subjects' who, having forfeited their Russian nationality 'by a longer absence than the laws of the Empire permit', had, under the Russian–British agreement of 1848, the right to British protection, but 'in Palestine only'. These 726 constituted about one in ten of the Jewish population of Jerusalem: more than 400 of them were children.

On 27 February 1866 Sir Moses Montefiore left England for his sixth and last journey to Jerusalem. He was 81 years old. As he approached the city on the morning of 26 March, 'the road and the adjacent hills', he wrote, 'became covered with a concourse of people of all different denominations'. The Governor of the city, Izzet Pasha, sent forty horsemen to escort him the last few miles, while the Chief Rabbi of the Sephardi congregation, Haim David Hazan, joined him for the final approach 'mounted on a beautiful Arab steed', together with Samuel Salant and other heads of the Ashkenazi congregation, 'all hailing my approach with the exclamation "Barookh Haba", "Blessed be he who cometh"', while hundreds of children stood by the roadside singing Hebrew hymns 'which had been specially composed for the occasion, and in which were recited the sufferings of Zion, and hope in Israel's future'.

Among the welcoming crowd, Montefiore particularly noticed forty boys from the Laemel school 'whose healthy and neat appearance, and beautifully harmonious voices, added greatly to the impressiveness of a scene not easily to be forgotten'.

Montefiore entered Jerusalem on this, his final visit, through the Jaffa Gate, being greeted there by a special prayer read by 'one of the chief officers of the synagogue', invoking God's blessing on the messenger from a distant land, a prayer to which the vast concourse of persons responded with what Montefiore recorded as 'a heart-stirring "Amen"'!'

Assisted by Louis Loewe, Montefiore spent much of his time in the city distributing funds which had been entrusted to him 'by several friends of Jerusalem, with a special request to dispense the same to the poor'. He also, at the Governor's request, provided £100 as a 'nucleus for further subscriptions' for a building beyond the city gates to house 'persons unhappily afflicted with leprosy'.

During the first and second days of the Passover, Montefiore visited 'the Touro almshouses', noting that they were situated 'in the most healthy part of the suburbs of the Holy City'. His account of what were soon to become known as the Montefiore cottages continued: 'scrupulous attention is paid to the preservation of order and cleanliness, and the inmates are cheerful and happy, devoting a portion of their time to religious observances and study; but nevertheless, not neglecting the following of industrial pursuits'. Montefiore added: 'I conversed with most of the inmates, who were mechanics, and found there was no hesitation or reluctance in doing the hardest work with the object of earning a sum, however small, towards their maintenance. The inmates apply themselves to a variety of trades. The evidences of the industrial activity of the Israelites afforded me much satisfaction. I was also gratified to observe the healthy appearance of themselves and their children, more especially as most of them are unable to incur the expense of providing themselves and their families with animal food, except on the Sabbath. These almshouses are so

Left: three elderly Jews on the porch of the Montefiore cottages (1870s). *Right:* the Montefiore cottages (1984).

highly esteemed that even many inhabitants of the city seek permission for a short sojourn there, for the recovery of their health; and I even found that some of the back offices, only intended for lumber rooms, had been actually, though without my knowledge, appropriated as dwellings for several families.'

During his visit, Montefiore received permission from the Governor of Jerusalem to set up an awning near the Wailing Wall, 'so as to afford shelter and protection from rain and heat to pious persons visiting this sacred spot'. Later in his visit, Montefiore noted: 'There are two Synagogues attached to the Touro almshouses, one of them for the Sephardim, which I had already visited, the other for the Ashkenasim; today I visited the latter. On my way thither, a young woman passed us with a large book in her hand, and, on my inquiring what it was, she informed me it was a Hebrew Psalm Book, with several Commentaries of ancient authors printed in Hebrew-German characters. I requested her to read one of the Psalms with the Commentary, this she did with great fluency and without hesitation. I have often had occasion to admire the ability of many females in our community of Jerusalem, not only in respect of their household duties and in needlework of every description, but also in

Hebrew lore. I was on one occasion addressed by the mother of two or three children who solicited aid, and, to my surprise, she spoke to Dr Loewe and myself in the Hebrew language with elegance and facility.'

On 14 April 1866 Sir Moses Montefiore left Jerusalem for the last time, wending his way towards the Jaffa road, leaving the Holy City 'more deeply than ever impressed with its sacred reminiscences and its perennial beauty, and more fervently than ever offering prayers for its future welfare'.

On 17 February 1867 a 27-year-old Royal Engineer, Lieutenant Charles Warren, reached Jerusalem, 'with eight baggage-mules heavily laden', as head of a second expedition mounted by the Palestine Exploration Fund. As a result of Colonel Wilson's expedition of the previous year, the Fund had set as its priority the excavations in Jerusalem aimed at answering the main questions still troubling biblical scholars. Where on the Temple Mount was the precise location of the Temple? Where were the three city walls described by the Roman-Jewish historian, Josephus? Where had the pre-Solomonic City of David been situated? What was the true site of the crucifixion?

Lieutenant Warren began his explorations on the region of the Temple Mount. Unable to excavate on the Mount itself, he was nevertheless allowed to study the structure of the Dome of the Rock, and to examine the many cisterns under the Temple platform. In all, Warren counted thirty-four reservoirs cut out of the solid rock. The largest of these reservoirs was forty-three feet deep, and could hold more than two million gallons of water.

On the western side of the Temple Mount, along the filled-in route of the Tyropoeon valley, Warren sank seven deep shafts. These revealed that the bedrock beneath the rubble was some seventy-five feet below the existing ground level. At the bottom of the shafts he discovered ancient remains: the foundations of a large pillar, and a tunnel hewn out of the rock.

Warren did not restrict his excavation to the area adjacent to the Temple Mount. He also sank shafts on the spur to the south of the Mount, the original City of David, and on the Ophel hill. Here, on 24 October 1867, fifty feet from the entrance to the tunnel at the Virgin's Fount, he discovered another passageway, coming from the north west. On being cleared out, it proved to be seventeen feet long, ending in a cave. From this cave a shaft, or chimney, hewn out of the solid rock, rose forty feet into the very heart of the hill: possibly the 'gutter', or conduit, mentioned in the biblical description of David's conquest of Jerusalem. 'And David said on that day, Whosoever getteth

Top: excavations near Robinson's Arch, next to the western wall of the Temple Mount (1867).
Above: excavations at Wilson's Arch, underneath the western wall (1867).

up to the gutter, and smiteth the Jebusites, and the lame and the blind, that are hated of David's soul, he shall be chief and captain.'

In memory of Warren's work, this conduit has been known ever since as 'Warren's shaft'.

Six years after his return to London, Warren published his book *Underground Jerusalem*, dedicated to the General Committee of the Palestine Exploration Fund. In his introduction he recalled how, when he was already in Palestine at the start of his work, and had asked for further funds, he had received the message: 'Give us results, and we will send you money!' In vain, he recalled, did he reply: 'Give me the tools, materials, money, food, and I will get you results.' Warren's plea had only elicited the further riposte: 'Results furnished, and you shall have the money!'

By November 1867 Warren was in debt to the sum of £1,000: five months unpaid salary. But he went on digging and questioning. Within three years he had examined fourteen different sites, among them Solomon's stables under the Temple Mount and remains of the Roman wall near the Citadel.

Warren's work frequently involved him in clashes with Muslim religious dignitaries, especially those responsible for the Mosque and Dome on the Temple Mount, around and below which so much of his digging was centred. 'Our progress through these passages had been rapid,' Warren wrote, of one of his underground explorations, 'but unhappily the hammer-blows, resounding

Excavations below the south-west corner of the Temple Mount (1867).

through the hollow walls in so unwonted a manner, alarmed the modern representative of the High Priest. Infuriate with anger, the fine old sheikh would listen to no reasoning: but repairing to the south-east angle of the old Temple enclosure, mounted its battlements and summoned the Sheikh of Siloam to stand forth and answer for his misdeeds. With full turban and long flowing robes, edges tipped with fur, the old man stood, on the edge of the steep masonry, stamping his feet with rage and bellowing imprecations.'

Warren's work was not all archaeological. He also made a study of the trades of Jerusalem, examining in all 1,320 shops, and noting down the trade, the number of men employed, and the men's religion. Of the 1,320 shops when he examined them, 278 were empty, but 'quite filled up during the Easter festivities by merchants from Damascus and other cities'.

According to Warren's enquiries, the single largest trade was that of shoemaker: there were 230 shoemakers in all, of whom 83 were Jews, 51 Muslims, 41 Greeks, 27 Armenians, 22 Latins and 6 Protestants. The next largest group of tradesmen, the grocers, included 86 Muslims and 51 Jews. The 88 greengrocers included 67 Muslims and 17 Jews. The 3 gunmakers were all Greeks. All 5 pottery kilns were worked by Muslims. Of the 22 money changers, all but 5 were Jews: these 5 were 3 Latins and 2 Armenians. There were no Muslim tailors, but 34 Jews, 10 Greeks, 10 Latins, 6 Armenians and 2 Protestants. All but one of the 9 sugar sellers were Jews, and all but 2 of the 34 tin smiths and 4 of the 19 watchmakers were Jews. There were 66 Muslim coffin makers, but no Jews: the Jews of Jerusalem did not bury their dead, as Jews elsewhere, in coffins, but in shrouds, tradition asserting that this would expedite their return to the Temple Mount on the Day of Judgement.

Surveying the bazaars, Warren observed that the Muslims and Jews 'appear to amalgamate with less difficulty than Muslims and Christians'. Of the Jews praying at the Wailing Wall he wrote: 'It is a most remarkable sight; these people all thronging the pavement, and wailing so intensely, that often the tears roll down their faces.' It was also, Warren noted, a 'great rendezvous' for European visitors, 'who walked about laughing and making remarks, as though it were all a farce, instead of realizing that it is, perhaps, one of the most solemn gatherings left to the Jewish Church'.

In reflecting on the future of Jerusalem, Warren was drawn to comment that, as far as the Jews were concerned 'for a long time the country must be governed for them', allowing the Jew 'gradually to find his way into its army, its law, and its diplomatic service, and gradually to superintend the farming

Jewish types: cotton workers (1880s); tinsmith (1880s); shoemaker (1860s).

operations, and work himself on the farms'. There was no need, he commented, 'to wait for him to find his way into the mercantile pursuits, he has done so already'. If, Warren added, this Jewish enterprise 'could be carried out for some twenty years, the Jewish principality might stand by itself, as a separate kingdom guaranteed by the great powers'.

Five years after the arrival in Jerusalem of the first Jews from the Russian province of Georgia, another group of non-Ashkenazi Jews from Russia reached the city. These were the Jews of Bukhara, a remote khanate east of the Caspian Sea, near the northern border of Afghanistan. Bukharan Jews, like their Georgian counterparts west of the Caspian, believed that they were descendants of one of the ten 'lost' tribes.

Many Bukharan Jews had been forcibly converted to Islam in the early nineteenth century: in 1844 a European Jewish convert to Catholicism, Joseph Wolff, in the course of a missionary journey to the east, found 300 such families of forced converts in Bukhara. He also found 'ten thousand Jews', who, to distinguish them from the Muslims, 'must wear a small cap and girdle around their waist'.

Jews from Bukhara (photographed in 1950); a 'Venerable taylor' from Bukhara (photographed in 1966).

The first Bukharan Jews to reach Jerusalem, in 1868, were soon followed by several wealthy families who wished to make Jerusalem the spiritual centre of the Bukharan community. Already, in Bukhara, they had heard of the work of Sir Moses Montefiore, and in Jerusalem they set up a small community, visually distinguished by the splendour of the women's ceremonial clothes and jewellery, and by the men's scull caps, heavily embroidered with coloured silk, or gold.

By the turn of the century there were an estimated 180 Bukharan Jewish families in the city.

Christian building was also in evidence during 1868. The wooden cupola over the Holy Sepulchre, which had been erected by the Greeks after the great fire, in 1809, had begun to fall out of repair. Since 1850 the question of its restoration had been discussed repeatedly, but had reached a stalemate during the struggle between Russia and Turkey. Following the Crimean War the matter was again taken up, and, in 1868, an arrangement was made between France, Russia and Turkey, in accordance with which a new cupola, supported on iron frames, was constructed. 'Whether it will be more lasting than its immediate predecessor', commented Colonel Wilson, 'remains to be proved, but it cannot be regarded as satisfactory from an architectural point of view, and it does not compare favourably with its rival in Jerusalem, the cupola of the Dome of the Rock.'

The wood needed for the cupola could not be found in Palestine, where the woods of ancient times had long been cut down, leaving barren, stony, treeless hillsides. It was brought therefore from France, going by sea from Marseilles to Jaffa, and carried up from Jaffa to Jerusalem by camel.

Church building was also in evidence on the Mount of Olives. In 1868 Princess Latour d'Auvergne, Comtesse de Bouillon, a wealthy relative of Napoleon III, provided the funds for the building of a church near the summit of the Mount of Olives. Called the Church of the Lord's Prayer, it was built next to the Place of the Ascension, which the Muslims had turned into a mosque after the defeat of the Crusaders. The new church had around its courtyard thirty-one slabs on which were inscribed the Lord's Prayer in thirty-two languages. The Princess herself moved to Jerusalem, living in a small house adjoining the church until her death eight years later.

In 1868, in his handbook for that year for travellers to Syria and Palestine, John Murray noted that in Jerusalem, despite 'much improvement within the last few years', nevertheless the houses in the city 'are bad, and the rents high'. Murray also commented that Noel Temple Moore, the British Consul, was 'well known for his courtesy and kindness to travellers, as for his extensive and thorough knowledge of the country and people. From him authentic information can always be obtained as to the state of the roads, and the practicability of excursions to remote, dangerous, or unfrequented localities.'

Of the Jewish quarter, Murray wrote that until the last few years its lanes and houses 'were in a wretched state of squalor and dilapidation; but a great change for the better has taken place, chiefly owing to the enlightened efforts and princely generosity of Sir Moses Montefiore.' Of Jerusalem's 'cleanliness' Murray noted: 'Vegetable and animal matter to an enormous extent is thrown into the courts, streets, and waste places within the walls, and there allowed slowly to decay. Most of the houses are destitute of proper sewerage, and badly ventilated; while not a few of them, especially in the Jewish quarter, are dripping with damp. The cisterns and reservoirs, both covered and uncovered, which abound in the city, are permitted to become stagnant and foul. These things combine to produce both malignant and intermittent fevers during the summer and autumn.'

Within the city walls, the pressure of the population was noted in 1869 by

Rebuilding the cupola of the Church of the Holy Sepulchre (1868). *Right:* The cloisters of the Church of the Lord's Prayer (Fiorillo, 1888).

a visitor from the United States, Andrew Thomson. 'The many-coloured population of modern Jerusalem', he wrote, 'with its many antagonist faiths, is far from sufficient to occupy the space which is enclosed within its walls. The impression which our every survey of it left upon our mind was that of a shrivelled old man, who had long ago seen better days, but who had somehow shrunken grievously within his dress. Its streets are in many places arcaded and gloomy, so narrow that it is with some difficulty that two loaded camels can pass each other, and rough almost as a mountain-path; and its houses with so few windows fronting to the street, that they unpleasantly remind you of a prison.'

A widely-travelled American, Thomson noted that the synagogues in Jerusalem 'are not adorned like many of those in our European capitals, such as we have seen at Leghorn and Frankfort, probably in order to avoid tempting the cupidity of unscrupulous Moslem rulers. It is indeed remarkable in how many ways the Jews keep hold of their country as with a trembling hand, and are reluctant to let go the traces and the records of a glorious past.' At Passover, Thomson visited the Wailing Wall, where he found the number of Jews assembled there 'unusually great, probably between eighty and one hundred – of

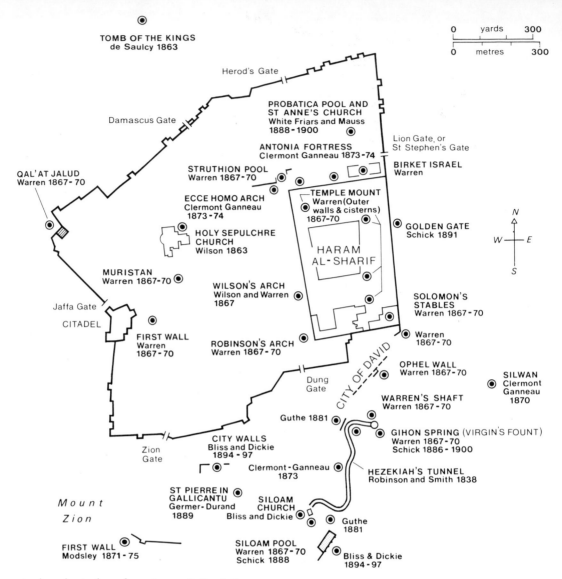

TOMB OF THE KINGS
de Saulcy 1863

0   yards   300
0   metres   300

Herod's Gate

Damascus Gate

PROBATICA POOL AND
ST ANNE'S CHURCH
White Friars and Mauss
1888-1900

Lion Gate, or
St Stephen's Gate

ANTONIA FORTRESS
Clermont Ganneau 1873-74

BIRKET ISRAEL
Warren

QAL'AT JALUD
Warren 1867-70

STRUTHION POOL
Warren 1867-70

ECCE HOMO ARCH
Clermont Ganneau
1873-74

TEMPLE MOUNT
Warren (Outer
walls & cisterns)
1867-70

HOLY SEPULCHRE
CHURCH
Wilson 1863

HARAM
AL-SHARIF

GOLDEN GATE
Schick 1891

N
W — E
S

MURISTAN
Warren 1867-70

WILSON'S ARCH
Wilson and Warren
1867

SOLOMON'S
STABLES
Warren 1867-70

Jaffa Gate
CITADEL

FIRST WALL
Warren
1867-70

ROBINSON'S ARCH
Warren 1867-70

Warren
1867-70

OPHEL WALL
Warren 1867-70

SILWAN
Clermont
Ganneau
1870

Dung
Gate

CITY OF DAVID

WARREN'S SHAFT
Warren 1867-70

Zion
Gate

CITY WALLS
Bliss and Dickie
1894-97

Guthe 1881

GIHON SPRING (VIRGIN'S FOUNT)
Warren 1867-70
Schick 1886-1900

Clermont-Ganneau
1873

HEZEKIAH'S TUNNEL
Robinson and Smith 1838

Mount
Zion

ST PIERRE IN
GALLICANTU
Germer-Durand
1889

SILOAM
CHURCH
Bliss and Dickie

Guthe
1881

FIRST WALL
Modsley 1871-75

SILOAM POOL
Warren 1867-70
Schick 1888

Bliss & Dickie
1894-97

Archaeological explorations, 1838-1898

every age, from the old white-bearded patriarch with shrivelled features and piping voice, to the beautiful melancholy boy of twelve. It was a touching sight. After the lapse of eighteen dreary centuries, Israel, represented there from almost every country in the world, was weeping over her ruined Temple, her ruined city, her ruined Church, her people scattered and reviled.' Jerusalem 'at this hour', Thomson added, 'is a Jewish poorhouse or prison, of which the Mohammedan holds the key'.

Even as Thomson wrote these words, further attempts were being made to break out of that 'prison'. For in that same year, 1869, seven Jewish families decided to move outside the city walls. They chose as the site of their new quarter a piece of land on the southern side of the Jaffa road, half a mile outside the Jaffa Gate. Known as 'Nahalat Shiva' – the quarter of the seven – it housed the printing press of one of its founders, Joel Moshe Salomon.

One of the seven was Beinush Salant, the son of Rabbi Salant, who had come to Jerusalem from Russia in 1841, and who greatly favoured the setting-up of Jewish quarters outside the crowded confines of the Old City, with its seemingly endless feuds and disputes.

Another of the seven was Joshua Yellin, then 26 years old, the son of the Ashkenazi Jew, David Yellin, from Russia and the Sephardi Jewess, Sarah Yehezkel, whose parents had come to Jerusalem from Baghdad.

The year 1869 saw the opening of a metalled road from Jerusalem to Jaffa. It was not a success, however. As Andrew Thomson noted: 'The Pasha has made his first attempt at road-making on this route. But, like all his other attempts in the direction of civilization, it has been spasmodic, fitful, reluctant, and has stopped short whenever his exchequer threatened to become a little shallow. You have, therefore, road-making in all its degrees on this first journey – some places finished, many more half-finished, and therefore intolerably rough and impassable, and others little more than marked off, and scarcely touched as yet by the spade or the mattock.'

The object of this road-building was to provide a welcome for the Austrian Crown Prince Rudolf, ill-fated heir of the Habsburgs, who was certainly the most noble of the city's visitors that year. Another visitor was Mark Twain, who wrote of how: 'Rags, wretchedness, poverty, and dirt, those signs and symbols that indicate the presence of Moslem rule more surely than the crescent-flag itself, abound. Lepers, cripples, the blind, and the idiotic assail you on every hand.' Jerusalem, Mark Twain added, 'is mournful, and dreary, and lifeless. I would not desire to live here.'

Those who did live in the city accepted myriad hazards. Of these Europeans, Charles Warren and the archaeologists were among the most sorely troubled. 'Showers of stones and streams of loose and treacherous shingle were common occurrences,' Andrew Thomson recalled, of an exploration with Warren. 'In some places the earth was so poisoned by sewage, that the hands of the workmen broke out into festering sores; in other places the air was found to be so impure, that the candles refused to burn.' In another instance, Thomson wrote, 'the water from a periodic spring so increased upon them, that they were obliged to flee before it; and when it swelled up to Captain Warren's neck, he could only preserve the candle from extinction by carrying it in his mouth'.

CHAPTER V

The 1870s: Advice for travellers

More than any other single excursion, a visit to 'the Jews' Wailing Place' had become a part of the tourist's itinerary. Each visitor was stirred to different reflections. Coming to the wall in 1870, the Reverend Richard Newton, Doctor of Divinity, and editor of the publications of the American Sunday-School Union, drew two lessons as he 'turned to go away': the first, that it was 'the sin of the Jews which brought upon them all the evil that they are suffering now, and that their fathers before them have suffered for hundreds of years', and the second, that 'the sin of neglecting Jesus is especially a dreadful thing'. That, Newton felt vividly at the Wailing Wall, 'was the great sin of the Jewish people: they neglected Jesus'.

Some Jews, Newton noted, would 'put their mouths to the opening on the stones, and repeat some of the lamentations of Jeremiah, or offer their prayers in a very sad and mournful voice, while the tears at the same time are running down their cheeks. It makes one feel very sad to see it: and I almost felt as if I could weep with those who wept in that interesting old place.'

It was not only at the Wailing Wall that ancient stones could be found. Many individual stones were also visible as part of recent dwellings. In the Muslim village of Silwan, as inside the city itself, it had long been the habit to strengthen and embellish a house with one or more of these sturdy relics of the past, which were to be found at almost any point where new foundations might be dug. In 1870 the French archaeologist Charles Clermont Ganneau, searching in Silwan, came across two such stones, with Hebrew inscriptions on them, set into an outer wall.

The Silwan inscriptions proved to be even older than those which had been found earlier in the Siloam Tunnel. They were, however, so badly defaced as

'Wailing Place of the Jews' (Bergheim, 1870s).

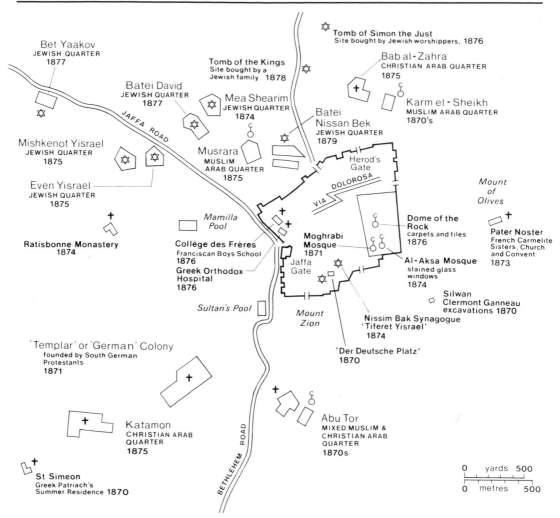

New Muslim ($\overset{\circ}{\underset{\circ}{\text{}}}$), Christian (✝) and Jewish (✡) building in the 1870s.

to be indecipherable. Clermont Ganneau wished to send them to Paris. But his discovery coincided with the outbreak of the Franco-Prussian war, and no one in Paris seemed interested in a relic of ancient days, or willing to bear the costs involved. Clermont Ganneau therefore approached the British Consul, who arranged for the inscriptions to be cut from the wall and sent to the British Museum: the expenses being born by the Museum.

Archaeological discoveries in Jerusalem created a stir in the scientific salons of Europe. Jews 'wailing' drew the eager interest of readers of the annual travel books. But in the city itself, it was the unobserved and unreported activities which marked the slow but steady emergence of Jerusalem into the 'Victorian' age. In 1870 the Hebrew-language newspaper *Havazzelet* began publication again. Among its contributors was Israel Frumkin, son-in-law of the printer, Israel Bak. At the age of nine, Frumkin had been brought to Jerusalem from White Russia. Now, at the age of twenty, he imposed a radical tone upon his father-in-law's newspaper, of which he eventually became editor.

Frumkin's causes were many: an end to financial corruption in the Jewish community, the inclusion of secular subjects and vocational training in the schools, and the striving for higher educational standards. He also advocated the establishment of Jewish agricultural villages in Palestine.

As Frumkin's influence over *Havazzelet* increased, so did the paper's outspokenness. Three years after he had joined it, it launched an attack on those who controlled the Jewish charitable funds. So determined was Frumkin to see Jewry freed from the corruption of overseas charity, that he openly criticized the principal benefactor of Jerusalem's Jews, Sir Moses Montefiore, on the grounds that Montefiore had shown 'excessive sympathy' towards those in charge of the charities.

In 1870, in the Silesian city of Breslau, a German Jewish professor, Heinrich Graetz, completed the ninth volume of his eleven-volume *History of the Jews*. These nine volumes had taken him seventeen years to write. The remaining two were to be the first in the chronology of his history: the biblical and Second Temple periods. Not having seen the lands of the Bible, Graetz had left these two volumes to the last, determined to see Palestine, and Jerusalem, with his own eyes, before writing them. He reached the city in 1870, at the age of 53. Shocked by what he regarded as the unenlightened nature of the Jewish schools and the evil influence of the predominant system of charity, and angered that with so many Christian orphanages there was no Jewish orphanage, he returned to Germany dispirited.

Making no reference in the text to his visit, Graetz completed his history, the biblical volume, to the death of Solomon, being published in 1874, and its successor, up to the revolt of the Hasmoneans, in two parts, in 1875 and 1876.

Within the walls, each quarter of Jerusalem was noted for its tracts of open and waste land, mostly overgrown. Both the north-eastern section of the Muslim quarter and the area inside the Dung Gate abounded with vast bushes of prickly pear. Another waste area lay to the south of the Jewish quarter, between the densely packed dwellings and the southern perimeter of the Ottoman walls. Here, in 1870, Jews from Germany began to build a series of elegant,

Top: The prickly pears inside the Dung Gate, with the Jewish quarter beyond (before 1914).
Above: The church at the entrance to the Templar Colony (photographed in 1984).

two-storey, red-tiled dwellings around a central courtyard: an area which soon became known as 'der Deutsche Platz'.

German influence in Jerusalem was not confined to Jewish activity. In 1871 a group of Protestants from Württemberg, in southern Germany, founded a residential quarter to the south of the city, in the Valley of the Giants – the reputed site of David's killing of Goliath. Known as the 'Templar' or 'German' Colony, this quiet haven of church, monastery, school, hospital and hospice drew a growing number of German missionaries to the city.

In 1871 the most comprehensive history of Jerusalem until that year was published in London. Its authors were Walter Besant and E. H. Palmer, the latter a former Professor of Arabic at Cambridge University. Their history, in 521 pages, went from the earliest times until the destruction of Crusader power by Saladin. But their conclusion was a negative one. Since Saladin's conquest of the city five hundred years before, they wrote, 'Jerusalem has been without a history', and they ended: 'Nothing has happened but an occasional act of brutality on the part of her masters towards the Christians, or an occasional squabble among the ecclesiastics. Perhaps, some time, the day may come when all together will be agreed that there is no one spot in the world more holy than another, in spite of associations, because the whole earth is the Lord's. Then the tender interest which those who read the Scriptures will always have for the places which the writers knew so well may have a fuller and freer play, apart from lying traditions, monkish legends, and superstitious impostures. For, to use the words which Cicero applied to Athens, there is not one spot in all this city, no single place where the foot may tread, which does not possess its history.'

Besant and Palmer completed their work in the year that the most recent Muslim construction, the Moghrabi mosque, was built on the Temple Mount. With the Dome of the Rock and the Al-Aksa mosque, it became a place of prayer and pilgrimage for Muslims as far away as Morocco and India. Christians, too, now regularly visited the Temple Mount, so recently a forbidden site. 'The Muslim guide', Besant and Palmer, noted, 'will wax eloquent' upon the connection between Al-Aksa and the Day of Judgement. After the 'anti-Christ' had been killed, 'the victors will then proceed to a general massacre of the Jews in and around the Holy City, and every tree and every stone shall cry out and say: "I have a Jew beneath me, slay him". Having done this, the Messiah will break the crosses and kill the pigs (Christians), after which the Millennium will set in.'

Top left: Tourists on the Temple Mount (Underwood and Underwood, 1897). *Top right:* The crusader façade of the Al-Aksa mosque (Francis Bedford, 1 April 1862). *Above:* Crusader columns inside the Al-Aksa mosque (1880s).

The Jews were for the most part unperturbed by such fulminations. From day to day, the mingling of peoples and religions proceeded without incident or danger, each community intent upon eking out a livelihood in a city which lay on no commercial crossroads, possessed no industry, and whose barren surrounding hills contained little to nourish and sustain a city. Yet the population grew from year to year. The Jews, from being predominantly newcomers, established through their children their own local family and patriotism.

Among the Jews born in Jerusalem in 1871 was Mazel Menace-Misraki. Seventy-two years later, on 2 March 1943, after being rounded up by the Germans in Paris, he was deported to Auschwitz. There, he perished.

The building of the metalled road from Jerusalem to Jaffa in 1869 had been a short-lived benefit. By 1872 its surface had so broken up that carriages could no longer use it. Nor did the Governor of the city since 1869, Kamil Pasha, have the funds to repair it. But better access to Jerusalem from the coast seemed again to be a possibility in the spring of 1873, when a railway route was surveyed through the Judaean hills. Not only was the route surveyed: its actual course was marked out on the ground by engineers. But although the Sultan had given approval, and a special Jaffa to Jerusalem railway directorate had been set up at Constantinople, the railway project was abandoned before any lines could be laid. Once more, travellers had to reach the city on horseback, their luggage being brought by mule over the ruins of the metalled road of 1869, ruins that gave no solace to their discomfort.

European explorers continued to search the ruins of Jerusalem for evidence of its ancient past. Most of them were equally drawn to describe the modern aspects of the city. Claude Conder, the 'officer in command' of the Palestine Exploration Fund survey expedition, was no exception:

'From my room in the Mediterranean Hotel I looked out at dawn. The orange-coloured light behind the Mount of Olives showed a black outline of mosque and tree and hill, with steel-coloured mountains to the right, capped by long wreaths of leaden vapour. The town lay in darkness below, its roofs shining wet with the heavy dew. Dimly visible the great dome of the Chapel of the Rock shone with its new coat of lead, and the tall minaret on the north wall of the Haram, together with the dark cypresses, was just distinguishable. A vapour went up over the whole city, and gave it a weird and dream-like aspect.

'Soon the town awoke, and the morning hubbub began. Long trains of camels came in, and the swarthy Bedawin wrangled with the soldiers at the gate. The market-girls from Bethlehem appeared under David's Tower, and, as the crowd thickened, black priests in saucepan-like hats jostled sickly Jews, with fur caps, long lovelocks, and dirty gabardines. The heavily-shod, unkempt Russian pilgrims mingled with sleek Rabbis, with Europeans, and German residents; Armenians with apple-cheeks and broad red sashes, and fierce Kurds with long moustachios and swords, were also numerous.

'So motley a scene as that which is presented daily in David Street and in the market-place under David's Tower, is perhaps to be found nowhere else. The chatter of the market-people, the shouting of the camel-drivers, the tinkling of bells, mingle with the long cry of the naked derwish, as he wanders, holding his tin pan for alms, and praising unceasingly "the Eternal God".'

Conder added: 'If it be Easter, the native crowd is mingled with the hosts of Armenian and Russian pilgrims, the first ruddy and stalwart, their women handsome and black-eyed, the men fierce and dark; the Russians, yet stronger in build and more barbarian in air, distinguished from every other nationality by their unkempt beards, the long locks, their great fur caps, and boots. Not less distinct are the Spanish, Mughrabee, Russian, and German Jews, each marked by a peculiar and characteristic physiognomy.'

Recording his visits to the Wailing Wall, Conder wrote of how the scene was 'striking from the great size and strength of the mighty stones, which rise without door or window up to the domes and cypresses above, suggesting how utterly the original worshippers are cast out, by men of alien race and faith …' His account of the Wailing Wall continued: 'Nearest to us stood the Pharisees from Germany, the Ashkenazi Jews, dressed in their best; the old men with grey locks and thin grey beards, on their heads the high black velvet cap edged with fur, their lovelocks curling on either side of their lank faces, their robes long gabardines of many colours; the younger men had blue-black hair, and pale strongly-marked features; here and there one saw a richly-dressed boy, a few little red-haired children, and occasionally an old woman, their faces all stamped with that subtle likeness which betrays the Jews in any country, and in any dress.

'There were bits of colour in these groups which would have delighted Rembrandt. An aged white-haired man, in a mulberry gabardine and black velvet cap, contrasted with the black satin and fur of his next neighbour, and in front of both was a third in a green dress. All these dark rich costumes were set in a warm background of tawny colour made by the great wall towering above.

Inside the Jaffa Gate, at the beginning of David Street (American Colony photograph, before 1914).

'Beyond the Ashkenazi were the Spanish and Mughrabee Jews, in quieter colours with black turbans, brown-eyed and more dignified in bearing. Presently came in a hulking fellow in citron-coloured coat and blue trousers, with a tall black pointed lambswool cap – a Russian Jew. The little Pharisees seemed to dwindle beside this giant, and his handsome, fresh-coloured face, blue eyes, and russet beard, seemed hardly to allow of his being one of the same nation; but it is the greatest peculiarity of the Jews that while never intermarrying, they yet approach in appearance most nearly the natives of the country in which they live, without entirely losing national traits of a distinctive character.'

Conder, determined to uncover further evidence of the biblical past, noted that explorations 'within modern Jerusalem' were made almost impossible 'by the fact that the foundations of the modern houses are laid not on the rock but on rubbish, so that even an unusually rainy winter is sufficient to cause many buildings to collapse; this was 'notably the case' in the last months of 1873 and the early months of 1874. Severe winters such as that one were common, accompanied by fierce winds, driving rain, and, as the temperature dropped below freezing, by heavy snow falls.

That same winter of 1874 a British civil engineer, Henry Maudslay, while making improvements in the Anglican bishopric school on Mount Zion, over-looking the Sultan's Pool, uncovered the bed rock, where it had been 'cut smooth and straight as a wall', to a height of some thirty feet, for a length of more than 130 yards. Under the school house itself, Maudslay discovered the foundation of an ancient tower, with a base forty-five feet square, standing on a broad ledge of rock. Below the tower were thirty-one steps cut out of the rock, leading to the base of a second, smaller tower: and below these towers, a system of eighteen water cisterns cut in the rock: a part of the water system of Roman Jerusalem. The water itself was brought by a covered, stone-carved conduit from the distant Hebron hills: the covered pipes following the tortuous line of the mountain contours, piercing in long tunnels both the ridge of hills to the south of the city, and the ridge on which Bethlehem was built.

For the Muslims, the middle of the decade saw a renewal of repair work on the Temple Mount, now graced by the imposing minaret of the new Moghrabi mosque. In 1874 the Sultan, Abdul Aziz, provided funds to repair the dilapi-dated ceiling, walls and floors of the Dome of the Rock, and to fit stained glass windows in the Al-Aksa mosque. Two years later, his successor as Sultan, Abdul Hamid II, provided the Dome of the Rock with carpets and tiles.

While the Dome and the Mosque were being in this way beautified, and Muslim Arabs able to feel once more a sense of pride in their Noble Sanctuary, outside the city walls the first Arab quarters were being built: Muslim Karm el-Sheikh and Christian Bab al-Zahra just to the north of Herod's Gate, Muslim Musrara four hundred yards north-west of the Damascus Gate, Christian Katamon a mile and a quarter to the south-west of the Jaffa Gate, and Abu Tor, a mixed Christian and Muslim quarter, on the hill half a mile south of Zion Gate, perched above the Hinnom and Kidron valleys.

For the Jews, the mid-1870s was also a time of renewed building outside the walls. On 18 March 1874 Joseph Rivlin presided over a meeting of Jews who wished to emulate those already living outside the city walls. The aim of those at the meeting was to encourage a hundred families to put their money into the most substantial building project to date. They would receive, so the founders proposed, a hundredfold return in their investment. 'Then Isaac sowed in that land, and received in the same year an hundredfold: and the Lord blessed him.' From the Hebrew for 'hundredfold', *mea shearim*, the new quarter received its name.

Within a few days of the first meeting to launch Mea Shearim, 140 families had applied to join. The rules of the quarter were drawn up by Rabbi Zalman Baharan, who stated that the quarter was being built for non-Hassidic Jews. Later, in answer to criticisms of the lack of greenery, Rabbi Baharan declared that there were no parks or gardens because these were prohibited by the Torah. Others believed that the prohibition was 'invented' to cover an oversight in the original plans. The religious tone was to be changed fifteen years later, when it was agreed to allow a Hassidic synagogue to be built in the quarter.

The early months of Mea Shearim went badly. The first ten houses were ready for occupation in March 1875. But a few days before the opening ceremony, a Jew was murdered by Arabs in the Nahalat Shiva quarter on the Jaffa road, and the opening was postponed for two months. Even then, all was not well: one rabbi, and the wife of another, were killed by Arabs, and there were frequent robberies. Families were frightened of the half-mile walk to the Jaffa Gate, or even of the path beyond the entrance way to their particular house.

Nevertheless, Mea Shearim was to grow beyond the original plan, reaching 147 houses, each with four apartments in it. These apartments were small: one or two rooms only. But a plethora of houses of prayer, synagogues and shops made the quarter self-contained for the three to four thousand inhabitants:

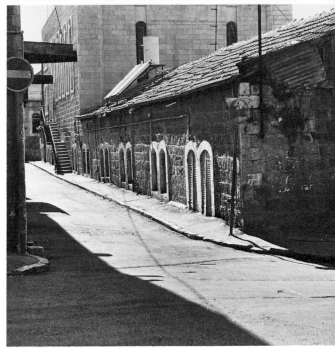

The religious school in Mea Shearim; a row of houses built in the 1870s; and, opposite, an outside staircase from the 1880s (photographed in 1984).

some 600 families in all. Each of the four sides of the symmetrical layout was entered by a single gate, closed at nightfall to protect the inhabitants from further intrusion.

Even as the first families were moving into Mea Shearim, other Jewish quarters were being built on either side of the Jaffa road: Even Yisrael and Mishkenot Yisrael in 1875, Batei David and Batei Yaakov in 1877.

In contrast to the single Arab houses, each with its own garden, built in clusters, the Jewish quarters were mostly set out in long squat rows, the entrances inside a courtyard, the side facing the street with no doors, as a protection against hostility.

European Christians continued to build inside the walls, the Franciscans setting up their Boys' School, the Collège des Frères, in the centre of the Christian quarter in 1876, and the Greek Orthodox Church opening its Hospital in the Christian quarter that same year. The Ratisbonne brothers, however, had built their monastery well outside the walls, west of the Mamilla pool.

Another of those who decided to move outside the walls in the 1870s was Rahamin Natan Meyuhas, whose family had come to Jerusalem in 1510, within

twenty years of the expulsion of the Jews from Spain. Many years later his son Joseph Meyuhas recalled how 'one bright day my father surprised us by announcing to the family that we were leaving our home inside the city walls once and for all'.

Rahamin Meyuhas had decided to establish his new home in the Arab village of Silwan, perched high above the Kidron valley immediately opposite the south-east corner of the Temple Mount, and within a few minutes' walk of the Jewish Cemetery on the Mount of Olives. The longest established Arab village in the immediate vicinity of Jerusalem, Silwan was built on ancient rock tombs which covered its hillside, and within sight of Absalom's monument.

By living in Silwan, Rahamin Meyuhas had told his wife and children, 'we will fill our lungs with fresh health-giving air instead of the bad air in the city; there we shall occupy ourselves with tilling the land; we shall plant vegetables with our own hands and eat them, especially we shall also drink fresh crystal clear spring water from the beginning of the year to the end of the year instead of the bad and cursed water of the cisterns of the old city'.

Meyuhas had no need to remind his family of how, with the coming of summer, the cisterns of the Old City would dry up for three and even four months, and where its inhabitants were 'forced to pay good money', as his son later recalled, in order to obtain water from Job's Fountain, the one freshwater spring in Jerusalem that flowed all year, and situated in the very same village of Silwan to which they were now to move. During those months when the Silwan fountain was the only source of water available to Jews, Christians, and Muslims alike, each family had to make do with a single goat skin, or at the very most two goat skins, of water each week; few could afford more. 'This little bit of water', Joseph Meyuhas later recalled, 'had to serve in the Old City for very limited drinking, only just enough water to quench one's thirst, as well as for washing hands – for which the correct name was "wetting" – from the remains of which one had to do one's laundry, and from the remains of that was done the floors, the so-called cleaning.' The use and re-use of this water 'served', as Joseph Meyuhas later recalled, 'as a faithful source for all sorts of illnesses and eye diseases'.

The Meyuhas family put to Rahamin Meyuhas every conceivable objection to leaving the Jewish quarter. But he was determined to make the move, telling his family: 'a village and tilling the soil is the desire of my heart, and that is where we shall go, and where we shall live!'

The Meyuhas family became the first Jews to live in Silwan village, growing vegetables and fruit on a small plot of land. But within four years, Rahamin Meyuhas died, leaving his 10-year-old son to carry on the family name. The young Joseph remained with his mother and sisters in Silwan, where he was to write down the stories told to him by his Arab neighbours, and to sit for many hours with some of the older Arab women, listening to and recording their own legends and parables. To earn money, he would sell tourists to the Old City examples of his miniscule handwriting: the words 'land of milk and honey' written on a single grain of wheat, or the whole of the Song of Songs written on an egg-shell.

In the late 1880s, Joseph Meyuhas moved to one of the new Jewish quarters which had been built along the Jaffa road. Later he became one of the leaders of the Jewish community of Jerusalem. A Sephardi Jew, he married one of the daughters of the Ashkenazi educationalist, Michael Pines, thus linking in his own family and offspring the two main branches of the Jewish diaspora. In 1898, at the time of the Kaiser's visit to Jerusalem, Jose Meyuhas was host to the Kaiser on behalf of the Jewish community of the city, providing the German Emperor with what a later generation recalled as 'a wonderful mixture' of Sephardi and Russian cooking at a sumptuous banquet: all the more remarkable because he was a man of frugal style.

Not all Christian visitors found inspiration in the holy sites and stones. On 17 November 1874, the 38-year-old William Henry Leighton wrote caustically in a letter to his brother: 'On Sunday we went to church at the English church on Mount Zion, where a nigger read the prayers and the Bishop did part of the Communion Service, and a German Jew preached.' Leighton added: 'We have seen the Church of the Holy Sepulchre, Calvary, the place where the rock was rent by the earthquake, the centre of the earth, and about thirty-five other things all conveniently brought together under one roof. I am sick of traditions.'

Fifty miles to the south-east of Jerusalem, at the limit of Kamil Pasha's authority, war had broken out in 1875 between the two largest Bedouin tribes of the Negev desert, the Tarabin and the Tiyaha. In the hills, wadis and encampments of the Negev, Jerusalem's authority was weak, with the result that the Bedouin struggle continued with little respite, and amid much bloodshed, for twelve years.

Several of the war poems of that desert conflict have survived, noted down

a century later by the orientalist Clinton Bailey. In one poem the Tarabin taunt
their enemies: 'We will grant you no peace, no peace will you see, until the
wolf recites rhymes at our night-time dances, or an ostrich-bitch suckles a
jackal'. But the Tiyaha poets were equally certain of victory. 'The Tiyaha', one
of them sings, 'will never cede their homeland to others, like a State standing
guard over all that is hers'.

Travellers in Palestine were warned by their consuls to avoid the risks of
crossing these warring regions. But Jerusalem, unaffected by such distant
battles, remained a tourist objective. In 1876 the publication of Baedeker's
guidebook to Palestine and Syria included 134 pages on the city: described not
only as a historic city, but as a modern traveller's destination.

Baedeker explained that, with the recent repair of the metalled road of 1863,
a horse-drawn 'omnibus' from Jaffa to Jerusalem had been started by the
German Colony: 'two vehicles run each way daily'. The journey time was
eleven and a half hours to twelve hours for the thirty-two miles. In case 'the
bad state of the road' should force this service to be closed down, as had
happened with the earlier carriage service, it would, Baedeker warned, be
necessary to go by horseback. Riders should start early from Jaffa, 'as riding
in the narrow, crowded and ill-paved streets of Jerusalem after dark is very
unpleasant'. It was advisable to make the ride in two days, spending the first
night either at Ramleh, or at 'the house of a Jew' at Bab el-Wad. One final
warning: 'Those who wish to make sure of having their luggage at Jerusalem
on arrival have no alternative but to accommodate their pace to that of the
baggage-mules, unless the latter are despatched at a much earlier hour than
that at which the travellers themselves start.'

There was good news for the purchaser of Baedeker's 1876 guidebook: two
years earlier, municipal taxes had been abolished throughout the Ottoman
Empire, so that there was now 'no examination of luggage at the gates of the
city'. Just inside the Jaffa Gate could be found the main hotels. At the Mediterranean Hotel (landlord Moses Hornstein) and the Damascus Hotel belonging
to his brother Aaron, food was 'generally good', the rooms small, 'but sufficiently large for ordinary travellers who are seldom indoors'. A third hotel, the
Casa Nova of the Franciscans, which had been 'greatly enlarged' three years
earlier, was chiefly patronized by Roman Catholics. The arrangements were
simple, but the dining rooms 'very handsome' and the beds 'good and clean'.
Poor visitors would be put up free for two weeks, 'but in a simpler manner
than those who pay'. The monks in charge were chiefly Italians.

Top: Landing at Jaffa (Robert M. Bain, 1894). *Above:* The Jewish-owned inn at Bab el-Wad, on the road from Jaffa to Jerusalem (1880s).

There were also an Austrian and a Prussian Hospice within the walls. But, Baedeker noted, in the height of summer many people, inhabitants as well as visitors, camped outside the gates 'for the sake of the purer air'. The traveller should not, however, camp outside the walls in spring 'as the weather is then often bitterly cold'.

Baedeker's practical guidance for the tourist included the location of two beer and coffee shops: Lendholdt 'in the lower part of the town' and Shrafft near the Casa Nova. He also gave the addresses of four shops selling wine and beer, including Bergheim in Christian Street who sold English beer. There was a reference to 'Arabian' – that is, Arab – cafes which abounded 'but are not frequented by travellers'. The location of three 'respectable' bankers was given, as was that of Bergheim the wine-merchant. Any visitor wishing to visit a mosque, Baedeker noted, would need to obtain permission from one of the consulates.

Baedeker also noted that there were two good shops for buying photographs of the city: Shapira in Christian Street, and, once more, Bergheim. Photographs could be bought of every part of Palestine, 'medium size, 18 francs per dozen'. A large choice of souvenirs could be found in the space in front of the Church of the Holy Sepulchre, including mother-of-pearl crosses from Bethlehem and objects carved in black 'stinkstone' from the Dead Sea. Some of the 'dealers' could be asked to bring their wares to the travellers' rooms. 'As a rule', Baedeker advised, 'one-half or a third only of the price demanded should be offered'.

A 'staple product' of Jerusalem was olive-wood carving – rosaries, rulers, letter weights, stamp boxes, cigar cases and glove boxes. These gifts could be bought at Vester's shop in the Via Dolorosa, Bayer's House of Industry, or at Faig's. Many of these articles, Baedeker noted, bore the name 'Jerusalem' in Hebrew letters.

Baedeker's last practical points concerned the physicians, chemists, tailors, shoemakers and, last but most essential, the dragomans or guides. Physicians whom he recommended were Dr Chaplin of the 'English Jewish missions', Dr Sandreczki of the 'German institutions' who was known as 'a skilful operator' – Dr Schwarz, an Austrian, of the Rothschild Hospital, and Dr Mazaraki of the Greek hospital. The one chemist recommended was Damiani in the Via Dolorosa; the two tailors, Eppinger and Silberstein, both in Christian Street; the two shoemakers, Schohn and Schlegel, likewise both in Christian Street. Finally, there were the dragomans, three of them Protestants – Bernard Hilpern,

Christian Street (Underwood and Underwood, 1897).

Abraham Lyons and Khalil Dhimel, and two of them 'Latins', Hanna Auward and Joseph Karam.

Despite the 'overwhelming interest' of Jerusalem, Baedeker warned that many travellers would at first sight be 'sadly disappointed'. It would seem at first, he wrote, 'that little was left of the ancient city of Zion and Moriah, the far-famed capital of the Jewish empire; and little of it indeed is to be discovered in the narrow, crooked, ill-paved, and dirty streets of the modern town. It is only by patiently penetrating beneath the modern crust of rubbish and rottenness which shrouds the sacred places from view that the traveller will at length realise to himself a picture of the Jerusalem of antiquity, and this will be the more vivid in proportion to the amount of previously acquired historical and topographical information which he is able to bring to bear upon his researches. The longer and the oftener he sojourns in Jerusalem, the greater will be the interest with which its ruins will inspire him, though he will be obliged to confess that the degraded aspect of the modern city, and its material and moral decline, form but a melancholy termination to the stupendous scenes once enacted here.'

Baedeker went on to explain that every traveller in Jerusalem would have forced upon his notice the 'chief modern characteristics of the city' – a combination of 'wild superstition' and 'the merest formalism', together into the 'fanatacism and jealous exclusiveness of the numerous religious communities of Jerusalem'.

Of the Jerusalem houses, Baedeker noted that, owing to the scarcity of wood, they were built entirely of stone, each room with its own vaulted chamber being 'pleasantly cool in summer'. The streets of the city, 'ill-paved and crooked, many of them blind alleys', were 'excessively dirty' after a rainstorm. Snow and frost were not uncommon in winter. The 'badness' of the city's water, together with the 'miasma' from unremoved rubbish, caused fever, dysentery 'and other maladies' which were a hazard in summer. Nevertheless, the sanitary arrangements were, he wrote, 'a degree better' than formerly.

'As might be expected from the religious character of the city', Baedeker added somewhat tersely, 'there are no places of public amusement at Jerusalem'. The British Consulate, however, was the guardian of a 'Literary and Scientific Society', of which the Prince of Wales was patron, and the Consul president: its library was 'open daily', from ten in the morning until four in the afternoon. Visitors staying any length of time in the city were welcome to subscribe to it 'by the month'.

In his guidebook Baedeker described the various Christian communities. The Greek Church was 'the most powerful in the city', with eighteen monasteries and foundations, two of which could accommodate up to 500 pilgrims each, with the others capable of putting up a further 2,000 pilgrims in all. The Greeks also possessed a printing office, 'a handsome new hospital', a girls' school with 'two female teachers and sixty pupils' and a boys' school with 'three masters and one hundred and twenty people'. The Old Armenian Church had a monastery 'said to be capable of accommodating upward of 1,000 pilgrims', a printing office, a seminary with about forty pupils, a nunnery, a small museum and a photographic studio. There were three other, smaller, eastern Churches, somewhat 'scantily' represented in the city: the Coptic, the Syrian Jacobite and the Abyssinian Churches, the latter numbering only '75 souls'. Those 'good-natured Abyssinians', Baedeker wrote, 'lead a most wretched life, and are more worthy of a donation than many of the other claimants'.

Two other even smaller eastern Churches were affiliated to the Roman Catholics. One was the Greek Catholic Church, with only thirty souls in all, under Father Elias. The other was the United Armenian Church, '16 souls'. By contrast the Roman Catholics, or Latins, numbered some 1,500: they had a printing press on which even Arabic text books were printed, a boys' school for 170 boys, an industrial school, a hospital for both sexes, its physician being Dr Carpani, and two girls' schools, with 320 pupils in all. The most important Latin institution, to which both the boys' school and the printing press were attached, was the Franciscan Monastery of St Salvator.

The ninth Christian Church was the Protestant Church, with its 'handsome English church', Christ Church, a boys' and a girls' school, a school in the city 'for proselytes and Jewish children', fifty in number, and an 'Arabic' church and school. The chief German protestant institutions were Dr Sandreczki's hospital, with 43 beds, the Talitha Kumi girls' orphanage, a children's hospital with eight beds, and the leper hospital.

Touring the city, Baedeker noted 'shreds of rags' suspended from the window gratings at many pilgrimage shrines. These shreds had been 'torn from the garments of the pilgrims and placed there by them in fulfilment of vows to the saint'. At the north side of the Temple Mount, the possible site of the Antonia Fortress of the Romans, then a Turkish army barracks, he remarked caustically that 'the execrable music of a Turkish military band is frequently heard'.

Inside the Dung Gate, through an open space partly planted with cactus hedges, were the 'miserable dwellings' of Muslims from North Africa, the Moghrebins. Just behind these dwellings was the 'Wailing Place of the Jews'. Since the early middle ages, Jews came 'to bewail the downfall of Jerusalem'. In Baedeker's opinion, 'This spot should be visited repeatedly, especially on a Friday after 4 p.m., or on Jewish festivals, when a touching scene is presented by the figure leaning against the weatherbeaten wall, kissing the stones, and weeping'.

Men often sat at the Wailing Wall 'for hours reading their well thumbed prayer books'. Many of them were barefooted. 'The Spanish Jews, whose appearance and bearing are often refined and independent, present a pleasing contrast to their squalid brethren of Poland'.

One of the Jewish prayers at the Wailing Wall was, Baedeker noted, 'May the kingdom soon return to Zion!' and he commented: 'These people adhere to their ancient traditions with marvellous tenacity, still expecting and earnestly longing for the establishment of the second "Kingdom of David".'

Of the most sacred of the Christian shrines, the Church of the Holy Sepulchre, Baedeker wrote: 'It is a humiliating fact that Muslim custodians, appointed by the Turkish government, sit in the vestibule for the purpose of keeping order, particularly during the Easter solemnities, among Christian pilgrims from all parts of the world; and yet the presence of such a guard is absolutely necessary; so completely do jealousy and fanaticism usurp the place of true religion in the minds of many of these visitors to the Holy City.'

In his guidebook, Baedeker was also critical of the focal point of Christian pilgrimage to Jerusalem, the celebration of Easter, when there were enacted, both in the Church of the Holy Sepulchre and throughout the city, 'many disorderly scenes which produce a painful impression'. These ecclesiastical ceremonies, he added, 'are very inferior in interest to those performed in Rome'. Graphically, Baedeker then described how one of the 'most disgraceful spectacles' was the 'so-called' miracle of the Holy Fire. Until the sixteenth century the Latins had taken part in this event, but since then it had been 'managed' by the Greeks alone. On this occasion, Baedeker explained, 'the church is always crowded with spectators. The Greeks declare the miracle to date from the apostolic age, and it is mentioned by the monk Bernhard as early as the ninth century.' According to one account, 'the priest used to besmear the wire by which the lamp was suspended over the sepulchre with resinous oil, and to set it on fire from the roof. Large sums are paid to the priests by those who are allowed to be the first to light their tapers at the sacred flame sent from heaven. Armenians, Copts, and Abyssinians also take part in the ceremony. The wild and noisy scene begins on Good Friday. The crowd passes the night in the church in order to secure places, some of them attaching themselves by chords to the sepulchre, while others run round it in anything but a reverential manner.'

On Easter Eve, Baedeker explained, at about 2 p.m., 'a procession of the superior clergy moves round the Sepulchre, all lamps having been carefully extinguished in view of the crowd. The patriarch enters the chapel of the Sepulchre, while the priests pray and the people are in the utmost suspense. At length the fire which has come down from heaven gleams from the Sepulchre, the priests emerge with a bundle of burning tapers, and there now follows an indescribable tumult, every one endeavouring to be the first to get his taper lighted. Even from the gallery tapers are let down to be lighted, and in a few seconds the whole church is illuminated. This, however, never happens without fighting, and accidents generally occur owing to the crush. The spectators do not appear to take warning from the terrible catastrophe of 1834. On that occasion there were upwards of 6000 persons in the church, when a riot suddenly broke out. The Turkish guards, thinking they were attacked, used their weapons against the pilgrims, and in the scuffle that followed about 300 pilgrims were suffocated or trampled to death.'

For the tourist of 1876 Baedeker offered many disappointments. The covered bazaars at the centre of the Old City 'are very inferior to those of Cairo and Damascus, and present no features of special interest'. The way from the bazaars to the Jewish quarter was 'a somewhat dirty street with brokers' stalls, shops for the sale of tin-ware manufactured by the Jews, and several uninviting wine-houses'. There were several synagogues, 'none of which are interesting'. The Armenian monastery merited a visit, but the monks there 'naturally dislike to see visitors tread on their carpets with dirty boots', while the beautiful garden of the monastery 'is unfortunately seldom shown'.

As for the 'ancient' olive trees shown to visitors by the Franciscans in the Garden of Gethsemane, Baedeker commented, it was 'well-authenticated that Titus and Hadrian cut down all the trees round Jerusalem, and that the Crusaders found the whole region absolutely destitute of wood'. The Greeks, Baedeker added, 'have also set up a "Garden of Gethsemane" of their own farther up the Mount of Olives'.

Baedeker drew his tourists' attention to some of the sites of the new Jerusalem. 'Hideously repulsive lepers', he wrote, 'are still met with on the Jaffa road, as many of them, particularly the Jews, have a great repugnance to being lodged in the hospital'. In the Russian buildings to the north-west of the walls the cells for the poorer pilgrims were 'rude and without beds', although the dwellings were 'a great boon to that class', accommodating 1,000 pilgrims at a time, and the divine service in the church was 'accompanied by good singing'.

Not to be outdone by Baedeker, Thomas Cook had also published a guidebook to Jerusalem in 1876. Unlike Baedeker, Thomas Cook offered his own facilities for the tourists, both inside the city and on the way to it. 'Travellers under the arrangements of Messrs. Cook and Son', he noted of the plain at the entrance to the Judaean hills, 'will be surprised to see the tents all pitched, and a "canvas town" ready for them to occupy'. People not using Cook's services, however, 'sometimes stay at an inn kept by a Jew' at the entry to the gorge. 'But as the lower part of the house is a stable, and there are only two sleeping rooms and a "parlour", nothing but great necessity should detain the tourist.'

Like Baedeker, Cook has little good to say of the first 'site' at the entrance to the city. 'The traveller', he warned, 'will be vexed to see a mass of ugly buildings erected by the Russians, principally for the benefit of pilgrims', while

Top: The women's hospice for Russian pilgrims (late 1880s). *Above:* Guest room for a wealthier Russian visitor (late 1880s).

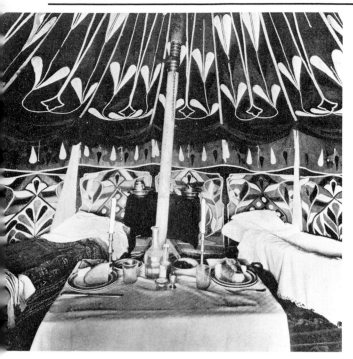

Inside a traveller's tent (1880s). *Right:* 'Tickets to All Parts of the World': Thomas Cook's office inside the Jaffa Gate (1880s).

once inside the city there were further vexations. At the Church of the Holy Sepulchre, for example, the traveller 'may, perhaps, see here how the hateful practice of scribbling upon the wall of even sacred buildings is persisted in by ignorant persons'. Even the Via Dolorosa was not, for Thomas Cook's patrons, quite what it seemed. 'No one can traverse its curious zig-zags', he wrote, 'and look at its "holy places" with indifference, as it is sacred with the tears of many generations of pilgrims, who, according to their faith, strove to follow in the footsteps of the Lord. As a mere hard and dry matter of fact, however, there is no historical evidence whatever for the sacred sites; the street was not even known until the fourteenth century.'

Not only the Baedeker and Cook guidebooks, but also an explorer's account of the city, was published in 1876: Captain Warren's book *Underground Jerusalem.* Warren had taken two photographs of a group of Ashkenazi Jews: one of which he published. 'There is an irrepressible pride and presumption', he wrote, 'about this fragile and wayward people of Ashkenaz that I could not help admiring; dressed in greasy rags, they stalk about the Holy City with as much dignity as though they were dressed in the richest garments, and give

Seven Ashkenazi Jews (Warren, 1876).

way to no one; years of oppression have in no way quelled their ancient spirit, and if they could only be induced to work and become united, they would be a very formidable race, for their courage and fortitude makes up for the want of stamina.' Warren added: 'They are among the most fanatical of mortals and can only believe in their own observances, and look with disgust upon the freedom from ceremony of even the strictest of Jews of our own country.'

Such 'fanatical' Jews were not always without supporters among the Europeans. Since the departure of Consul Finn thirteen years before, his successor, Noel Temple Moore, had frequently intervened to support the Jews against British missionary activity. In October 1876 he asked the Governor of Jerusalem to act against the Reverend E. B. Frankel, a Jewish convert to Christianity, who, while in temporary charge of the English Mission Church, had pasted placards to the wall of the Church enclosure – placards which sought to prove to the Jews, from Old Testament quotations, that 'they were in error in holding that the Messiah had not yet come into the world'. Moore noted, in reporting his action to the Foreign Office, 'that the number, influence and strong religious sentiment of the Jewish population of Jerusalem render them much less tolerant of any offence, or what they conceive to be such, than may be the case with their co-religionists in other cities of Turkey'.

In September 1876, as if to show both Baedeker and Thomas Cook that Jerusalem was, after all, on the way to modernity, *The Times* announced in London that Signor Pierotti, the Vatican's representative in Jerusalem, had obtained pontifical sanction to build a port at Jaffa, and a railway from Jaffa to Jerusalem. There were to be a hundred 'foundation members'. Their names would be published in a prospectus, inviting Roman Catholics all over the world to become shareholders, and, as a result of their investment, to 'draw their dividends in the form of feelings of satisfaction at having assisted by their subscriptions'.

The scheme failed. The lure of a purely spiritual dividend had not been enough to finance the much-needed railway.

Since 1872, a number of Jerusalem Jews, among them the printer, Joel Moses Salomon, and the Jerusalem-born Joshua Yellin, had hoped to set up a Jewish village, far from the city, in which Jews could till the soil, grow crops, raise cattle, and live by the strength of their own brow, and plough. The first site chosen was twenty miles east of the city, in the Jordan valley, not far from Jericho. Salomon was among those who, in 1872, discussed this Jericho land purchase with the Arab dignataries, but the negotiations failed. The group then turned their attentions westward, to Petah Tikvah in the coastal plain. The local Arabs were helpful, and in 1878 the sale went through.

In Jerusalem, many Jews mocked at the decision of the group to set up an agricultural village. Outside the newly built Tiferet Israel synagogue, derisive voices were raised when Salomon tried to explain the project.

'What will you do if your cow runs away on the Sabbath?' asked one pious Jew.

'First of all', Salomon replied, mimicking the traditional plaintive chant of a Talmudic scholar, 'I have to acquire a cow. Next, I have to make sure to fence her in properly. And then, if she runs away, God forbid, on the Sabbath' – he lifted his thumb in Hassidic fashion – 'I'll do what Moses our Rabbi, and Saul the King did in such a case. . . .'

The onlookers paused. Salomon stretched out his hands and continued, '. . . I'll go and look for the cow'.

Among those who had negotiated this land purchase was a Hungarian-born Jew, David Meir Gutman. In 1848, at the age of 21, Gutman had fought in the Hungarian War of Independence. Disillusioned by Hungarian hostility towards those Jews who had sought only to be patriotic Hungarians, in 1876 he had sold his property in Hungary and travelled to Jerusalem. On arrival, he had given substantial sums of money to charity, supported projects for Jewish suburbs outside the city walls, and joined those who had, for the past four years, been searching for the site of a Jewish agricultural village.

From the first days of the village's existence, debts grew and with them a sense of uncertainty, and fear. Gutman now sold all his property in Jerusalem in order to pay the village's debts, and to pay for the lawsuits which had continued with the previous Arab landowners.

Another of the Jerusalem Jews who had been active in the Jericho and Petah-Tikvah land-purchase schemes was Israel Lapin, born in Russian Poland in 1810. As contractor for the building of the Grodno railway in western Russia, he had become a wealthy man before leaving for Jerusalem in 1863. As well as seeking Jewish land purchase for agricultural and rural settlement, in 1877 Lapin had bought the land for one of the new Jewish quarters astride the Jaffa road, Bet Yaakov: one of his sons, Bezalel, was to set up the first coach service from Jaffa to Jerusalem, in place of the mules and donkeys on which, hitherto, travellers had travelled to the city from the coastal plane. To this end, the road, which had been metalled in 1869, but had quickly disintegrated, was re-metalled, this time more carefully, in 1881, after which the coach, or 'diligence', quickly replaced the four-legged method of ascent or descent.

It was also in 1878 that Michael Pines arrived in Jerusalem as the representative of the Moses Montefiore Testimonial Fund. Pines quickly became a controversial figure. Born in White Russia in 1843, by the age of 28 he had established himself as a leading exponent of the need for cautious reforms in

Jewish life: a fusion of traditional religious practice with science and modern languages. Holding such ideas in Jerusalem, Pines found himself in dispute with many sections of the Jewish community, including the Hassidic and the Sephardi Jews: so much so that the ultra-religious proclaimed him 'excommunicated'.

Pines did not bow to these hostile forces. Instead, he urged the Montefiore Fund to continue to sponsor new houses and new quarters outside the walls, and to establish artisan and industrial projects. Pines also put his own money into these projects.

Among those who were most fiercely opposed to Michael Pines was Moses Diskin, who had only arrived in the city in the previous year. But Diskin, a child prodigy in his Russian birthplace, had long before achieved fame as the rabbi of Brest-Litovsk, and on reaching Jerusalem was accepted at once as one of the leaders of orthodoxy. For the next twenty years Diskin fought against all manifestations of modernity and modern culture in Jerusalem, arguing in favour of the complete separation of religious and non-religious Jews.

Jerusalem gossip alleged that Moses Diskin's wife Sonia was the true zealot of the pair, and that it was her domineering personality which had pressed him into the more extreme assertions of orthodoxy.

In 1879 a German Jew, Wilhelm Herzberg, reached Jerusalem, after two years as director of the Mikveh Israel agricultural school near Jaffa. Born in 1827, in the Baltic port of Stettin, in an assimilated family, it was not until his early forties that he turned to Judaism. On reaching Jerusalem, he became director of the first Jewish orphanage to be set up in the city: an orphanage founded by Baron Rothschild, at the suggestion of the historian, Heinrich Graetz, who had been so shocked at the absence of such an orphanage during his visit in 1870.

With the founding of this orphanage, a fierce feud broke out between the ultra orthodox Jews and their less orthodox brethren. The cause of the feud was the desire of the founders to teach Arabic and Turkish to their Jewish pupils. There were immediate protests against this 'breach' of orthodoxy. But Rabbi Samuel Salant, the recently appointed Chief Rabbi of the Ashkenazi Jews – who was to remain Chief Rabbi until his death in 1909 – not only supported the teaching of Arabic to Jewish boys, but received money from Jews in England to set up such teaching.

A teacher was engaged, and Arabic and Turkish lessons began. But soon afterwards, as the British Consul, Noel Temple Moore, explained to the British

Ambassador in Constantinople on 11 June 1879, 'A violent opposition was manifested by a faction, numerically small, who ill-treated the teacher and threatened to wreck the room in which the teaching was carried on'. The Jewish opponents of Arabic teaching went so far as to obtain a decree from the Sultan. This decree, Moore reported, declared the teaching of 'foreign languages' to be unlawful. By these means, Moore noted, 'the opponents of the scheme carried their point, and the lessons were discontinued'.

Consul Moore sought to intervene in the 'foreign'-language dispute, discussing it with Rabbi Salant. 'He told me – as has already appeared from what has been stated – that he and the large majority of his fellow Rabbis were in favour of instructing Jewish boys in the Arabic and Turkish languages, and appreciated the advantages that would result to them therefrom, but that he had discontinued the teaching of Arabic which had been begun rather than that it should be the cause of dissensions and disturbances, which, moreover, he was powerless to repress – a view concurred in by the donors of the funds, to whom he had reported the circumstances.' As a further proof of Rabbi Salant's own 'good-will in the matter, he informed me that he had refused to allow the decree to be published to the people in the Great Synagogue, as was strongly desired by its authors'.

It appeared, Moore commented, 'that the opposition proceeds from a small minority of Rabbis, mostly of the sect of Khasidim, or "the Pious", which is characterised by intense fanaticism, and composed chiefly of Hungarian Jews. Their motive seems to be a fear that the study of foreign languages would lure away the Israelitish youths from the study of their own sacred literature and imbue them with gentile ideas, which, in its turn, would interfere with the flow of charitable donations from Europe, whose raison d'être is the supposed piety, and consequent efficacy of the vicarious prayers, of the Jews of Jerusalem.'

The language dispute proved an intractable one. Rabbi Salant's authority as Chief Rabbi of the Polish and German Jews was not recognized by the Turkish authorities in Jerusalem. In addition, the Russian-born Rabbi Diskin, the main opponent of Arabic lessons, was a naturalized French subject. As a result of Diskin's hostility, 'intolerant and unreasonable proceedings of the foreign rabbis', so the British Ambassador to Constantinople reported, 'are strongly condemned by the leading Jews in England'.

To resolve the dispute, the new orphanage was put under British protection. In this way, the authority of a Protestant sovereign served to advance the education of Jewish children in a Turkish and Muslim land. In a final protest,

Hezekiah's Pool with, beyond, the restored cupola of the Church of the Holy Sepulchre, and the minaret of the Sidna Ali mosque (Bonfils, 1877).

Rabbi Diskin founded a special 'orthodox' orphanage in the city, dedicated to 'save' Jewish orphans from the 'contamination' of the modern world.

The decade, which was coming to an end, had seen a rapid growth in photographic studios in Jerusalem. One of the most successful of the photographers was Félix Bonfils, a French bookbinder who had first visited the Near East in 1860 and who had settled in Beirut in 1867. Ten years later, his 17-year-old son, Adrien, began a comprehensive photographic study of Jerusalem, while his father concentrated on the commercial aspects of their business. More than 800 Bonfils photographs are known. They were sold as photographic prints to all visitors to the city, and appear in virtually every album compiled by visitors on their return home.

A second successful photographer, whose work was also quickly to figure in the tourists albums, was the Italian, L. Fiorillo. Between them, Bonfils and Fiorillo photographed more than a thousand of Jerusalem's sites and vistas, enabling the traveller to take home with him a record of almost everything he had seen.

CHAPTER VI

The 1880s: Battles ancient and modern

It was now the turn of Swedish Protestants to add their energies to the growth of Jerusalem. In 1880 a small mission from Sweden, working together with an American family, the Spaffords, founded a small hospice and school to the north of the Damascus Gate. Known first as the 'American Quarter', later as the 'American Colony', it quickly became a focus for Protestant missionary activity: and a centre of photographic enterprise.

American Colony photographs were soon to provide visitors to the city with the most comprehensive of all collections of city 'views': archaeological, modern, and human. Among these 'human types' of the enlarging city were the Jews from Georgia, whose small community was much increased in 1880 by the arrival of several hundred more families. The reason for this sudden exodus from Georgia was a 'blood libel' accusation in a small village near Kutaisi, the main town of Georgian Jewry. As in Damascus in 1840, so in Kutaisi in 1878, Jews were accused of using Christian blood in the baking of their Passover bread. In this instance, the death of a 6-year-old Christian girl was blamed on the Jews amid an upsurge of anti-Jewish feeling. A trial was held, Russian lawyers defended the accused, all of whom were declared innocent. But the original accusation, revealing as it did deep and ugly prejudices, acted as a spur to as many as four hundred Georgian Jews to join their fellow-Georgians in Jerusalem.

In June 1880 a 16-year-old boy was exploring Hezekiah's tunnel with a friend. Entering at the Pool of Siloam end, the two boys were almost twenty feet inside the tunnel when the 16-year-old stumbled and fell into the water. On rising to the surface he noticed some marks, like letters, on the rock wall in

The arcade of the Muslim religious school on the Haram al-Sharif, or Holy Sanctuary (photographed in 1984).

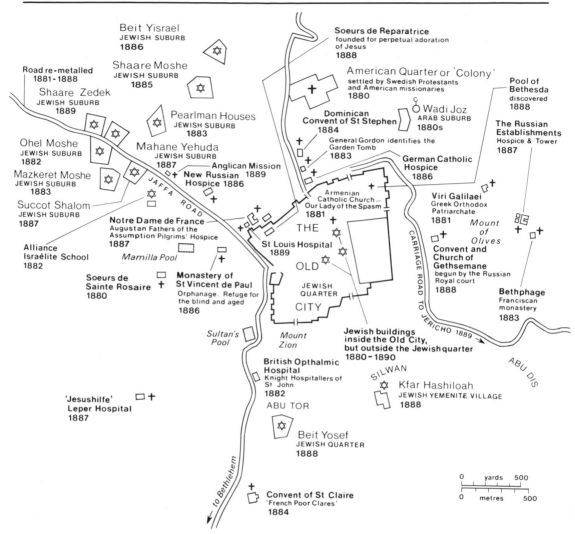

New Christian (✝), Jewish (✡) and Muslim (☿) building in Jerusalem in the 1880s.

front of him. The boy was Jacob Eliahu, the son of Sephardi Jews who had come to Jerusalem from Turkey. The boy had been born in Jerusalem. His parents had been among the first Jews converted to Christianity by the London Mission to the Jews. He too was a Christian.

Jacob Eliahu reported his find to Conrad Schick, his headmaster, and a dedicated scholar of the city's hidden past. Shick went to the tunnel, where he studied the rock writing by lamplight. Four months later he published a description of the writing in the Quarterly Statement of the Palestine Exploration Fund. The inscription was in Hebrew letters, Schick reported, written in an elegant classical Hebrew, and recording the moment when the tunnellers, starting from different ends, had first heard 'the voice of a man calling his fellow'. They had then struck through towards each other 'pick-axe against pick-axe' until the two tunnels met, 'and the water flowed from the spring towards the reservoir'.

The discovery of this ancient inscription gave historic life to Captain Warren's efforts thirteen years earlier, and was a landmark in the rediscovery of biblical Jerusalem. The description of the tunnel-cutters' meeting also constituted the longest single document ever found in ancient Hebrew: and remains so to this day. Shortly after being discovered, the inscription was removed by a treasure hunter who hoped to sell it to some wealthy visitor. While being prized from the rock face it broke up into several pieces.

Shortly afterwards, these pieces appeared in the shop of a Jerusalem dealer in antiquities. They were for sale. The Ottoman authorities were quick to act, confiscating the pieces, and taking them from Jerusalem to Constantinople. There, in the Museum of the Ancient Orient, they can be seen today, one of Jerusalem's most precious documents in stone.

A year after making his chance discovery, Jacob Eliahu left Schick's school and went to live with the Spaffords at the American Colony. Soon afterwards he was adopted by them, taking the name Jacob Spafford.

In the search for new sites to adorn, the Armenian Catholics established in 1881 their Church of Our Lady of the Spasm on the Via Dolorosa. That same year, the Greek Orthodox Patriarchate built the Viri Galilaei church and monastery, on the upper slopes of the Mount of Olives.

The 'Men of Galilee' thus immortalized were those who, having seen Jesus 'taken up' and received by a cloud 'out of their sight', were then addressed by two men 'in white apparel' who stood by them: 'Ye men of Galilee, why stand ye gazing up into heaven? This same Jesus, which is taken up from you into heaven, shall so come in like manner as ye have seen him go into heaven.'

In 1881 the Russian-born Abraham Luncz, who had been living in Jerusalem since he was 15 but had become blind at the age of 24, published, while still only 27, a Yearbook 'for the diffusion of an accurate knowledge of ancient and modern Palestine'. The book revealed many facets of the Jerusalem of 1881. There were now more than twelve hospices and hotels for visitors, including two 'houses for Strangers' in the Jewish quarter. At the Austrian Hospice, every pilgrim could stay for thirty days, during which time 'he has free board and lodging'. There were eleven synagogues as well as seventeen Houses of Prayer and study for Sephardi Jews, fifteen for Ashkenazi Jews of the more secular persuasion, six for Ashkenazi Jews of the Hassidic sects, and nineteen for Jews from Morocco and North Africa.

Abraham Luncz was fascinated by the occupations of the Jews in Jerusalem. His enquiries were considerably helped by a questionnaire which had been sent out to Jerusalem five years earlier by the Board of Deputies of British Jews, to which he had access. From this, he discovered that there were many Sephardi Jews working as unskilled labourers, as porters, water carriers and cesspool cleaners. But the success of the Valero Bank was, he commented, 'a striking instance of what may be made of true Oriental Jews, when they are educated according to a rational mode', the father of the two Valero brothers having taken care 'to have his children so brought up, that by their general knowledge and specially their knowledge of various European and Oriental languages they take rank with European bankers'.

Most Sephardi Jews, Luncz commented, were traders living 'very comfortably and quietly, counting very few poor persons among them'. He himself had made a special enquiry into their specific trades under what he described as 'very difficult circumstances, owing to the wellknown Oriental prejudice against all attempts at a census'. Overcoming the prejudice, Luncz itemized the trades, among them forty-nine grocers, four tobacconists, five brokers of old furniture, two dealers in old iron, three booksellers, two cotton dealers and fifteen pedlars; but the largest number, fifty-eight in all, were tailors.

Luncz also noted, among the Sephardi Jews, thirty-three cobblers 'sitting in the streets of Jerusalem or itinerating the villages', most of these being Jews from North Africa. There were also, in the Sephardi community, goldsmiths, blacksmiths, coppersmiths and gunsmiths, as well as three auctioneers, three hatmakers and three musicians. Among the 6,660 Ashkenazi Jews, most of whom came like Luncz himself from Russia, but others from the Austro-Hungarian Empire, Germany and Holland, there were, he noted, two classes: Talmudic scholars and the aged, and tradespeople. The majority of the first class, he wrote, 'are the aged who, weary of this life's troubles, have given up all business and have come to Jerusalem to die here in peace and to be buried on the Mount of Olives in view of the site of our holy temple. They bring generally with them their younger children from whom they do not like to separate. There are also to be found people of middle age who, being childless

A Jewish bank in Jerusalem: the 'stocks and shares' and 'deposits' section (before 1914).

and suffering from some disease know that their days on earth cannot be long, and come to Jerusalem for the same purpose of concluding here peaceably the remaining years of their life. All people belonging to this class spend their time in religious exercises of all kinds, study of the Talmud, prayers and all good works in general.'

The tradespeople included many grocers and bakers, shoemakers and scribes, as well as 'one looking-glass maker, two upholsterers, two potters, four umbrella makers, one saddler, two painters and three hat makers'. In several trades, among which Luncz noted the painters, glaziers and saddlers – trades which in Europe provided a good livelihood – in Jerusalem 'their work is not much wanted' being more necessary for luxury than necessity, 'and they remain often literally without a morsel of bread'.

There were also, among the Ashkenazi Jews, 215 families whose livelihood came from labouring, some as porters, others as day labourers, twenty-five as 'regular beggars' and 120 as 'odd-jobmen or idlers, as the case may be'.

Luncz pointed out that the beggars earned their living going from house to house in the Jewish quarter 'and it is, therefore, clear that they have a right to be classed among the hardest-worked people in Jerusalem'. As for the 120 odd-jobmen or idlers, Luncz commented: 'There are idlers and idlers; – many people count the class which we have described under Nr. 1 – the beggars – as idlers, but unjustly so; for though they ply no regular trade, they do employ their time usefully in study or pious works for which purpose they have indeed come here; – but the idlers here mentioned are quite of a different stamp. They are people who grew up at a time when all parents thought it a matter of course that their children must be Talmudical scholars and to learn a trade was considered a disgrace here, – to devote themselves to study they had however no adaptation and thus they were idlers living as best they could from their Haluka. But when their wants on account of their having married, increased and the income from Haluka decreased they had to betake themselves to whatever kind of work they could get, and thus they are now no more idlers, but their work is naturally not worth much, as they have not learned anything regular, and they are now in a very pitiable plight.'

'Haluka', the dependence of Jerusalem Jews on charity, remained, throughout the 1880s, a marked feature of the more 'pious' communities.

Luncz also studied the Muslim and Christian trades, noting among the Muslim Arabs a total of 23 coffee-shop-keepers and among the Christian Arabs 48 'vendors of eatables' and eight vendors of mother-of-pearl work, and among the European Christians four chemists, ten teachers, three hotel keepers, eight 'medicalmen' and thirty-six employees 'of Governments or European societies'. One of the most illuminating of the statistics set out by Luncz in his Yearbook of 1881 was the town of origin of the Russian Jews who retained while in Jerusalem their congregations based upon their place of origin. The largest of these congregations, more than 1,000 in all, was of Jews from Vilna, Kovno and the Lithuanian region of Russia. The next largest, 830, was of Jews from Minsk and the Minsk region. Other communities were made up of Jews from White Russia, from the Slonim region, from Grodno and Warsaw, as well as two smaller groups from Hungary – 440 Jews – and Holland and Germany combined, 100 Jews. The largest Hassidic group were the 770 Jews from western Russia: others were from White Russia, Minsk, Austria and Rumania. There were also in the city, Luncz noted, 235 converts to Judaism 'who, as a matter of course, did not belong to any one congregation in particular'.

It was not only Jews from the Russian Empire who sought physical and spiritual sanctuary in Jerusalem. In 1881 several hundred Jewish families from the Yemen reached Jerusalem. They came from communities from which a few individuals had earlier, from time to time, gone to Jerusalem. But this was the first mass migration. It was made easier by the opening of the Suez canal in 1869, and the re-imposition of Ottoman control over the Yemen tribesmen in 1872; despite the enormous distance, the Jews of Yemen were 'merely' travelling from one part of the Ottoman Empire to another.

These Yemenite Jews were from one of the poorest and most remote of the world's Jewish communities. On reaching Jerusalem, they hardly mixed at all with either the Ashkenazi or the Sephardi Jews. At first they tried to live as agricultural workers at 'Rama', a hillside below the Tomb of the Prophet Samuel, several miles to the north of the city. This experiment failed: but the Yemenite Jews soon found a niche in Jerusalem's economic life, many of them as stonecutters, stonemasons, building workers and plasterers; others as silver-smiths, coppersmiths and embroiderers. As the city grew outside the walls, their work as stonecutters was particularly in demand.

Six years after their arrival in Jerusalem, many Yemenite Jews moved out of the Old City to their own stone-built houses at the southern edge of the Arab village of Silwan, overlooking the ancient City of David, and the Kidron valley.

British influence in Jerusalem was strengthened in 1882 with the British conquest of Egypt. Henceforth, most travellers to the city were to come through the Egyptian port of Alexandria, either by sea to Jaffa or overland across the northern coast of the Sinai desert, through Gaza and Beersheba. Many travellers going by sea from Britain to India stopped in Egypt, to make a brief visit to the Holy Land. With Britain having become the ultimate master of Egypt, there was a new security for travellers; and a new incentive, as 'Cairo and Jerusalem' became a tourist catch phrase.

Among the visitors to Jerusalem in 1882 were two of Queen Victoria's grandsons, the 18-year-old Prince Albert Victor, known as 'Prince Eddy', who died ten years later, shortly after his twenty-eighth birthday, and his younger brother, the 16-year-old Prince George. In 1910 Prince George was to succeed his father, Edward VII, as King, as George V.

The two Princes were on a world tour on board HMS *Bacchante*, accompanied by their tutor, the Reverend J. N. Dalton. The cruise had begun in September 1879. In 1882 the two Princes had sailed from Australia to Fiji and Japan, where they were received by the Mikado, then on to Hong Kong, Shanghai, Singapore and Colombo, before reaching Suez on 1 March 1882. After spending almost a month in Egypt, they sailed from Alexandria to Jaffa.

Like his father, Prince George kept a journal, and like his father he first saw Jerusalem from the tomb of the Prophet Samuel, noting in his journal that 'one of Mr Cook's sons is travelling with us to see that everything is right'. Outside Jerusalem, Prince George noted, the camping ground was 'the very same that Papa camped on when he was here, it is under olive trees and is between the town and the Mount of Olives, it is a capital place'.

Shortly after the arrival of the two Princes, the Governor of Jerusalem called upon them. They then dined early, at six, and went to bed at 9.30, rising early on April 1 to begin their first visit to the city. Just as the Prince of Wales had been accompanied twenty years earlier by the knowledgeable Canon Stanley, so the two Princes had as their guide Captain Conder, whose explorations as 'Officer in Command' of the Palestine Exploration Fund survey expedition eight years earlier had done so much to establish many new sites of biblical Jerusalem.

Their first visit took the two Princes to the Church of the Holy Sepulchre, the Hospice of St John, the Citadel, the Jaffa Gate, Bishop Gobat's school, the English cemetery on Mount Zion and, descending into the Hinnom valley, the pool and village of Siloam. Mr Dalton, the Princes' tutor, noted, of the Siloam pool: 'the Jews still bathe here to cure rheumatic stiffness in the back or limbs, standing in their clothes in the pool "waiting for the troubling of the waters"'. 'The flight of steps is a long one', he added, 'for a cripple to get down unaided.'

Writing to his mother, the Princess of Wales, later Queen Alexandra, Prince George noted of the Siloam pool: 'it is quite true about it bubbling up because while we were there it was rising fast'. From the pool, the two Princes walked up the Kidron valley to Absalom's Tomb, their tutor commenting that he 'longed for a few thousand pounds and trucks and tramway to cart away (after sifting) all the debris here, accumulated right down the Kidron valley to the Dead Sea, and so uncover the natural slopes of Zion, Ophel, and the Temple Hill, once more to the light of day'.

Climbing the slopes of Kidron, the two Princes then saw the massive wall of masonry which made up the south-east corner of the Temple Mount 'with old stones still on the wall', and then returned to their camp. That evening, Prince George noted, 'I was tattooed by the same man that tattooed Papa with the 5 crosses, and I bought a few curios.'

That night there was little sleep for the royal visitors; 'a dreadful night', Prince George noted in his journal, 'blowing a gale of wind and pouring, a squall struck us at about 1.30 and nearly blew all the tents down but the muleteers clapped onto the tent ropes and put stones on top of the pegs and saved the tents, not a drop of water got inside'. In a separate account of the incident, Dalton noted that the two tents occupied by thirty-eight sailors from *Bacchante*, who had come up to Jerusalem that evening, 'were blown completely over'.

On Palm Sunday, April 2, the Princes rose at 7.30 but, as Prince George noted, 'had a lay-in on account of it being Sunday'. They then prepared for their second visit to the city. Dalton later recalled that 'the mud and pouring streams of water made the streets like stone watercourses of filth', an impression confirmed by Prince George in his journal as the royal party walked through the narrow streets to the Protestant Church. During the walk, the Prince added, 'we saw Russians and other sorts of pilgrim walking about with palm leaves as it is Palm Sunday'.

At Church, two Bishops were present, the Bishop of Ballarat, in Australia, and the Bishop of Nelson, in New Zealand, the latter preaching the sermon. After the service, the Princes went to the English Consulate where the Reverend Kelk showed them a large wooden model of the Church of the Holy Sepulchre with, as Prince George noted, 'the various parts apportioned to the different sects in different colours'. From the consulate, the two Princes returned to camp, Prince George writing in his journal: 'Mr Dalton and others have gone to Bethany but we did not, it is too wet.' On their way from the consulate to the camp, the Princes had hoped to visit the Garden of Gethsemane but could not do so, as it was 'locked and closed'.

During the journey to Bethany, Dalton, passing the Sultan's Pool, commented: 'into this the Turks have lately given orders that all are to shoot their rubbish in order that it may be filled up and planted out as a garden'. This intention, however, remained, like so many of the Ottoman plans, an aspiration unfulfilled.

It was cold on the morning of April 3: '48 degrees fahrenheit', Prince George noted in his journal. At 7 that morning the Princes walked through St Stephen's Gate, as their father had done twenty years before, to the Dome of the Rock. They were shown over it by both Captain Conder and Sir Charles Wilson. The custodian of the Haram allowed the visitors to close the doors of the Dome in order, as Dalton noted, 'to examine the mosaics in the roof by help of a magnesium wire lamp'.

Prince George noted that the Dome of the Rock was 'beautiful'. Unlike his father, he made no comparison with the mosque in Cairo. The two Princes likewise then saw one of the large underground cisterns and visited the Convent of the Sisters of Zion. Their tutor noted that the founder of this convent was 'a Jew by birth, who, since his conversion to Christianity, has devoted all his means to its establishment and support'. Dalton added that the nuns were mostly French, 'though some few are English'. In the basement of the convent, the royal visitors saw the paving stones of the old Roman street, the slabs furrowed by deep parallel lines cut in their surface to prevent horses from slipping.

While still in the city, the Princes went, as their father had done, to the

Wailing Wall, but, as Dalton noted, 'it was empty and void'.

After lunching at their camp, the Princes walked back to the English Consulate 'to buy some curios which they had for us to see'. They then returned to their camp to write letters. That night they dined early, at 5.45, and an hour later 'we went in the town', Prince George wrote, 'to the Chief Rabbi's house to see the "Passover" eaten. It was a very curious ceremony, it lasted for an hour and a half. Sir Charles Wilson and Captain Conder were there also.'

The Princes' host during the Passover meal was the Chief Sephardi Rabbi, Raphael Mayer Panigil, whom Dalton recalled as 'a venerable old man with a white turban and long coat trimmed and lined with fur, which he wore over his flowing under-dress'. Rabbi Panigil was accompanied by Rabbi Nissim Baruch, 'nearly as old and venerable as himself'.

Two tables had been laid, and, in the midst of Rabbi Panigil's family celebration of the exodus from Egypt, the Princes and their tutor witnessed their first Passover. Dalton recalled how, during the preliminary prayers, those assembled 'chanted in a monotone in the original Hebrew', and that the prayer over the wine was sung in 'a sort of monotonous chant'. But the visitors were 'much impressed', he added, 'by the complete domesticity of the feast', the men, women and children all 'conversing and chatting together at intervals, as at a happy family gathering'.

After the meal there were further prayers, including those for Queen Victoria, for the Prince and Princess of Wales, and for 'other members of their family'.

After nearly two hours the meal and prayers came to an end, whereupon the two Princes returned to their encampment. 'As we walked home through the streets of the Jewish quarter', Dalton recorded, 'we heard other families celebrating the Passover with closed doors.' Leaving the city by the Damascus Gate, he commented on how 'the full Pascal moon was overhead, showing through the rifts of heavy black clouds which were still drifting from the west'. Just such a night as this, Dalton reflected, 'was Christ's last before His death, when He, having eaten the Passover, left the city, and went forth to the Garden of Gethsemane'.

The Princes were in bed by 10 o'clock that night. Two days later, Prince George described their encampment to his mother. It consisted, he wrote, of eleven tents in all, two big ones 'for sitting and writing in', two more for eating in, and seven for sleeping in, as well as a kitchen tent and sleeping tents for the servants. The Princes were accompanied, Prince George added, by about

The Ophthalmic Hospital, and, on Mount Zion beyond, Bishop Gobat's school (1880s).

ninety-five animals – horses to ride and mules and donkeys for the baggage – and sixty people, 'so all together we are a very nice caravan'.

On the morning of 4 April the Princes were up at 5.30, their Jerusalem visit at an end. That morning they set off on the long journey to Bethlehem, Mar Saba, Jericho, Amman, Salt, Nablus, Jenin, Nazareth, Tiberias, Banias, Damascus and Beirut, retracing their father's steps of twenty years earlier, and covering in all, from leaving the *Bacchante* at Jaffa to rejoining her at Beirut, a total of 585 miles.

Travelling south from the Jaffa Gate, the Princes passed below Bishop Gobat's school, on the roof of which, as Dalton noted, 'a number of native boys were gathered who sang the English National Anthem as we rode by'.

The road which Prince Albert Victor and Prince George took southwards was the road which a growing number of travellers to and from Egypt were taking. It could be traversed southward beyond Hebron to Beersheba, the Sinai desert and Suez. As it left Jerusalem, the road passed the site of a new building under construction, the Ophthalmic Hospital, built with British charitable funds by the Knight Hospitallers of St John, and soon ministering to hundreds of Muslim and Christian Arabs, many of them from Bethlehem, who were suffering from the eye disease, trachoma.

From the new Ophthalmic Hospital the road continued southward, rising gently towards the Monastery of St Elias, and passing above the Valley of the Giants, where German missionaries were steadily expanding their own Templar Colony, with its church, its missions and its hospital.

For forty years, philanthropy had been one of the main spurs to the growth of Jerusalem. In 1882 a Jewish philanthropic organization based in Paris, the Alliance Israélite Universelle, made its own first contribution to the life of the Jews of Jerusalem. Hitherto, for the previous twenty years, its charitable, and above all its educational, work had been focussed on the Jews of North Africa. In 1870 it had set up the Mikveh Israel agricultural school just outside Jaffa – a landmark for travellers on the Jaffa to Jerusalem road. Now, it brought its zeal for secular Jewish education and practical apprenticeship to the Holy City.

The man chosen to set up the new school was Nissim Behar, himself Jerusalem-born, who for the previous nine years, as head of the Alliance School in Constantinople, had pioneered the teaching of modern Hebrew as the language of everyday life. In search for funds for the new project, Behar travelled to London, Cologne, Frankfurt, Berlin, Vienna, Budapest and Bucharest. His quest was successful, particularly in London. On 1 February 1882 he reached Jerusalem with the money needed to begin. Five weeks later, on 9 April 1882, the Alliance School opened, with a single pupil. Within two months there were fifteen pupils, including the sons of several rabbis.

One of Nissim Behar's first decisions as head of the Alliance School was to appoint a recently arrived Russian Jew, Eliezer Ben Yehuda, to teach modern Hebrew, according to the principles Behar had already developed in the Ottoman capital. Ben Yehuda believed in his task with a revolutionary passion. He began at once to introduce Jewish pupils, whose languages at home were Yiddish, Russian, Spanish or Arabic, to the unifying tongue of the ancient Jewish prophets, brought up to date.

Those Jerusalem Jews who already spoke Hebrew among themselves were delighted with Ben Yehuda's teaching. But the orthodox rabbis were scandalized that the 'holy' language should be taught, and heard, as a work-a-day language. Rabbi Diskin led the orthodox Ashkenazi rabbis not only in condemning the teaching of Hebrew as the language of daily life, but in declaring a formal rabbinical ban on attending Hebrew classes.

Inside one of the Jerusalem synagogues (1893).

Ben Yehuda was personally convinced that Hebrew should, and could, become the first and 'native' language of all Jews living in Palestine. He was supported in this belief, and in his teaching of modern Hebrew, by Michael Pines, whose own knowledge of the Hebrew language was soon to establish him as one of its leading writers. Working together, Ben Yehuda and Pines founded the Hebrew Language Committee dedicated to the introduction of Hebrew as a spoken language.

One rabbi who encouraged spoken Hebrew was Jacob Meir, a Sephardi Jew born in Jerusalem of a wealthy merchant father. In 1882 Meir went as an emissary of Jerusalem to Bukhara, the remote central Asian Khanate, then under Tsarist rule, and the home of tens of thousands of Jews. Later he was to travel as an emissary to the Jews of Tunisia and Algeria. In 1911 he became Chief Rabbi of Jerusalem, and in 1921, at the age of 65, the first Sephardi Chief Rabbi of Mandatory Palestine.

Interest in Jews from remote and distant communities was widespread. One of Nissim Behar's early decisions at the Alliance School was to offer a chance to the newly arrived Yemenite Jews to learn trades and skills unknown to them in their remote Yemeni villages. Special arrangements were made so that Yemenites who could not attend regular classes because they already had to support their families, could study after school hours, in the afternoon or evening. Thus it was that many of the Yemeni Jews, whose work as manual labourers was all that they had been taught they could aspire to, left the Alliance workshops as skilled craftsmen.

Among the first boys to be entered into the Alliance School was David Yellin, the 17-year-old son of Joshua Yellin. As a result, father and son – who had both been born in Jerusalem – became the first members of the Ashkenazi community to ignore the rabbinical ban on studying at the school. As a punishment, he and his family were refused any part of the European 'halukah', or charities.

David Yellin, who had earlier studied at the Tree of Life religious academy, and was deeply versed as a young man in both the religious and secular traditions, was later to become a teacher at the Alliance himself. Like his father, he was fluent in Arabic, and was to publish the first text books in Arabic for the use of Arabic-speaking Jewish children: the growing number of Jews from Arab lands who were to make Jerusalem their home. David Yellin was also a forceful advocate of Hebrew as the spoken language of Palestine Jewry, and was one of the first Jerusalem-born Jews to join his own teacher, Eliezer Ben Yehuda, and Michael Pines, on their Hebrew Language Committee. Later, David Yellin was to marry Pines' daughter Itah.

The influence of David Yellin on Jewish Jerusalem was to be considerable, both in the last decade of the nineteenth century, and in the first four decades of the twentieth. By the time of his death in 1941, at the age of 77, he had become a symbol both of the integration of the Ashkenazi and Sephardi communities, and of the use of spoken Hebrew. His achievements were, however, only a small part of the legacy of Nissim Behar, who maintained close links with the Turkish authorities, in order to ensure that his school, his workshops, and his pupils were allowed to progress without obstacles. The principal obstacles did not come from the Turks, however, but from the orthodox rabbis, whose resistance to the teaching of modern Hebrew and secular Jewish education continued unabated, so much so that in 1897 Behar was forced to give up his headmastership. For the next thirty years, until his death in 1931, he lived in New York, an exile from the city of his birth and his greatest achievements; and in New York he died.

Many nations were to feel the impact of the anti-Jewish violence which erupted throughout Tsarist Russia in the early 1880s. Hundreds of thousands of Jews abandoned their homes and way of life, leaving Russia for ever. For most of them, the United States was the first goal: the 'Golden Land' of legend and dreams. England, too, held attractions for many: were there not Jewish Members of Parliament, even Jewish Lords? But for a minority it was Palestine, and Jerusalem, which beckoned.

On 21 January 1882 a group of young Jews met in Kharkov to discuss their responses to the upsurge of anti-Jewish violence in Russia. One of their number, Israel Belkind, urged them to go to Palestine. Fourteen of them agreed to follow his lead.

On 29 June 1882 these fourteen young Russian Jews, having set off earlier by ship from Odessa, took ship again from Constantinople, on the last lap of their journey to Palestine. That same day, the Ottoman authorities telegraphed to the Governor of Jerusalem, forbidding any Russian, Rumanian or Bulgarian Jews from landing at Jaffa or Haifa. Nor were they to be allowed to go to any of the four holy cities of Judaism, Jerusalem, Hebron, Safed or Tiberias.

This order was in direct conflict with the Capitulations, which assured Russian subjects the right of unrestricted travel in all the provinces of the Ottoman Empire, with the sole exception of Arabia. A correspondence ensued between Jerusalem and Constantinople. For the time being at least, Jewish pilgrims and businessmen were to be allowed to visit Palestine, but settlers were not.

While Constantinople and Jerusalem exchanged telegrams about whether or not Russian Jews could enter Palestine, a Professor of Mathematics at the University of Heidelberg, Hermann Shapira, published a series of articles in St Petersburg, in the Hebrew-language journal *Hamelitz*, arguing in favour of the establishment of a Hebrew University in Jerusalem. Professor Shapira pointed out that Jewish students all over the western world suffered from various forms of discrimination in higher education. What could be more sensible, then, than a university of their own, for Jews from any land, in the spiritual centre of the Jewish people? This idea, launched from the Tsarist capital, was to be realized forty years later.

On 6 July 1882 the fourteen young Russian Jews who had left Russia with Israel Belkind landed at Jaffa, filled with dreams of the return of Jews to the soil of Palestine. This tiny group took its name 'Bilu', from the initial Hebrew letters of the biblical verse, 'House of Jacob, come ye, and let us go.' At first they settled at the agricultural school of Mikveh Israel, near Jaffa, where they were joined by some forty more young enthusiasts, mostly from Kharkov and Odessa. Within a year, some of them moved to Jerusalem, where they were befriended by Michael Pines.

On behalf of the young immigrants from Russia, Pines established a society for them in Jerusalem, the 'Return of the Craftsmen and the Smiths'. He also purchased some 800 acres of land for them in the Judaean foothills, at Gederah. There, growing grain and grapes, the Bilu pioneers survived, and flourished. A few later returned to Russia, or moved on to the United States. But the experiment succeeded, and the Bilu farmers, as they became, joined with Ben Yehuda and Pines in speaking Hebrew among themselves, singing Hebrew songs, and meeting on Jewish festivals, determined to transform the language of liturgy into the language of daily life.

With the influx of so many Jews from Russia, converted Jews were to figure much less in the history of Jerusalem. In 1882 a Society for the Relief of Distressed Jews was set up by Anglican missionaries in London: it did not undertake any specifically proselytizing work, but its Jerusalem agent was Mary Hornstein, the daughter of one of Consul Finn's first Jewish converts, Aaron Hornstein, a watchmaker. Mary Hornstein, although raised as an Anglican, was said to speak all the languages of the Jewish quarter, and was still carrying out her charitable work at the end of the First World War.

It was a telegram from Sir Moses Montefiore that first informed Jerusalem of the attempt to assassinate Queen Victoria in 1882. In his telegram, Montefiore asked for prayers for the Queen's safety to be said in all the synagogues of Palestine. In Jerusalem, Consul Moore attended the service in the main Ashkenazi synagogue.

It was only some while after these prayers, Moore informed London, that the English papers arrived with 'accounts of the dastardly attempt', whereupon 'I requested our minister, the Rev. A. Hastings Kelk, to return thanks to Divine Providence for the preservation of Her Majesty, in our Church on Mount Zion, and that the National Anthem should be sung by the Choir on the occasion, Mr Kelk most readily acceded to my request, and on Sunday last the thanksgiving service was held'. It happened, Moore added, 'that just at this time the largest number of British travellers is gathered at Jerusalem, and there could not have been less than one hundred of these present on the occasion. I attended in uniform with Captain Conder and Lieutenant Mantell, Royal Engineers, whom I had invited to accompany me in uniform, and the Staff of the Con-

Gordon's Calvary on 'Skull Hill', looking north from the city walls (an American Colony photograph, before 1914).

sulate. The entire congregation heartily joined in singing the National Anthem with which the service commenced, and the event was touchingly and eloquently alluded to in the sermon, which was preached by the Rev. Mr Friedlander, of the London Jews Society.' Friedlander was a Jewish convert to Christianity.

Battles in Jerusalem were of long-standing. Jerusalem's fiercest biblical-archaeological debate had opened in 1842, when it had been suggested that the site of the crucifixion was not the rock subsequently enclosed by the Church of the Holy Sepulchre, but a site outside the northern Ottoman wall, Jeremiah's Grotto. The first to put forward this view was an archaeologist, O. Thenius. But it was only forty-one years later, in 1883, that this theory received popular support, when General Gordon announced that this was indeed the true site of the crucifixion.

Gordon called the site at Jeremiah's Grotto 'Skull Hill', not, as some thought, because of what it looked like from the ground, but because the 2,549-feet contour line on the map, as drawn by the 1864 Ordnance Survey of Jerusalem, resembled a skull at this very location. When a rock-hewn tomb was discovered at the western front of this same hill, Gordon declared that this was indeed the tomb of Joseph of Arimathea.

For the next twenty years the claims of Skull Hill were to be much contested in learned journals, more words being expended on this single location than on any other. Clearly, if the Church of the Holy Sepulchre were to be displaced as the holiest of the Christian sites, pilgrims, priests and the whole pattern of Jerusalem life would be put severely out of joint.

The balance of argument was against Gordon, culminating, on 6 June 1901, with an article by Dr Conrad Schick, in which he too was to put the weight of his formidable authority against the General. But to this day Skull Hill has its adherents, and its pilgrims, who venerate it in their minds with no less fervour, and no less sincerity, than the still paramount Hill of Calvary to which most feet still wend, within the Church of the Holy Sepulchre.

The building activities of all communities were visible throughout 1882 and 1883; the Franciscans establishing their monastery at Bethphage, site of Jesus' raising of Lazarus, and starting point of his final return to Jerusalem, on the eastern slope of the Mount of Olives; the Muslim Arabs building new stone houses north-east of the city, in the Wadi Joz with red tiled roofs; and the Jews building two new quarters on either side of the Jaffa road, Mazkeret Moshe and the Pearlman Houses.

Observing all this, Maggie Lee, a newly arrived missionary at the American Colony, wrote, on 17 January 1883: 'The activity of rebuilding is by no means confined to the Jews. Catholics, Greeks, Mohammedans and Protestants are all taking part in it. There are at the present time more than one hundred buildings going up, all of stone, and most of them of carefully cut stone. The new method is to use iron girders to support the ceiling. This is then covered with French tiles instead of the older and more picturesque dome roof.'

The year 1884 saw yet more building north of the Damascus Gate, where the Dominicans built the Convent of St Stephen. South of the city, just off the road to Bethlehem, with a spectacular view over the Jordan valley to the mountains of Moab, the French Poor Clares built their convent. And on the eastern slope of the Kidron valley, the first small stone houses – some of only a single room – were built for poor Jews from the Yemen: a charitable venture to help those families who, after four years in the city, had failed to find any secure livelihood. In a further effort to help these Yemenites, a committee was organized in London, the Yemenite Refugees Relief Fund, to collect money for yet more such houses.

The Grand New Hotel, built in 1885 (photographed in 1984). *Right:* the Tenth Legion column, used for more than a century as the base of a street lamp (photographed in 1984).

Not all projects prospered: 1884 saw the winding up of the American Palestine Exploration Society, founded fourteen years before. It had been unable to match the funds, or zeal, of its British counterpart.

In the late autumn of 1885 the foundations were laid of a modern hotel just inside the Jaffa Gate. The site chosen for the hotel was over an ancient pool, known locally as Bathsheba's pool, in the belief that Uriah's wife was bathing there when first seen by King David.

To build the hotel, a roof was put over the pool, turning it into a cistern for the hotel itself. In excavations nearby, several remains from the Roman period were found: a section of the so-called 'second' wall, which enclosed Jerusalem on the north side in Roman times, several Roman tiles with the stamp of the Tenth Legion, and, most intriguing of all, inside the area enclosed by the wall, part of a column erected by the Tenth Legion in honour of Marcus Junius Maximus, the legate of the Emperor Augustus.

This column, which was turned into the base of a street lamp set up close to the spot where it was dug up, created considerable excitement among biblical scholars and historians. According to the Jewish historian, Josephus, when

Jerusalem was captured in AD 70, and reduced to ruins, Titus left the Tenth Legion to garrison the city, instead of sending them back to their camp in the Euphrates valley. Josephus adds that Titus left a part of the west wall of the city standing, in order to provide protection for the garrison.

According to Josephus, the Tenth Legion's camp was inside the city walls. This was now confirmed by the location of the column, and the line of the newly discovered wall: once more, a two-thousand-year-old account was found to be accurate.

For Christian pilgrims, each archaeological discovery increased the lure of the city. To cater for the growing numbers of pilgrims, a new Russian hospice was opened in 1886 in the Russian compound. That same year, Christian charitable and missionary work was also advanced with the founding by German Catholics of a hospice and college – later Schmidt College – immediately opposite the Damascus Gate, and the establishment of the St Vincent de Paul monastery, orphanage, and refuge for the blind and aged just outside the north-western corner of the walls. Within three years, three further Christian foundations were to be built at that same north-western corner, a pilgrim's hospice, Notre Dame de France, in 1887, by Augustan Fathers of the Assumption; the Soeurs de Reparatrice convent 'for the perpetual adoration of Jesus' in 1888; and the Hospital of St Louis of France in 1889.

Nor were these buildings alone: in 1887 the 'Jesushilfe' Leper Hospital was built by German Protestant missionaries just to the north of the Templar Colony while, on the facing crest of the Mount of Olives, the Russian Orthodox Church constructed, also in 1887, a hospice and a tower: the tower, known as the Belvedere, being to this day the tallest structure on the Mount, visible not only from every vantage point in Jerusalem, but from the Tomb of the Prophet Samuel to the north, from Mount Gilo to the south, and, incredibly, from across the Jordan valley twenty miles to the east, and 3,900 feet below. From the top of the Belvedere, the waters of the Dead Sea can be seen, appearing as if only a few miles away: they were, however, a seven-hour ride away, across barren, uninhabited hills, fifteen miles from hill-top to water's edge.

The journey through those hills had continued to be a hazardous one. On 7 August 1885 one of the senior dragomans in Palestine, Rolla Floyd, an American from Maine, had written home of how 'some friends of mine (Muleteers, that is owners of horses) had 8 horses and mules stolen from them three days ago. They were on their way from the Jordan to Jerusalem and only about 12 miles from Jerusalem when about 20 Bedowins attacked them and took the

Top left: Schmidt College (before 1914). *Top right:* Notre Dame de France (photographed in 1984). *Above:* St Louis de France (photographed in 1984).

'Bedouin Robbers, Wilderness of Judaea, near the Road to Jericho', No. 51 in the Underwood and Underwood series of stereoscopic slides (1896).

horses and mules. The way they did it was to catch hold of the most courageous man in the lot, and throw him on the ground. Then 3 of the robbers – one put a sword across his neck, one a long knife to his breast and one his gun cocked to his head and told him if any of his party fired a shot or cried aloud they would kill him at once. Then they stripped the clothes from all the party, took the 8 horses and mules and left, and up to the present time have not been heard from.'

Despite such incidents, the tourists continued to flock to Palestine. 'At one time', Rolla Floyd wrote home on 19 May 1887, 'I had a party of 55 persons in Jerusalem, while Cook had only 17.' On 6 July 1887 Floyd wrote again: 'The Russian Consul told me last Monday night that 2 very rich men have started for Constantinople to get a firm to build a railroad from Jaffa to Jerusalem. He says it is a sure thing now. I only hope it is'; and on 10 August 1887 Floyd wrote home from Jerusalem: 'The Turkish government have started up a new program to repair and mend their ways. They have nearly completed the carriage road between here and Jaffa – have also commenced to make a carriage road from Nablus to Jaffa – 40 miles. And one from Jerusalem to

Hebron, 25 miles.' All the principal streets in Jerusalem, Floyd added, 'have been very nicely paved with stones well trimmed and smoothed for the purpose. The government also had new drainage put in under the whole city of Jerusalem. People who were here 15 or even 10 years ago would hardly know the city and its surroundings now. There are now some of the finest buildings being put up just outside the city wall – 3, 4 and even 5 stories high, all built of nice white limestone.'

Five years after the first influx of Russian Jews escaping pogrom and persecution, the Governor of Jerusalem received orders 'inhibiting foreign Jews from coming to reside at Jerusalem, or in Palestine generally'. As Noel Temple Moore reported to the British Ambassador in Constantinople on 5 March 1887, 'The reasons given for this unusual measure are that the great majority of the Jews that come here are of the indigent class, whilst numbers are old and infirm who come to end their days in the Holy City. Both these categories have no means of subsistence and live in much misery and want, depending on a dole of a few pence a week from the charitable collections received from Europe, the amount of which of course decreases as the demand on those funds increases, and flocking to the already over-crowded Jewish quarter of the city – adding to its squalor and unhealthiness and thus jeopardizing the public health, and are also the cause of dearth.' Moore commented: 'That there is truth in these assertions is not to be denied; I imagine, however, that besides these considerations, a certain feeling of uneasiness must have entered the minds of the authorities at the large influx of Jews into the country within recent years, with their rights and privileges as foreign subjects, and they desire to check this influx.'

It was understood 'for some time', Moore commented, 'that this regulation was especially directed against the Russian Jews'. The Russian, German and Austrian Consuls, Moore added, 'seem to have acquiesced in the regulation in question'.

From Constantinople, the British Ambassador noted that it was not only the Ottoman Government which was imposing such restrictions. 'It appears', he wrote, 'that both at the port of New York and also at Hamburg stringent rules have been lately laid down under which persons without sufficient means are not allowed to land and which are evidently due to the same desire to exclude paupers of the Jewish persuasion who come without any means of support.'

The restriction on Jewish immigration remained in force, modified only

A cast-iron manhole cover, cast in Jerusalem by pupils at the Alliance Israélite school before 1914 (photographed, still covering its manhole, in 1984). The Hebrew letters stand for 'All Israel are brothers'.

slightly in October 1888, when the Governor of Jerusalem received orders from the Sublime Porte to apply the measures only 'in cases when such immigration should take place en masse'.

In 1887 Consul Moore prepared a report on the schools of Jerusalem, a city, he wrote, 'more plentifully endowed with schools than, perhaps, any other town of equal size in the Ottoman Empire'. Moore enumerated German, Roman Catholic, and English missionary schools, also the Jewish schools, the best three of which, he noted, taught Hebrew, and two of them also Arabic. The foremost Jewish school, he wrote, was the Alliance School, 'a superior and excellent institution under efficient direction', with two Hebrew, three Arabic, two French and one English master, one 'mechanician', and seven masters 'for teaching arts and trades'. Among the trades taught were carpentry and shoemaking.

For the Jewish communities of Jerusalem, 1887 saw the setting up of a Joint Ritual Slaughter Board of the Ashkenazi Jews, the Hassidic Jews, and the Perushim, or non-religious Ashkenazim. The Board was headed jointly by the Chief Rabbi of the Ashkenazim, Samuel Salant, a noted moderate, and Moses Diskin, a more severe zealot. Abolishing the separate Ritual Slaughter authorities of the three Jewish communities, it quickly reduced frictions which had become intolerable. Salant was also active in the work of improving relations between the Ashkenazi and Sephardi communities, working in harmony closely with his 'opposite number', the Sephardi Chief Rabbi.

Among the individuals who were able to bridge the Sephardi-Ashkenazi gap was Joseph Meyuhas, the young Sephardi Jew, born in Jerusalem, and speaking Ladino, the Jewish tongue of Asia Minor and Greece, whose father had left the confines of the city for Silwan in the 1870s. Meyuhas was one of the first Sephardi Jews to marry an Ashkenazi girl: Margalit, the daughter of Michael Pines. He and his wife were also one of the first Jewish couples in Jerusalem to speak only Hebrew in their family circle.

A teacher, Meyuhas taught for a while in the Evelina de Rothschild school: later he was headmaster of a Teachers' Seminary, and of the municipal school for boys. In 1889 he was one of the founders of Shaare Zedek, one of eight new Jewish quarters built outside the walls, mostly on the Jaffa road, between 1882 and 1889.

Joseph Meyuhas also participated, in 1888, in the establishment of the Jerusalem Lodge of the B'nai B'rith, a Jewish philanthropic organization founded in New York's Lower East Side in 1843. The new Lodge was named 'Jerusalem'. Its library, of which Joseph Meyuhas was a leading supporter, became the nucleus of the Jewish National and University Library of later years. 'Jerusalem' was the first B'nai B'rith Lodge in which Hebrew was spoken. It was also a pioneer organization in the bringing together of Ashkenazi and Sephardi Jews in a common social purpose. It was active, too, in fighting the continuing efforts of the Christian missions in the city to convert Jewish children, and, as part of this fight, it set up the first Jewish kindergarten in the city.

To the south-east of Jerusalem, in the Negev desert, the Bedouin war had continued with only one short pause since 1875. As one of the poets of the war had written, after a particularly fierce battle in 1882: 'Many bones have been crushed; ground into the dust. Many riders have fallen; many well-groomed lads have died.' But now the Governor of Jerusalem, Rauf Pasha, decided that he must bring the conflict to an end, and restore his authority. He therefore summoned twelve of the leading Bedouin warriors from their Negev encampments to Jerusalem, where he immediately imprisoned them.

These warriors would only be released, the Governor announced, if the fighting stopped. The fighting came promptly to an end.

Jerusalem had at times to spread its authority deep into the countryside. On 20 October 1888 a Bedouin girl was gathering wood in the fields near the village of Beth Fajar. Two young men of the village met her in the field, and tried to rape her. The girl, shrieking at the top of her voice, rushed back into the Bedouin camp. 'To arms!' she cried. 'Your honour is soiled!' 'In daytime your girls are violated!'

A crowd of young Bedouin immediately rushed to Beth Fajar, seized the belongings of the 'guilty' family, and severely wounded four of the family as they fled. Herds, flocks, camels and donkeys were carried off. Property was destroyed. The Bedouin avengers, returning to their camp, lived for several weeks on their booty.

As soon as news of the incident reached Jerusalem, soldiers were sent to Beth Fajar, and the Bedouin forced to give up what was left of their booty. At the same time, the two young men who had assaulted the Bedouin girl were taken from Beth Fajar to Jerusalem, and imprisoned.

In 1888 one of the most successful, and controversial, of the British administrators in India, Sir Richard Temple, visited Jerusalem. He was impressed, as he approached the city, by the 'fresh buildings' which were, as he wrote, 'springing up year by year', and he noted that several of the European consuls now lived outside the walls in these new, 'light-coloured' stone buildings. These new buildings, Temple added, occupied the western approach to the city 'where no sacred associations, no historical remains, exist. Consequently, their construction has spoiled nothing, while ministering to the health and convenience of those whose duty compels them to reside close to Jerusalem.'

Like many British visitors, Sir Richard Temple commented, of the location of the biblical sites, that 'some are fanciful, some unproved, and some plainly wrong, being contrary to the language of Scripture'. There were nevertheless, he added, some identifications that were 'undoubted'.

Sir Richard Temple drew attention to a number of changes that were taking place, among them the clearing and exploration 'under German auspices' of the Muristan, a structure built in crusading times by the Knights of the Order of St John, but now 'crumbling masonry'. He was particularly impressed during his visit by the work of the British missionaries and doctors. 'In the fulfilment of this evangelizing work, imposed upon us as an obligation by Divine Command', he commented, 'we may be thankful to reflect that Britain, despite all failures and shortcomings, is striving to perform her part, and that while among all nations her sphere is, in this respect, the widest, her resources the largest, and her responsibility the strictest, so are her efforts the most strenuous and her work the most effective.'

Among the visitors to Jerusalem at the end of the 1880s was a British Jew,

The Russian Church of Gethsemane, St Mary Magdalene, with the Golden Gate beyond (Underwood and Underwood, 1897). *Right:* St Peter's Prison in the Muristan (photographed in the early 1880s).

Isaac Levinsohn, who had converted to Christianity and then set forth on a pilgrimage to Jerusalem. His joy at seeing Jerusalem for the first time was tempered by the thought that he had once been 'as bigoted and fanatical as the rest of my poor brethren'; so it was that he entered the city 'full of sorrow and sadness when I thought of the children of Israel, who, alas! are still in darkness, ignorance and superstition'. He was therefore surprised on entering the Jewish quarter not only to find several of his own relatives, one of whom was a rabbi, but to receive from them a friendly welcome, 'for I knew how great is the prejudice of Jews towards those who embrace Christianity'.

Levinsohn had visited the Wailing Wall, touched 'to see some of the stones wet with tears!' A devout Christian, he found himself impressed, in spite of his conversion, by those Jews of Jerusalem who clung so tenaciously to the faith of their forefathers. 'It is often said', he wrote, 'that Jews live to make money, and that they worship Mammon. Although this is true of many in Europe, the charge certainly cannot be brought against the Jews of Palestine. Most of the Jewish inhabitants of the Holy Land are very poor. Many of them have left

Europe, where they lived in comfort and luxury, and have given up *all* for the sake of spending the remainder of their lives in *prayer and fasting*. Many Jews fast regularly on Mondays and Thursdays. Some appoint for themselves other special fast days, which they spend in devotion and in mortifying the flesh, believing that this will be accepted as an atonement for their sins. Besides these special days of fasting, the Jewish inhabitants in Palestine observe the regular fast days . . .'

Levinsohn noted during his walks about Jerusalem how Jews, Muslims and Roman Catholics were often to be seen 'walking about, reading their respective books of creeds'. On several occasions he met Jews in the Kidron valley near to Absalom's Pillar reading from their Hebrew bibles who solemnly assured him in their conversation 'that they daily expect the Messiah to appear in that valley, and from that place He will proclaim Israel's freedom and judgment upon their oppressors'. His account continued: 'Jews, Roman Catholics, and Mohammedans look forward for the world's greatest conflict to take place in this valley, and believe that here will be the scene of the last judgment. In this lonely place, we are impressed with a group of rock-hewn sepulchres situated in the narrow ravine. These monuments are objects of interest and of veneration.'

One day, having spent many hours 'walking about and riding on a mule over hills and valleys' together with a group of other Christian pilgrims, Levinsohn returned to his hotel where, to his surprise, he found a number of Jews waiting for the pilgrims, 'all of whom, however, had one object, and that was begging'. Levinsohn's account continued: 'As M. Rothschild, of Paris, was at the time staying at a neighbouring hotel, I advised them to pay him a visit, assuring them that he was much more able to help them than I was. Their cries were, however, so piteous, and certainly their faces seemed to tell of much suffering and starvation, that I gladly gave them enough to purchase a loaf each, and their gratitude was most touching. They eagerly kissed my hand, and invoked all the blessings of Jacob on my head. This was a splendid opportunity, of which I gladly availed myself, of distributing portions of Scripture, particularly the Epistles to the Hebrews and Romans. They accepted them most willingly.'

The convert was particularly moved by the Via Dolorosa. 'The zigzags', Levinsohn wrote, 'all added charm to our observations of the holy places which the Master trod, and which now we walked on, with delight remembering the story of His redeeming love.'

In 1888 the idea of a railway from Jaffa to Jerusalem was revived. That

'View in the Valley of Jehoshophat' below
the Mount of Olives, showing Absalom's
Pillar, Jewish rock tombs of the pre-
Roman era, and, in the foreground, tombs
of the Jewish cemetery (early 1880s).

Right: Baron Edmond de Rothschild
leaving the Kaminitz Hotel (1887).

Christian pilgrims in the Via Dolorosa (before 1914).

October, the Sultan granted Joseph Navon, a Jerusalem Jew, permission to seek the funds with which to build one. While Navon travelled to Europe to find the necessary money, the Russian royal court was establishing its own presence in the city, a convent and church on the Mount of Olives, above the Garden of Gethsemane. The church, with its distinctive onion domes, was to be much photographed on completion: a touch of Muscovy in the Levant.

Archaeological work also continued without interruption. 'The great discovery of the year', the Palestine Exploration Fund's Quarterly Statement for 1888 declared, 'has been that of the Pool of Bethesda. There seems to be very little doubt that we have here the ancient pool itself.'

The new discovery was to the north of the crusader Church of St Anne, within the grounds of the church. Henceforth, to this quiet haven near the Lion Gate, a stream of pilgrims was destined to wend. The pilgrim routes themselves were about to be transformed by the building of three metalled roads, the first, in 1889, to Bethlehem and Hebron, the second to Jericho, and the third to Ain Karim, the birthplace of John the Baptist.

Christian missionary work in Jerusalem was further enhanced in 1889 when

The Greek Orthodox Patriarch, a consular Kavass, and the Armenian Patriarch (1900s).

Bishop Blyth opened an Anglican Mission Home for Jewish women and girls in the city. Three times a week, classes were held for about sixty women; there was a free school for girls, and an orphanage in which, after six years, thirteen orphan girls had been received. The money for the first phase, $5,000, was a gift from an Anglican in the United States.

These missionary activities were small by comparison with those of forty years before: by 1889 Jerusalem's population had risen to an estimated 25,000 Jews, with a further 7,000 Christian Arabs, and 7,000 Muslim Arabs, making up a total population of nearly 40,000. Of the Christians, the Greek Orthodox predominated with 4,000, followed by the Roman Catholics, or Latins, with 2,000. The other Christian sects were all smaller: 500 Armenians, 300 Protestants – including Bishop Blyth and his Mission – 150 Greek Catholics, 100 Copts from Egypt and the Sudan, 75 Abyssinians and, the smallest Christian sect of all, 50 Armenian Catholics.

Photographers, whose work was now an integral part of travellers' Jerusalem, delighted in portraying, in their souvenir portfolios, the different faces and costumes of these many communities.

CHAPTER VII

The 1890s: Strangers and patriots

The Christian presence in Jerusalem was much enhanced in 1890 when a Dominican monk, Father Vincent, was active in the setting up of the Ecole Pratique d'Etudes Bibliques – known in the city as the 'Ecole Biblique'. This biblical academy organized public lectures on archaeology, and published its own journal. It also had its own photographer, Savignac, who recorded the daily life of the Dominican order in Jerusalem.

The Benedictine order was also active, establishing in 1890 a convent on the Jericho road, while Jewish building was likewise much in evidence that year: the Torat Hayyim synagogue just inside the Damascus Gate, to minister to the growing number of Jews who had bought houses inside the Arab quarter, and two new Jewish suburbs off the Jaffa road, followed in 1891 by four more, and a further two in 1892.

The Bedouin conflicts which had ended in 1887 with the imprisonment of the warring leaders in the Jerusalem prison broke out again, three years later, when the victors disputed the spoils. It was now the turn of the Azazma, former allies of the Tarabin, to feel aggrieved at being denied some of the conquered territories. In the friction that followed, the Tarabin occupied some Azazma lands. Fighting intensified. The Azazma were beaten back towards the Judaean hills, and then defeated ten miles south-west of Hebron, on the road from Beersheba to Jerusalem.

Faced with the loss of all their lands, the Azazma appealed to the Ottoman Governors in Jerusalem and Gaza. But neither Governor was willing to intervene. The Azazma then appealed to the Greek Orthodox Patriarch in Jerusalem. He too could offer no assistance.

Russian Orthodox priest and Russian pilgrims (before 1914).

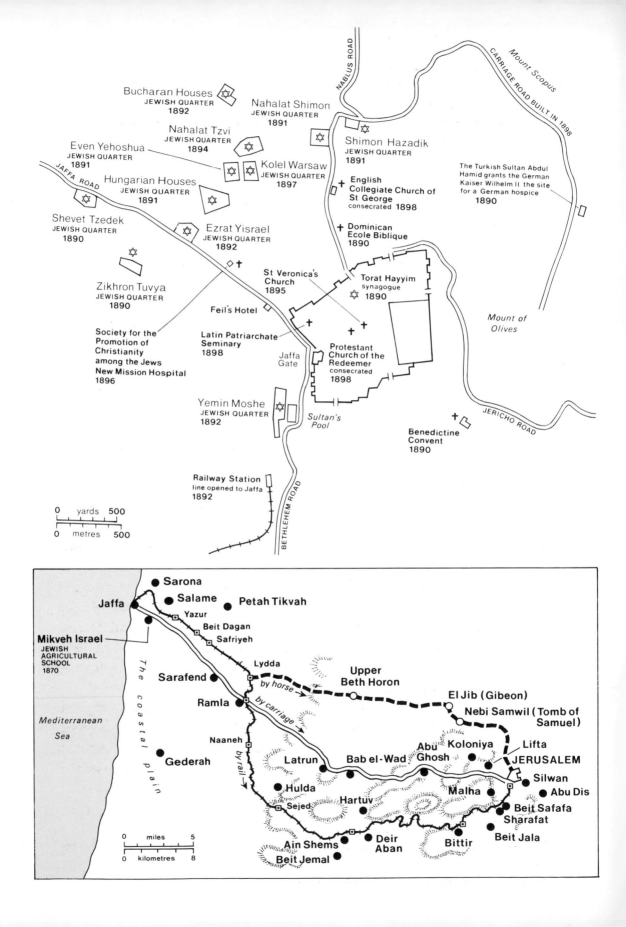

Bucharan Houses
JEWISH QUARTER
1892

Nahalat Shimon
JEWISH QUARTER
1891

Nahalat Tzvi
JEWISH QUARTER
1894

Even Yehoshua
JEWISH QUARTER
1891

Kolel Warsaw
JEWISH QUARTER
1897

Hungarian Houses
JEWISH QUARTER
1891

Shimon Hazadik
JEWISH QUARTER
1891

NABLUS ROAD

CARRIAGE ROAD BUILT IN 1898

Mount Scopus

The Turkish Sultan Abdul
Hamid grants the German
Kaiser Wilhelm II the site
for a German hospice
1890

English
Collegiate Church of
St George
consecrated 1898

Shevet Tzedek
JEWISH QUARTER
1890

JAFFA ROAD

Ezrat Yisrael
JEWISH QUARTER
1892

Dominican
Ecole Biblique
1890

St Veronica's
Church
1895

Torat Hayyim
synagogue
1890

Zikhron Tuvya
JEWISH QUARTER
1890

Mount of
Olives

Society for the
Promotion of
Christianity
among the Jews
New Mission Hospital
1896

Feil's Hotel

Latin Patriarchate
Seminary
1898

Jaffa
Gate

Protestant
Church of the
Redeemer
consecrated
1898

JERICHO ROAD

Yemin Moshe
JEWISH QUARTER
1892

Sultan's
Pool

Benedictine
Convent
1890

Railway Station
line opened to Jaffa
1892

BETHLEHEM ROAD

0   yards   500

0   metres   500

Sarona

Salame

Petah Tikvah

Jaffa

Yazur

Beit Dagan

Safriyeh

Mikveh Israel
JEWISH
AGRICULTURAL
SCHOOL
1870

Lydda

Upper
Beth Horon

El Jib (Gibeon)

Nebi Samwil (Tomb of
Samuel)

Sarafend

by horse

Ramla

by carriage

Lifta

Mediterranean
Sea

The coastal plain

Naaneh

by rail

Latrun

Bab el-Wad

Abu
Ghosh

Koloniya

JERUSALEM

Gederah

Hulda

Hartuv

Malha

Silwan

Abu Dis

Sejed

Beit Safafa

Sharafat

Bittir

Beit Jala

Ain Shems

Deir
Aban

Beit Jemal

0   miles   5

0   kilometres   8

With Jerusalem unable to assist them, the Azazma looked to Constantinople for redress. Nor was the visit of their paramount chief, Hasan al Malta'a, to the Ottoman capital in vain. The authorities in Constantinople listened to his complaint, and then ordered the new Governor of Jerusalem, Rashid Pasha, to send troops from the city to the Negev, to 'remand' the Tarabin chiefs, to punish them, and then to effect a reconciliation between the former allies.

An account of the sequel was recorded by the British archaeologist, W. M. Flinders-Petrie, then excavating an ancient site at Tel el-Hasi. On reaching the excavation site he was told of 'a skirmish' a few miles away between the Tarabin and the Azazma. There were already, as a result of Constantinople's order, 'some 150 soldiers down in the Gaza district'. Their mission was successful, for, as Flinders-Petrie noted, they 'seized and carried off thirteen shaykhs in irons to Jerusalem'. The thirteen leaders were kept in prison for seven years. Four of them died in gaol.

Deprived of their leaders, the Tarabin made peace with the Azazma, as they had done three years earlier with the Tiyaha. So successful was their reconciliation that within two years they were once again allies, fighting alongside each other against a coalition of Bedouin tribes east of the Dead Sea, far from the authority or concern of Jerusalem. The Negev, scene of so much disturbance and bloodshed in previous decades, returned to the calm which archaeology required for a successful season: 'the tribes are at peace', noted the British archaeologist F. J. Bliss in 1891, as excavations at Tel el-Hasi resumed.

On Good Friday, 1890, a British traveller, Mrs Oliphant, already well-known as the author of books on Venice and Florence, walked along the Via Dolorosa watching the Easter pilgrims on their way from the Antonia fortress to the Church of the Holy Sepulchre. On that walk, she wrote, 'it was impossible not to feel that just so must the surging masses have closed upon that fatal procession, the soldiers clearing the way, the wandering spectators gazing over each others' shoulders, pressing upon the sufferer, as He made his way up the toilsome steep, His bodily frame worn with the night's vigil....'

Of all Jerusalem's sacred sites, the Via Dolorosa retained its primacy for pilgrims, and, despite the many Jewish and several Muslim holy places, marked out Jerusalem as a city of Christian predominance. Ruled by Muslims, the majority of its inhabitants Jews, Jerusalem seemed, nevertheless, and especially when viewed from Europe, a Christian city.

By 1890 the Jerusalem of 1838 was a remote memory and a world apart.

New Christian (✝) and Jewish (✡) buildings and suburbs in Jerusalem in the 1890s, and the railway station.
Three routes to Jerusalem, by horse, carriage, and train.

Christian pilgrims at the Tomb of the Virgin (before 1914).

'For the last quarter of a century', Consul Moore noted in February 1890, 'the condition of this city has been one of progress and improvement, for the first half of that period the progress was slow; it has proceeded much more rapidly during the latter half. Amongst the indications of this may be enumerated the very considerable increase of the population from 20,000 to 40,000 of whom more than half are Jews.'

Fear of the arrival of more Jews was considerable among the Muslim Arabs. Moore's successor as British Consul, John Dickson, informed the Foreign Office on 16 July 1891, in one of his first reports, that, 'news having been spread' that 'large numbers' of Jews were about to come to Jerusalem, 'the leading Moslems of this city telegraphed, on the 24th ultimo, to His Highness the Grand Vizier, praying that the entry of such Jews into the Country should be prohibited, as, not only was the labour market overstocked, but also the Moslems themselves would be greatly the sufferers, as, the European Jews being skilled in all the different kinds of trades, the Moslems could not compete against them.'

The decision of the Grand Vizier, Dickson noted, was to allow the Jews 'to

A new Jewish suburb to the south of Jerusalem (before 1914).

visit Jerusalem temporarily', but not to stay more than three months at the longest. Dickson added: 'The influx of Jews into Palestine has, of late years, become very considerable, and the Jewish population in Jerusalem now numbers from 35,000 to 40,000 out of a total of 60,000 inhabitants. Most of these Jews come from Russia and Germany, and many of them are in indigent circumstances, and the tenants of the various almshouses erected through the benevolence and charity of the Rothschild and Montefiore families, and of Baron Hirsch.'

Baron Hirsch, an Austrian Jew, was putting most of his charitable energies into the settlement of Russian Jews, not at Jerusalem, but in the Argentine. A minority always sought Jerusalem. 'It is not possible', Dickson wrote, 'to give correct figures as to the number of Jews who have arrived in Palestine since the beginning of the present year, for no statistics are kept, and even the Russian Steamboat Agency at Jaffa does not enter their names in its books; but, as far as I have been able to ascertain, about 1,600 from Russia alone have come into the country, during the six months ended the 30th ultimo. Of this number about 400 – probably the more well to do – have again quitted Jerusalem, leaving about 1,200 as permanent settlers.'

Also arriving in Jerusalem in 1890 were more Jews from the Yemen – 180 families in all – 'their settlement here', Dickson explained, 'being the result of certain religious beliefs, such, for instance, as the conviction that the Messiah will very shortly appear in Jerusalem. They form a colony of themselves, and are very poor.'

Each visitor to Jerusalem pondered the future of a city in ferment. 'What is to be her future?' asked one Christian visitor, the Reverend Hugh Callan, in 1891, and he went on, with more questions: 'Shall the Russians rule through their Greek Church (as they are like to), or shall the Jews, possess her? This at least is sure, while the rest are strangers, the Jews are still the only patriots there.'

Among those Jews reaching Jerusalem in 1891 was the 32-year-old Shalom Ben Joseph Alsheikh from Sana in the Yemen. Alsheikh had preached and taught for several years at the Great Synagogue in Sana. In Jerusalem he soon became involved in organizing the Yemenite community, for which he set up several educational and charitable institutes. Four years after reaching the city, Alsheikh was one of the founders of a study house for Jewish mysticism. In 1908 he became Chief Rabbi of the Yemenite community. He died in 1944, at the age of 85, having written an account of the first stirrings of Yemenite Jewry for their return to Zion.

Renewed Jewish building outside the city walls reflected in part the continuing hostility between the orthodox Jews and their more secular fellow-Jews. In 1891 the 'Hungarian Houses' were built just north of the Jaffa road. Their founder, Joseph Sonnenfeld, had come from Slovakia in 1873, at the age of 24, and was by 1891 one of the leaders of the orthodox struggle against Jewish secular education. Sonnenfeld, with Moses Diskin, was an uncompromising advocate of the complete separation of the orthodox and non-orthodox communities. In later years, with the advent of the British Mandate, he was to urge moderation towards the Arab population. In contrast to many ultra-orthodox Jews, Sonnenfeld accepted Hebrew as his 'national' language.

As well as the Hungarian Houses, eight other Jewish quarters were opened between 1890 and 1894, outside the city walls. 'One of the features of modern Jerusalem', Ellen Miller wrote in 1891, 'is the multitude of houses which have been erected for Jewish families outside the walls.' Formerly, she noted, 'it was death to a Jew found trying to intrude into a Turkish quarter; he was restricted to close, unwholesome limits, and compelled to wear a specific European dress; now he is left pretty well to himself, and permitted to erect his own hospital, schools for women and children etc. However, Mohammedan, Christian, and Jew each still prefer to keep to their own quarter'.

The hub of Jerusalem life outside the walls was the Jaffa road. Here, Jewish suburbs, Arab merchants, Bedouin women selling trinkets and vegetables, Christian pilgrims intermingled. The Reverend James Kean commented in 1891, how he would walk down the street, 'avoiding toes of squatting women and heads of leg-tied fowls, and standing to let a string of camels pass'.

In 1891 a group of Jewish residents, members of the 'Jerusalem' Lodge of the B'nai B'rith, acquired the land for a Jewish village just outside Jerusalem. The site chosen was a hillside overlooking the road to the coast. The village was called Motza, the name of one of the cities of the tribe of Benjamin. Thirty-two years earlier, Joshua Yellin had bought land on this same hill for a Jewish farming community, but it had failed. Now two men, William Herzberg, the director of Jerusalem's only Jewish orphanage, and Joseph Meyuhus, gave expression, and funds, to their faith that such a farming village could succeed.

Success came only slowly, however. In 1894 two Jewish labourers and their families moved to the site, followed by three more families in 1895. They lived in houses rented from the Arabs of the nearby village of Koloniya, in watchmen's huts, and even in caves. Keeping cows and goats, these families went to Jerusalem, a forty-five minute walk on foot, to sell milk and cheese. They also planted vineyards, the first wine being made in 1898, and soon sold in the city. But even then, only ten families lived in the village. Only after the turn of the century, when a factory for roof tiles was built, did success come; more than ten years after the first eager expectations.

'The government is Turkish; most of the inhabitants are Jews; the chief Powers of Europe have resident agents; most of the branches of Christendom have some representation; and through its gates stream countless visitors from all parts of the globe.' Thus began Charles Biggs' account of his six months in Jerusalem, as chaplain to Bishop Blyth, beginning in the last months of 1892.

The influx of visitors was made much easier during 1892 with the opening of the railway from Jaffa. Single track and narrow gauge, the railway marked a revolution in access to Jerusalem. Fearing Muslim opposition, the builders had approached the sheikh of the first prominent hill-top village, Malha, above the valley leading out of the city. No, he would not oppose the railway, he said, provided he received some token of the railway builders' esteem. His

Top left: Jerusalem railway station, photographed on inauguration day, on 27 September 1892, with Montefiore's windmill, far left. *Top right:* Russian pilgrims at Jerusalem railway station (before 1914). *Above:* Russian visitors at Jerusalem railway station, from the album of the Russian Consul (before 1914).

wish: some European furniture and a piano. These were duly provided. The sheikh fitted up his principal room with these symbols of modernity, where-upon the villagers of Malha allowed the railway to be built in peace. It was opened on 27 September 1892.

The railway made access to Jerusalem easier than it had ever been before. But the new Ottoman rules against Jewish mass immigration remained in force, nor did they affect only Russian Jews. At the end of 1891 a group of Jews from Persia, likewise driven by persecution to seek a new home, reached Jerusalem. They were warned that they could stay in the city only as pilgrims, and must leave after three months. This, they refused to do, and on 8 February 1892 the Turkish police removed them by force.

One witness of this expulsion was a Jewish convert to Christianity, the Reverend A. Ben Oliel, of the Presbyterian Alliance Mission in the city. Three days after the event, he set down his account of it. 'Last Tuesday at 3 p.m.', he wrote, 'there was a large crowd of Jews and others before the new stores, or shops, on the Jaffa road, in front of Feil's Hotel, and in coming near I heard piteous female cries issuing from one of those stores. Those inside were trying hard to force the doors open, while police and a set of Moslem roughs were piling big stones against the doors, the police striking any who succeeded in putting head or hands out. I at once realised what the violent scene meant.' Ben Oliel's account, written to the British Consul, continued:

'As you know, several groups of Persian Jews, driven away, it is avowed, by persecution, have, within the last two months arrived in Jerusalem, via Jaffa. They are computed at 50, 80 and 100 families but I have found no evidence to warrant an estimate exceeding 50 to 60 at most, of over 150 individuals, children included.

'The Jewish Community offered these exiles a plot of land near Siloam to settle upon, but not satisfied with it, they had an altercation with one of the acting Rabbis, who imprudently called the police to quell the tumult. This came to the knowledge of the Pasha, who thereupon telegraphed to the Porte, and received orders to expel them from the Country.

'Accordingly the police had been all day and were still hunting for the Persian Jews on every side and driving them by blows into that extemporized store-prison, to be kept penned up like wild beasts, till all could be collected and marched away back to Jaffa to be shipped off.

'I was told of a woman caught in the street and marched off by brute force, and she was shrieking piteously for the baby she left in her miserable hovel.

Another, I was assured, being "enceinte" was taken with pains under the blows which hurried her to the prison store. The scene was heart-rending and outrageous to all humane feelings.

'I remonstrated with the police against this inhuman, cruel treatment of these poor exiles, particularly the women and girls, but they were too excited and infuriated, and replied roughly that they were acting by superior orders. To the question had they committed any crime, there was no reply except that it was no business of mine.

'Feeling sure you would generously interpose your good offices to mitigate their sufferings, I decided to call on you at once; but on the way I learnt that you had already sought an interview with the Pasha, who put you off with the plea that it was a matter of internal administration; as also that you were from home.

'I therefore called on Mr. Nessim Bachar, superintendent of the "Alliance Israélite's" Schools and Industrial Manufactories, a Hebrew gentleman of great influence and sound judgement. I found three of the leading Rabbis waiting to see him on the same distressing subject. He came soon, and fully an hour was spent in Conference and consultation. It was decided to seek to obtain a respite, that they might not be marched off on foot, in a cold night, men, women and young children, goaded on by mounted soldiers; to provide them with lodging and food; and to arrange to send them off in batches on carts. It was understood that over 80 had already been collected forcibly in the prison-store. I offered to shelter them in my house, at least that night, till some other accommodation could be found, as also to supply their immediate wants; but it was judged best to lodge them in the precincts of the principal Synagogue. As the Pasha was known to be irritated with solicitations for these persecuted exiles, efforts were made to communicate with the Chief of the Police, who, however, was found to be away at Jaffa. By my advice two Rabbis were sent to the prison-store to try and stop the shrieks and bitter crying of the distressed women with the tranquillizing assurance that efforts would be made to alleviate their hardships; and this had the desired effect.

'Night came on and nothing had been accomplished and so Mr. Nessim and some Rabbis summoned courage and called on the Pasha, and they happily succeeded in obtaining the requisite respite and delay by becoming guarantees for the execution of the Porte's orders, pledging themselves to send the exiles out of the Country. Yesterday some 30 were sent off in carts, and the remainder will be sent off on Sunday or Monday.'

'One aggravating circumstance', Ben Oliel added, 'is that these Jews speak Persian and not Arabic; another that they are mostly poor, having spent their little all in defraying the expenses of their long journey by sea and land. They are a robust, and hardy set, these Persian exiles, and even the women are remarkably muscular. They would therefore have proved an acquisition in this land of slothful and lazy people.'

Those Jews who still sought to settle in Jerusalem had to face formidable obstacles. But the majority of Jews throughout the world saw the city as a spiritual goal rather than an actual destination. In 1892 Israel Zangwill, the London-based Jewish writer, who had not then visited the city, described in moving terms his own picture of Jerusalem through the eyes of one of his fictional characters, Mendel Hyams: 'Mrs Hyams died two years after her honeymoon, and old Hyams laid a lover's kiss upon her sealed eyelids. Then, being absolutely alone in the world, he sold off his scanty furniture, sent the balance of the debt with a sovereign of undemanded interest to Bear Belcovitch, and girded up his loins for the journey to Jerusalem, which had been the dream of his life.

'But the dream of his life had better have remained a dream. Mendel saw the hills of Palestine, and the holy Jordan, and Mount Moriah, the site of the Temple, and the tombs of Absalom and Melchitzedek, and the gate of Zion, and the aqueduct built by Solomon, and all that he had longed to see from boyhood. But somehow it was not his Jerusalem, scarce more than his London Ghetto transplanted, only grown filthier, and narrower, and more ragged, with cripples for beggars and lepers in lieu of hawkers. The magic of his dream-city was not here. This was something prosaic, almost sordid; it made his heart sink as he thought of the sacred splendours of the Zion he had imaged in his suffering soul. The rainbows builded of his bitter tears did not span the firmament of this dingy Eastern city, set amid sterile hills.

'Where were the roses and lilies, the cedars and the fountains? Mount Moriah was here indeed, but it bore the Mosque of Omar, and the Temple of Jehovah was but one ruined wall. The Schechinah, the Divine glory, had faded into cold sunshine. "Who shall go up into the mount of Jehovah?" Lo, the Moslem worshipper and the Christian tourist. Barracks and convents stood on Zion's hill. His brethren, rulers by Divine right of the soil they trod, were lost in the chaos of populations – Syrians, Armenians, Turks, Copts, Abyssinians, Europeans – as their synagogues were lost amid the domes and minarets of the Gentiles. The City was full of venerated relics of the Christ his people had lived – and died – to deny, and over all flew the crescent flag of the Mussulman.

'And so every Friday, heedless of scoffing onlookers, Mendel Hyams kissed the stones of the Wailing Place, bedewing their barrenness with tears, and every year at Passover, until he was gathered to his fathers, he continued to pray, "Next year – in Jerusalem".'

In December 1891, even as Zangwill was busy polishing the scathing portrait of his 'dingy' Jerusalem, a group of Jews from Bukhara purchased a large tract of land to the north-west of the city, on which they were to build houses of considerable affluence and splendour. Indeed, their code of ordinances expressly set out their aim, 'to erect a fine residential quarter, and in the most stately manner', aimed at creating 'streets and street markets, as in the important cities of Europe'. But in the minds of the Jews of Europe, the Jews of Jerusalem, for all their achievements and aspirations, remained the stereotype students in the religious schools with their black robes, side curls, and shuffling gait: the slaves to tradition, and to charity. They might be scholars, but they were neither men of the world, nor men of the future. When, two years after the publication of Zangwill's novel, the Warsaw journalist, Nahum Sokolow, learned that several hundred Palestinian Jews were working as farmers in the Galilee he wrote approvingly: 'Our point of gravity has shifted from the Jerusalem of the religious schools to the farms and agricultural schools, the fields and meadows.'

But it was not only in the religious academies of Jerusalem that Jews studied: nor were Jewish studies in Jerusalem confined to prayers and acts of piety. In 1893, in his house behind the Street of the Consuls, Eliezer Ben Yehuda began work on his ambitious task, a Hebrew-language dictionary. He had neither grammar books nor text books to help him. The spoken Hebrew of Jerusalem possessed no literature of explanation or example. The first word he coined was the word for dictionary – 'milon'.

That same year two British explorers, F. J. Bliss and A. C. Dickie, began a three-year excavation of the city. This was also a productive period for photographers. In 1893 Robinson Lees illustrated a volume on Jerusalem with twelve of his own photographs. A year later an American photographer, Robert Bain, was active in the city, while an Armenian photographer, H. Mardikian, opened his photographic studio, and a second American, Alfred Underwood, took sixty slides of the Holy Land for use with special stereoscopic glasses.

Bain's photographs were among those used by Bishop Vincent to illustrate his book *Early Footsteps of the Man of Galilee*. Bain and Vincent, like all

A stereoscopic slide: 'Cattle market day in the Lower Pool of Gihon', Underwood and Underwood, No. 13. (1897).

Christian visitors, were drawn, with camera and pen, to the Wailing Wall. 'One cannot help but observe in Jerusalem today', Vincent wrote, 'the devotion of the Jews to their city. All the years of change and war and bloodshed and fire and persecution have not been able to destroy the affection which this ancient people of God have for their Holy City. They have been scattered all over the world, but continue to love Jerusalem, the city of the Great King.'

Bishop Vincent, and his co-author, the Reverend James Lee, also wrote about the Arabs. 'Every Jew and every Christian who makes a visit to Palestine', they declared, 'resents in his own feelings the presence of an alien people in the land of the Hebrews and Christians.'

In 1894 George Adam Smith, one of the most distinguished scholars of his age, published his book on the historical geography of the Holy Land. Adam Smith's 713-page survey included, amid its otherwise serene and scientific observations, a scathing reference to the 'war' between the Greek Orthodox and Russian Catholic Churches – the Greeks and the Latins – 'for the possession of holy places, real and feigned'. These two Churches, he noted from personal observation, 'have disfigured the neighbourhood of Jerusalem, and threaten to cover most of the land with rival sanctuaries, planted side by side as they are even at Gethsemane'.

Each winter, Jerusalem, on its mountain-tops, was swept by gales and rain-storms of unexpected ferocity. During the winter of 1894 one such storm, lashing around the Zion Gate, blew down the heavy mediaeval door. An ancient stone was revealed, on which could be read an inscription dated from AD 116. It was a memorial stone to a Roman soldier, fallen in battle.

Each year, at least one book, and sometimes as many as five or six, were published in Europe and the United States about Palestine and Jerusalem. By the 1890s, most of these books were being illustrated with photographs, often lavishly. Several institutions and photographic studios could now offer a comprehensive collection of photographs for authors, travellers and pilgrims, the large format of the prints being convenient for rolling up and fitting into a rigid cardboard tube, or laying flat at the bottom of a cabin trunk.

In 1896 the population of Jerusalem reached 45,000. Of these, 28,000 were Jews, 8,600 Muslim Arabs, and 8,760 Christian Arabs and European Christians. The Jews were divided into 15,000 Ashkenazim – in 1838 the minority Jewish group – 7,900 Sephardim from Asia Minor and Greece, 2,420 North Africans, 1,288 Yemenites, 670 Georgians, 530 Bucharans and 230 Persian Jews.

Acknowledging this Jewish expansion, and seeking to derive some profit from it, in 1896 the Turkish Post Office opened a Jewish Quarter branch office, using a special cancellation, 'Quartier Israélite'. Also in 1896, the London Society for the Promotion of Christianity amongst the Jews opened a new hospital, for converts and sick Jews alike.

Friction between Jerusalem's Jews and the Christian missionaries broke out anew a year later, when five Jewish children being educated in Bishop Blyth's school were seized by their parents in the street, 'the police', as Consul Dickson reported in June, 'siding with the parents and refusing to hand the children back to the English lady teacher'. Five days later, Dickson gave details of a series of incidents involving the hospital opened in April 1896 by the Society for the Promotion of Christianity amongst the Jews. As Dickson reported: 'several hostile demonstrations against the work of the Society have been made by the Jews in Jerusalem in the vicinity of the Hospital, but more particularly before the Dispensary of the Society situated within the city walls. Placards have been posted up, signed by the Rabbis, containing false and defamatory expressions respecting the Society and patients going to and from the Dispensary have been assaulted and ill-treated on several occasions by a Jewish mob.'

The British Consul protested to the Turkish Governor. But his protests were to no avail. Four months later, in October 1897, Dickson reported that the Jewish demonstrations against the hospital 'have recently been renewed. Jews visiting the hospital as out-patients have, on issuing from the building, been beaten and their medicines taken away from them and destroyed by groups of Jews on the watch outside the gates; the friends and relatives of in-patients are persecuted and annoyed by the Rabbis and their agents; and lately no Jewish meat has been permitted to be sold to the hospital for the use of the patients.'

In August 1897, at the first Zionist Congress in Basle, held under the Presidency of an Austrian Jew, Theodor Herzl, several delegates had proposed that the Jews would offer themselves, both to the Ottomans and to the Christians, as special guardians of Jerusalem's holy places. Still, however, the image of the decrepit, stinking, oriental city survived. Karl Baedeker, reissuing his guidebook in that same year, wrote of the traveller to the city: 'The longer and the oftener he sojourns in Jerusalem, the greater will be the interest with which its ruins will inspire him, although he will be obliged to confess that the degraded aspect of the modern city, and its material and moral decline, form but a melancholy termination to the stupendous scenes once enacted here.'

In 1897 an American company, Underwood and Underwood, completed a series of a hundred stereoscopic slides of Palestine. Many of these slides showed scenes of Jerusalem. In the same year an Englishman, R.W. Fisk, toured the country making several hundred lantern-slides for a special lecture set entitled 'Manners and Customs of Palestine'. Fewer and fewer of the photographs were now archaeological: people had come to predominate. The United States Consul, Edwin Sherman Wallace, gave his account of that most mesmeric of sights, Jews in their homes. 'The residences', he wrote, 'are small, ill-ventilated and poorly lighted. In the poorer Jewish quarters humanity has not breathing-room, and apparently does not desire it. I have found ten persons sleeping in one small room with every door and window tightly closed; it was a room to be looked into for curiosity, but not to be entered voluntarily.'

From his own observations, Wallace added, 'made by day and by night in those wretched holes, misnamed houses, I think I have learnt one of the secrets of the indestructibility of the Hebrews: they can survive and increase and seem to thrive amid conditions that could be fatal to the average mortal'.

CHAPTER VIII

1898: Towards the twentieth century

In Karl Baedeker's 'revised and augmented' edition of his handbook for travellers, published in 1898, the new Jerusalem was clear for all to see. 'One train daily in each direction' between Jaffa and Jerusalem was the most striking revolution since Baedeker's first handbook issued twenty-two years earlier. Leaving Jaffa at 1.20 p.m., the journey took three hours and thirty-five minutes. 'The railway carriages are not very comfortable; ladies should always travel first class, but gentlemen may use the second-class carriages, which correspond to 3rd cl. carriages on European lines.'

On reaching Jerusalem station, Baedeker's traveller was told of the Restaurant Lendhold, in the nearby Templar Colony. This restaurant 'has a brewery of its own', producing Bavarian beer.

Hotels abounded: chief of them the Grand New Hotel, recommended by Thomas Cook, inside the Jaffa Gate, and the Hôtel de l'Europe in the Jaffa road. The Jerusalem Hotel, just outside the Jaffa Gate, offered 'excellent wine'. Among hospices, the Prussian Hospice of St John was recommended 'for a prolonged stay', but during the season it was wise to secure rooms in advance. The Austrian Hospice and the Casa Nuova of the Franciscans were 'plainly but well fitted up; clean beds and good food'. Among cafes was the European Casino, opposite the Citadel.

Numerous doctors were listed, as well as chemists, and the times of Divine Service. 'The beautiful masses in the Russian church are at 4 p.m.' Those 'inexperienced in oriental towns' were still advised to take a dragoman. One of the dragomen listed was Jakob Riske, 'a Russian, speaks German, English and French'. Karl Williams, a German, spoke French and English.

Jerusalem, Baedeker averred, was 'not a town for amusement'. Even from

The Kaiser and his entourage leave the Church of the Redeemer (2 November 1898).

'a religious point of view', the impressions which the traveller would receive 'are anything but pleasant'. The native Arab Christians, of all sects, 'are by no means equal to their task, the bitter war which rages among them is carried on with very foul weapons, and the contempt with which the orthodox Jews and Mohammedans look down on the Christians is only too well deserved'.

Inside the city, Baedeker noted the 'absolutely new structure' of the German Protestant Church of the Redeemer, completed that year, its bell tower commanding 'a beautiful view', and the space around the church 'now freed from a huge mass of debris, 25 feet deep, which formerly covered it': the rubbish had been removed 'to the space outside the Jaffa Gate', thus enlarging 'considerably' that particular plateau. The Jewish quarter contained 'several uninviting wine-houses': the Arab bazaar, as in 1876, presented 'no features of special interest', being 'very inferior to those of Cairo and Damascus'. There was no change, either, in the synagogues, 'none of which are interesting'. The space in front of the Jaffa Gate, however, was 'generally enlivened by processions of arriving and departing pilgrims'. Arab saddlers and farriers were also to be found there immediately outside the Jaffa Gate, as well as European shops. 'On Friday and Sunday, the scene is especially lively, the Jaffa road being the favourite promenade of the natives.'

A visit to the summit of the Mount of Olives was recommended, although 'the paths are stony and the afternoon sun very hot'. The Arab village on the summit, et-Tur, 'consists of poor stone cottages, whose inhabitants are sometimes importunate'.

Baedeker had passed no judgement on the new Church of the Redeemer, limiting his praise to the view from its bell tower. This tower was now the highest structure in the Old City. One of those who saw it immediately after its construction, and before the Kaiser's visit, was a British architect, Beresford Pite. 'The Emperor designed the tower himself', Pite wrote later. 'It is manifestly amateurish and does not fit well with the simplicity of the main building.' The bell tower certainly fulfilled 'an ambition to be ugly', Beresford Pite added, and served as a monument 'only to the Emperor William's arrogance'.

This acerbic comment was written on the last day of July 1916, while British troops were failing in their Somme offensive against the German army. 'It would be a benefit to Jerusalem', Beresford Pite added, 'if the allies should pull down this useless tower....' The tower remains to this day.

The 'new Jerusalem', wrote the American Consul, Edwin Wallace, in 1898, 'grows by accession from every part of the globe. On its streets "all sorts and conditions" of Jews and Gentiles meet and pass one another. They may be strangers to each other and ignorant of the part they are playing, but I cannot resist the belief that each is doing his part in God's plan for the rebuilding of the city and its enlargement far beyond the borders it has occupied in the past.'

Wallace also noted the attitude of the Muslims of the city. 'They look', he wrote, 'with a measure of scorn upon Jews and Christians, and, were it not for the financial benefit to them resulting from the presence of these representatives of despised religions, would gladly be rid of them.'

Wallace wrote his observations at a time when the new regulations against Jewish immigration were being rigidly enforced. 'The worst sufferers at the hands of the officers of the law', he wrote, 'are the Jews. These people are not wanted in this city by the Government, and those who have government affairs in charge make it difficult for them to get here and still more difficult to remain.'

Such a situation, Wallace believed, ought to change, or to be changed. 'Once the Turk gets over his animosity towards his elder brother, the Jew', he reflected, 'there will be nothing in the way of the increase of the new city. The Jew wants to come. He is anxious to buy a plot of ground and build him a home in or near the city of his fathers. He simply asks to be let alone, freed from oppression and permitted to enjoy his religion. The land of the new city is ready for him.'

Unlike Consul Finn fifty years before, Wallace had no missionary vision of conversion and redemption through Christianity. Instead, he understood the newly articulated Zionism, launched at Basel a few months earlier. 'The Jew has national aspirations and ideas, and a national future', Wallace wrote, and he went on to ask: 'Where, if not here, will his aspirations be realised and his idea carried out?'

Throughout the summer of 1898, two Jewish vigilante 'patrols', led by Nissim Varon and Abram Albukrak, had sought to disrupt the work of the new Mission Hospital of the London Society for the Promotion of Christianity amongst the Jews. The hospital's medical superintendent, Percy d'Erf Wheeler, a fellow of the Royal College of Surgeons, wrote on 14 July 1898 of how, that same week, 'the wife of Mr Metzger an employee of the Society, had her life endangered by not getting at once the medicine prescribed for her, for serious Uterine hemorrhage, the delay having been caused by the Jewish patrol who actually detained Mr Metzger's servant from going to the Hospital Dispensary. Again, yesterday, a deliberate attack was made on a Jew who was robbed and beaten, because he was carrying Kosher meat which they declared was for the Hospital patients; this meat was purchased and paid for in the usual way.'

Wheeler added, in submitting his complaint to the British Consul: 'Further, only this morning there was a scrimmage between one of these Jewish patrols, and a Jewish patient who was coming to the Hospital.' 'Such illegal acts', he wrote, 'are not only disgraceful, but a menace to the peace of the community at large.'

On 23 June 1898 the British Consul, John Dickson, had reported that the orders 'against the entry of Jews into Palestine' were still being put in force. British Jews, and even Ottoman Jews, were being refused entry at Jaffa. Despite official British protests, the ban continued; on 24 August 1898 the Governor of Jerusalem informed the British Consul 'that he had received strict orders from the Grand Vizier to prohibit the entrance into Palestine of all foreign Jews without distinction of nationality', unless they were to give assurance 'to leave the country within 30 days'.

The rules forbidding Jews to settle in Jerusalem came direct from Constantinople, and were rigorously applied. On 25 August 1898 the British Consul in Jerusalem reported that, eight days earlier, the police authorities at Jaffa had tried to stop Joseph Douek, the British Vice-Consul at Antioch in Syria, 'who had arrived with the intention of visiting Jerusalem, from landing, on account of his being a Jew'.

A month later, on 15 September 1898, nine Jews from Aden, all British subjects, were prevented from landing, beaten by the police, and forced to re-embark on the steamer from which they had landed. One of the Jews, Moshe Shemaiel, was with his two sons, his three daughters, and his wife, who had been born in Jerusalem. Two weeks later, two naturalized British subjects, Moses Magid from the Cape of Good Hope and Abraham Snowman from London, were detained, Magid with his wife, Snowman with his two sons. Magid, the Consul reported, 'succeeded in inducing the Police Authorities at Jaffa to connive at the fact that he is a Jew, by paying a bribe of seventeen napoleons; and he is now in Jerusalem'.

It was the 'forcible expulsion' of the nine Jews from Aden that led to British intervention: 'I have strongly protested', the British Ambassador to Constantinople, Sir Nicolas O'Connor, telegraphed to Dickson, 'against action of Turkish authorities which is direct violation of Treaty rights'. But it was only when the nine Jews gave assurance that 'they would not settle in the country' that they were allowed to land, on 8 October 1898, and to go to Jerusalem.

Those born in Jerusalem in 1898 were to reach adulthood in the twentieth century. One such baby, a Jewish boy named Haim Hatem, was born in Jerusalem on 17 September 1898. As an adult, he was to emigrate to France. It was in France that, on 12 September 1944, five days before his forty-sixth birthday, he was shot by the Gestapo for his part in the French resistance.

Forty days after the birth of Haim Hatem, the leader of the newly established Zionist movement, Dr Theodor Herzl, reached Jaffa by sea from Alexandria. 'We approached the land of our fathers with mixed feelings', he wrote in his diary. 'It is strange what emotions this desolate country evokes in most people: in the old German pastor from South Africa, in the Russian moujik in the vile-smelling steerage, in the Arabs who have been travelling with us from Constantinople, in Zionists like ourselves, in the poor Rumanian Jewess who is going to visit her sick daughter in "Yerushalayim", and who has reason to fear she will be turned back on account of her Rumanian passport.'

Herzl's visit had been carefully timed, to coincide with Jerusalem's event of the decade, the visit of the German Kaiser. Ostensibly going to Jerusalem to dedicate the Protestant Church of the Redeemer, the Kaiser's visit was to be Germany's display of power in the Near East.

The Kaiser had already been to Constantinople, as the guest of the Sultan. Indeed, Theodor Herzl had met him in the Ottoman capital on 18 October, when the Kaiser had offended the Zionist leader by talk of Jewish 'usurers' in Germany proving 'more useful citizens' if they were to take their money and settle in Palestine. 'That he should identify the Jews', Herzl wrote, 'with a few money lenders, irritated me.'

Now German Kaiser and Austrian Jew were to meet again, during the Kaiser's Near Eastern triumph. Lest the Turks should try to 'keep him out' of Palestine, Herzl had prepared a telegram to the Kaiser, 'recounting the difficulties raised against us'. But no such difficulties occurred for him, or for his four Zionist companions. 'When we got into the big Cook's landing boat', Herzl wrote, 'where I had the Rumanian woman sit with us – I learned that German police would be at the pier. I jumped ashore, and while the Turkish police were sniffing through our documents, I took the German official aside and told him that we were here at the Kaiser's command: they should let the five white cork-helmets pass through at once. This was done. I gave the

Theodor Herzl, with beard and pith helmet, next to the carriage, prepares to leave his hotel for sightseeing. *Right:* Herzl at the centre of the five-man Zionist delegation, on its way to see the Kaiser (2 November 1898).

Rumanian woman over to Mme Gaulis, the wife of a French journalist, sitting in the next boat: she was to pass off the Rumanian as her servant. Mme Gaulis complied, the poor old woman clung to the French lady's skirt and thus slipped through the cordon – happy beyond words at being in Palestine and able to visit her daughter who was at death's door. What forms of happiness there are!'

With the visit of the German Kaiser, the city of Jerusalem entered the modern age. The Kaiser was a grandson of Queen Victoria. In his diplomatic actions, he seemed determined to show himself, and the German Empire, superior to his nephew, the Prince of Wales, and to the British Empire of which the Prince would soon be the ruler. Victoria was in the sixty-first year of her reign. The Kaiser was a relative newcomer to power.

In preparation for the Kaiser's visit, and to enable him to enter the city on horseback, a breach had been made in the low wall, next to the Jaffa Gate. At the same time, a metalled road was built from the Damascus Gate to the crest of Mount Scopus, and to a site on the crest granted by the Sultan to the Kaiser for a German hospice, the Augusta Victoria, named after the Kaiser's wife. Here, from a tower almost as tall as the Russian Belvedere of 1889, a similar spectacle could be observed: the barren hills of the Judaean desert, the waters of the Dead Sea glinting 3,900 feet below, and, on the horizon, the mauve mountains of Moab, among them Mount Nebo, from which Moses looked across the Jordan valley to this very crest, the guardian of a Jerusalem he was never to see.

Beyond the city walls, 1898 saw the consecration of the Anglican Collegiate Church of St George, and the foundation of the American Colony Photographic Department by Elijah Meyers, a Jew from India who had converted to Christianity, and Frederick Vester, a German Protestant born in Jerusalem of missionary parents. That same year, the first bicycle was seen in the city – being pedalled courageously along the Jaffa road.

The Kaiser's entry into Jerusalem took place on 29 October 1898. A hundred photographs, professional and amateur, recorded the scene: William, mounted on a black charger, wearing white ceremonial uniform, his helmet surmounted by a burnished gold eagle. 'Revolting,' wrote the mother of the Russian Tsar. 'All done out of sheer vanity, so as to be talked about!' The whole visit, she wrote, was 'perfectly ridiculous, and has no trace of religious feeling – disgusting!'

For the Kaiser, however, the entry into Jerusalem was more than theatrical: more even than a display of Germanic power. 'The thought', he wrote in a letter to the Tsar, 'that His feet trod the same ground is most stirring to one's heart, and makes it beat faster and more fervently.'

Theodor Herzl's heart had also beaten faster, at the thought of putting the case for Zionism to the Kaiser personally, and in Jerusalem itself. But at first he and his delegation were denied an audience. Herzl fumed; changed hotels to be nearer the Jaffa Gate; watched from his hotel window as the Kaiser entered the city, through the Jewish and then the Turkish 'triumphal' arches.

While awaiting word that he could speak to the Kaiser, Herzl explored Jerusalem. 'When I remember thee in days to come, O Jerusalem', he wrote in his diary, 'it will not be with delight', and he went on to explain: 'The musty deposits of two thousand years of inhumanity, intolerance and foulness lie in your reeking alleys. The one man who has been present here all this while, the lovable dreamer of Nazareth, has done nothing but help increase the hate.'

Herzl added: 'If Jerusalem is ever ours, and if I were still able to do anything about it, I would begin by cleaning it up. I would clear out everything that is not sacred, set up workers' houses beyond the city, empty and tear down the filthy rat-holes, burn all the non-sacred ruins, and put the bazaars elsewhere.

Top left: The Jewish arch of welcome to the Kaiser. *Top right:* the Kaiser leaving the Dome of the Rock. *Above:* the Kaiser leaving Jerusalem for Bethlehem (November 1898).

Then, retaining as much of the old architectural style as possible, I would build an airy, comfortable, properly sewered, brand new city around the Holy Places.'

On 1 November 1898 Herzl wrote in his diary: 'We have been to the Wailing Wall. Any deep emotion is rendered impossible by the hideous, miserable, scrambling beggary pervading the place. At least such was the case, yesterday evening and this morning, when we were there. We inspected a Jewish hospital today. Misery and squalor. Nevertheless I was obliged, for appearance sake, to testify in the visitors' book to its cleanliness. This is how lies originate.'

The meeting between the Zionist leaders and the Kaiser took place on 2 November 1898, at the Imperial tent. 'The Kaiser awaited us there', Herzl noted, 'in grey colonial uniform, veiled helmet on his head, brown gloves, and holding – oddly enough – a riding crop in his right hand. I halted a few paces before the entrance and bowed. The Kaiser held out his hand to me very affably as I came in.' During the course of their discussion, Herzl noted in his diary, 'I managed to allude to my idea of restricting the old city to humanitarian institutions, cleaning it up, and building a New Jerusalem which could be viewed from the Mount of Olives as Rome from the Gianicolo.'

During the audience between the Kaiser and Herzl, Herzl was emphatic that the Zionists could find and develop the water needed to modernize Palestine. 'It will cost millions', Herzl told the Kaiser, 'but it will produce millions.' 'Well', the Kaiser replied jovially, tapping his boot with his riding crop, 'you have plenty of money, more than all of us.'

In the heat of a Jerusalem morning Herzl did not argue against this view of Jewish wealth; he spoke instead of 'what could be done with the water power of the Jordan', to the Kaiser's evident approval. The audience was then at an end. On the following day Herzl wrote the final diary entry of his Jerusalem visit; 'I am firmly convinced that a splendid New Jerusalem can be built outside the old city walls', he confided. 'The old Jerusalem would still remain Lourdes and Mecca and Yerushalayim. A very lovely beautiful town could arise at its side.'

Herzl was never to see his dream: he died eight years later, at the age of 42. But Jerusalem, already transformed, already showing so many of the signs of a modern city, was now an integral part of the political conflicts and emotional longings of the new century. Jew, Arab and European, Christian and Muslim, inhabitant and visitor, had built up the city, and given it its character. None were to find it perfect; each was to seek to change it; few were to leave it in peace; but all were to cherish its golden glow.

Bibliography

Chronological list of books published during the years covered by this volume, and consulted by the author:

1838   Lord Lindsay, *Letters on Egypt, Edom and the Holy Land*, 2 volumes (London)

1841   E. Robinson and E. Smith, *Biblical Researches in Palestine, Mount Sinai and Arabia Petrea: A Journal of Travels in the year 1838*

      J. Kitto, *Palestine, Its physical and Bible History*, 2 volumes (London)

1843   W.H. Bartlett, *Walks About the City and Environs of Jerusalem* (London)

      The Rev. George Fisk, *A Pastor's Memorial of Egypt, the Red Sea, the Wilderness of Sinai and Paran, Mount Sinai, Jerusalem, and other principal localities of the Holy Land visited in 1842* (London)

1844   J.T. Bannister, *A Survey of the Holy Land: Its Geography, History and Destiny* (London)

      Robert Curzon, *Visits to Monasteries in the Levant* (London)

      J.W. Johns, *The Anglican Cathedral Church of St James, Mount Zion, Jerusalem* (London)

1845   Lieutenant-Colonel George Gawler, *Observations and Practical Suggestions in Furtherance of the Establishment of Jewish Colonies in Palestine: The Most Sober and Sensible Remedy for the Miseries of Asiatic Turkey* (London)

      John Lowthian, *A Narrative of a Recent visit to Jerusalem and Several Parts of Palestine in 1843–44* (London)

      The Rev. George Williams, *The Holy City: or Historical and Topographical Notices of Jerusalem* (London)

      Ernst Gustav Schultz, *Jerusalem, eine Vorlesung* (Berlin)

1846   The Rev. John Blackburn, *A Hand-book Round Jerusalem* (London)

      W. Krafft, *Die Topographie Jerusalems* (Bonn)

      The Holy Land, Syria, Idumea, Arabia, Egypt and Nubia after lithographs by Louis Haghe from drawings made on the spot by David Roberts, R.A., and with historical descriptions by William Brockendon, 6 volumes (London)

      Rev. Joseph Wolff, *Narrative of a Mission to Bokhara in the Years 1843–1845* (London)

1847 Dr John Kitto, *Modern Jerusalem* (London)
      The Rev. John Wilson, *Lands of the Bible Visited and Described* (Edinburgh)
      James Ferguson, *An Essay on the ancient Topography of Jerusalem* (London)
1849 W.F. Lynch, *Narrative of the United States' Expedition to the River Jordan and the Dead Sea* (Philadelphia)
      George Williams and Robert Willis, *Jerusalem*, single sheet map based on the Royal Engineers map of 1841 (London)
1850 The Rev. Moses Margoliouth, *A Pilgrimage in the Land of My Fathers*, 2 volumes (London)
1851 W.H. Bartlett, *A Pilgrimage Through the Holy Land* (London)
      H.B. Whitaker Churton, *Thoughts on the Land of the Morning: A Record of Two visits to Palestine* (London)
1852 J. Finn, *Opening Address, Jerusalem Literary Society* (Beirut)
1853 Abbé Mariti, *Histoire de L'Etat Présent de Jérusalem* (Paris)
      Titus Tobler, *Denkblätter aus Jerusalem* (St Gallen and Konstanz)
      Titus Tobler, *Topographie von Jerusalem und seinen Umgebungen*, 2 volumes (Berlin)
1854 *Shrines of the Holy Land Contested by the Russian and the Turk* (London)
      C.W.M. Van de Velde, *Narrative of a Journey Through Syria and Palestine in 1851 and 1852*, 2 volumes (Edinburgh and London)
1855 W.H. Bartlett, *Jerusalem Revisited* (London)
      The Jerusalem Miscellany (London)
1856 Hanmer L. Dupuis, *The Holy Places: A Narrative of Two Years' Residence in Jerusalem and Palestine*, 2 volumes (London)
      Arthur Penrhyn Stanley, *Sinai and Palestine in connection with their History* (London)
      The Jerusalem Miscellany, No. 2 (London)
      Edward Robinson, *Later Biblical Researches in Palestine and the Adjacent Regions: A Journal of Travels in the Year 1852*
      Auguste Salzmann, *Jerusalem: Etude Photographique des Monuments de la Ville Sainte* (Paris)
1858 Horatius Bonar, *The Land of Promise: Notes of a Spring Journey from Beersheba to Sidon* (London)
      John Murray, *A Handbook for Travellers in Syria and Palestine*, 2 volumes (London, Paris, Malta)
      James Graham, *Jerusalem, Its Missions, Schools, Convents, etc under Bishop Gobat* (London)
1862 Frederika Bremer, *Travels in the Holy Land*, translated by Mary Howitt, 2 volumes (London)
      Captain Gelis, *Nivellement de Jérusalem*, single sheet map, scale 1:5,000, Paris, 18 November to 22 December 1863
      Mr F. Bedford's Photographic Pictures taken during the Tour in the East, in which, by command, he accompanied H.R.H. The Prince of Wales (London)
1863 Arthur Penrhyn Stanley, *Sermons preached before the Prince of Wales during his Tour in the East in the Spring of 1862, with Notices of some of the Localities visited* (London)
1864 Ermete Pierotti, *Customs and Traditions of Palestine, illustrating the Manners of the Ancient Hebrews* (Cambridge)
      Ermete Pierotti, *Jerusalem Explored* (London)

1865   Robertson and Beato, *Jérusalem Album Photographique* (Constantinople)

        Ch. Sandreczki, *Account of a Survey of the City of Jerusalem* (Jerusalem)

        Captain Charles W. Wilson, *Ordnance Survey of Jerusalem*, single sheet maps, 1:2,500
        (city) 1:10,000 (environs) and 1:500 (Temple Mount area) (Jerusalem)

1866   William Hepworth Dixon, *The Holy Land*, 2 volumes (London)

        Mrs Finn, *Home in the Holy Land: A Tale Illustrating Customs and Incidents in
        Modern Jerusalem* (London)

1867   Religious Tract Society, *Pictorial Journey Through the Holy Land, or Scenes in Palestine*
        (London)

1870   Ermete Pierotti, *Plan de Jérusalem, Ancienne et Moderne*, single sheet map, Paris and
        Lausanne

1871   Walter Besant and E.H. Palmer, *Jerusalem, the City of Herod and Saladin* (London)

1873   Committee of the Palestine Exploration Fund, *Our Work in Palestine* (London)

1874   The Rev. Samuel Manning, *Those Holy Fields* (London)

1875   Isabel Burton, *The Inner Life of Syria, Palestine and the Holy Land*, 2 volumes (London)

        K. Baedeker, *Palestine and Syria, Handbook for Travellers* (Leipzig and London)

1876   Thomas Cook, *Cook's Handbook for Palestine and Syria* (London)

        Charles Warren, *Underground Jerusalem* (London)

1878   James Finn, *Stirring Times, or Records from Jerusalem Consular Chronicles of 1853 to
        1856*, 2 volumes (London)

        Colonel Wilson, *Picturesque Palestine, Sinai and Egypt*, 4 volumes (London)

1881   James Neil, *Palestine Explored: with a view to its present natural features* (London)

1882   Felix Bovet, *Egypt, Palestine, and Phoenicia: A Visit to Sacred Lands* (London)

        A.M. Luncz (editor), *Jerusalem Year-Book for the Diffusion of an Accurate Knowledge
        of Ancient and Modern Palestine* (Vienna)

1883   The Rev. Andrew Thomson, *In the Holy Land* (London)

1884   Col. Sir Charles Warren and Capt. Claude Reignier Conder, *The Survey of Western
        Palestine: Jerusalem* (London)

        Henry Carr (and others), *Our Journey through Bible Lands* (Carlisle)

1885   Claude Reignier Conder, *Tent Work in Palestine: a Record of Discovery and Adventure*
        (London)

        Rev. J. King, *Recent Discoveries in the Temple Hill at Jerusalem* (London)

1886   Prince Albert Victor and Prince George of Wales with additions by John N. Dalton,
        The Cruise of Her Majesty's Ship Bacchante, 1879-1882, 2 volumes (London)

        Walter Besant, *Twenty-One Years' Work in the Holy Land* (London)

1887   Cunningham Geikie, *The Holy Land and the Bible*, 2 volumes (London)

        J.L. Porter, *Jerusalem, Bethany, and Bethlehem* (London)

        Mark Twain, *The New Pilgrim's Progress* (London)

1888   Sir Richard Temple, *Palestine Illustrated* (London)

1889   Major C.R. Conder, *Palestine* (London)

1891   The Rev. Hugh Callan, *The Story of Jerusalem* (Edinburgh)

        The Rev. James Kean, *Among the Holy Places* (London)

        Isaac Levinsohn, *Wanderings in the Land of Palestine* (London and Glasgow)

        Ellen E. Miller, *Alone Through Syria* (London)

        Mrs Oliphant, *Jerusalem, Its History and Hope* (London)

1893   G. Robinson Lee, *Jerusalem Illustrated* (London)

W.M. Thomson, *The Land and The Book* (London)

L. Valentine (editor), *Palestine Past and Present, Pictorial and Descriptive* (London and New York)

1894   Bishop John H. Vincent, (Photograph Artist, Robert E.M. Bain), *Earthly Footsteps of the Man of Galilee: Our Lord and his Apostles Traced with Note Book and Camera* (St. Louis, Missouri, and London)

George Adam Smith, *The Historical Geography of the Holy Land* (London)

Notes by English Visitors to Abraham's Vineyard, near Jerusalem (London)

Conrad Schick, 'Jerusalem Notes – a colony of Bokhara Jews', *Palestine Exploration Fund Quarterly Statement* (London)

1896   Rev. Charles Biggs, *Six Months in Jerusalem: Impressions of the Work of England in and for the Holy City* (Oxford and London)

1898   Edwin Sherman Wallace, *Jerusalem the Holy* (Edinburgh and London)

Alphabetical list of historical works, biographies and memoirs consulted by the author:

Aaronsohn, Ran, 'Building the Land: Stages in the First Aliya Colonization (1882-1904)', *The Jerusalem Cathedra*, Volume 3, Jerusalem and Detroit, 1983

Abramowitz, Leah, 'A landmark' (the Schneller Orphanage) *Jerusalem Post*, Jerusalem, 22 April 1979

Abramowitz, Leah, 'Historic Israeli personality' (Joshua Yellin), *Jerusalem Post*, Jerusalem, 6 August 1979

Abramowitz, Leah, 'Yoel Moshe and the Salomon's Printing Press', *Jerusalem Post*, 7 September 1983

The Architecture of Islamic Jerusalem, Jerusalem 1976

Aref-el-Aref, *Dome of the Rock*, Jerusalem 1964

Bailey, Clinton, 'The Negev in the Nineteenth Century: Reconstructing History from Bedouin Oral Traditions', *Asian and African Studies: Journal of the Israel Oriental Society*, volume 14, number 1, Haifa, March 1980

Bailey, Clinton, 'Bedouin War Poems from the Negev, perspective on pre-Islamic Poetry', in *Jerusalem Studies in Arabic and Islam*, volume 3, Jerusalem 1982

Baldensperger, Phillip J., 'Women in the East', *Palestine Exploration Fund Quarterly Statement*, January 1901, page 176

Ben-Arieh, Y., *A City Reflected in its Times: Jerusalem in the Nineteenth Century*, Part One: The Old City, Jerusalem 1977; Part Two, New Jerusalem, its beginnings, Jerusalem 1979

Ben-Eliezer, Shimon, *Destruction and Renewal, The Synagogues of the Jewish Quarter*, Jerusalem 1975

Ben-Yaacob, Abraham, *Jerusalem Between the Walls*, Jerusalem 1977

Blumberg, Arnold, *A View from Jerusalem, 1849-1958: The Consular Diary of James and Elizabeth Anne Finn*, Cranbury, New Jersey, 1980

Cannan, T., *Mohammedan Saints and Sanctuaries in Palestine*, London 1927

Chouraqui, André, *L'Alliance Israélite universelle et la renaissance juive contemporaine; cent ans d'histoire*, Paris 1960

Cohen, E., *The City in Zionist Ideology*, Jerusalem 1970

Comay, Joan, *The Temple of Jerusalem*, London 1975

Coquerel, Athanase Josué, *Topographie de Jérusalem au Temps de Jésus Christ*, Strasbourg 1843

Corti, Egon Caesar Count, *Maximillian and Charlotte of Mexico*, 2 volumes, New York 1928

Costello, C., 'Nineteenth Century Irish Explorers in the Levant', *Irish Geography*, Number 7, Dublin 1974

Cromer, Ruby, *The Hospital of St John in Jerusalem*, London 1961

Druyan, Nitza, 'The Immigration and Integration of Yemenite Jews in the First Aliya', *The Jerusalem Cathedra*, volume 3, Jerusalem and Detroit 1983

Duncan, Alistair, *The Noble Heritage: Jerusalem and Christianity*, London 1974

Duncan, Alistair, *The Noble Sanctuary: Portrait of a Holy Place in Arab Jerusalem*, London 1972

Egan, M.J., *Our Lady's Jew, Father M.A. Ratisbonne*, London 1953

Elon, Amos, *The Israelis, Founders and Sons*, London 1971

Finn, E.A., *Reminiscences of Mrs Finn, Member of the Royal Asiatic Society*, London 1929

Finnie, David H., *Pioneers East, the Early American Experiences in the Middle East*, Cambridge Massachusetts, 1967

Furneaux, Rupert, *The Roman Siege of Jerusalem*, London 1973

Gitlin, Jan, 'Tales of Mea Shearim', *Jerusalem Post*, Jerusalem, 13 October 1978

Goodman, Paul, *Moses Montefiore*, Philadelphia 1943

Graham, Stephen, *With the Russian Pilgrims to Jerusalem*, London 1913

Greenstone, Julius H., *The Messianic Idea in Jewish History*, Philadelphia 1906

Grindea, Milton (editor), *Jerusalem, a literary chronicle of 3,000 years*, Rochester, New York 1968

Guini, B., *Jerusalem, Section No. 3*, single sheet map, scale 1:2,000, Jerusalem, 14 November 1921

Guini, B., *Western District of Jerusalem*, single sheet map, scale 1:2,000, Jerusalem, 21 March 1921

Hanauer, The Rev. J.E., *Walks in and around Jerusalem*, London 1926

The Hebrew University, Jerusalem: its History and Development, Jerusalem 1948

Hopwood, Derek, *The Russian Presence in Syria and Palestine 1843-1914; Church and Politics in the Near East*, Oxford 1961

Hyamson, Albert M., *The British Consulate in Jerusalem in relation to the Jews of Palestine 1838-1914, Part I, 1838-1861; Part II, 1862-1914*, London 1939

Hyamson, Albert M., *Palestine: The Rebirth of an Ancient People*, London 1917

Israeli, Yael, *Jerusalem in History and Vision*, Jerusalem 1968

James, E.O. (foreword), *Jerusalem, A History*, London 1967

Join-Lambert, Michel, *Jerusalem*, London 1958

Kenyon, Kathleen M., *Jerusalem: Excavating 3000 Years of History*, London 1967

Kollek, Teddy, and Pearlman, Moshe, *Jerusalem Sacred City of Mankind: a history of forty centuries*, London 1968

Kollek, Teddy, and Pearlman, Moshe, *Pilgrims to the Holy Land: The Story of Pilgrimage through the Ages*, London 1970

Kroyanker, David, and Wahrman, Dror, *Jerusalem Architecture, Periods and Styles: The Jewish Quarters and Public Buildings outside the old city walls, 1860-1914*, Jerusalem 1983

Lauterpacht, Elihu, *Jerusalem and the Holy Places*, London 1968

Leighton, Douglas (editor), *The Letters of William Henry Leighton to his brother Robert*, London 1947

Leven, Narcisse, *Cinquante Ans d'Histoire, L'Alliance Israélite Universelle, 1860-1910*, 2 volumes, Paris 1911, 1920

Loewe, Dr Louis (editor), *Diaries of Sir Moses and Lady Montefiore*, London 1890

Lowenthal, Marvin (editor), *The Diaries of Theodor Herzl*, London 1958

Macalister, R.A.S., *A Century of Excavation in Palestine*, London 1925

Magnus, Phillip, *King Edward the Seventh*, London 1964

Mandel, Neville L., *The Arabs and Zionism before World War I*, Berkeley and Los Angeles, 1976

Mazar, Benjamin, *The Mountain of the Lord: Excavating in Jerusalem*, New York 1975

Meyer, Herrmann M.Z., *Jerusalem, Maps and Views*, Jerusalem 1971

Newton, Frances E., *Fifty Years in Palestine*, London 1948

Nicolson, Harold, *King George the Fifth, His Life and Reign*, London 1952

Oesterreicher, Monsignor John M., and Sinai, Anne (editors), *Jerusalem*, New York 1974

Onne, Eyal (editor), *Photographic Heritage of the Holy Land 1839-1914*, Manchester 1980

Parkes, James, *The Story of Jerusalem*, London 1949

Parsons, Helen Palmer (editor), *Letters from Palestine: 1868-1912, written by Rolla Floyd*, Maine 1981

Pollack, F.W., *The Turkish Post in the Holy Land*, Tel Aviv 1962

Prawer, Joshua, *The Latin Kingdom of Jerusalem: European Colonialism in the Middle Ages*, London 1972

Raphael, Chaim, *The Walls of Jerusalem: An Excursion into Jewish History*, London 1968

Reiner, Elchanan, *The Yochanan Ben Zakkai Four Sephardi Synagogues*, Jerusalem 1970

Rozin, Mordechai, and Landau, Julian L., *Mishkenot Sha'ananim*, Jerusalem 1974

Samuel, Viscount Edwin, *A Lifetime in Jerusalem*, London 1970

Schick, C., *Nähere Umgebung von Jerusalem*, single sheet map, 1:10,000, Leipzig 1905 (drawn in 1894-5)

Schiller, Ely (editor), *The Heritage of the Holy Land, Illustrated Periodical of the Landscape of the Holy Land*, No. 1, Jerusalem, December 1982

Schneider, Peter, and Wigoder, Geoffrey (editors), *Jerusalem Perspectives*, Arundel 1976

Shanks, Hershel, *The City of David, a guide to biblical Jerusalem*, Tel Aviv 1973

Smith, George Adam, *Jerusalem*, 2 volumes, London 1907

Spyridon, S.N., 'Father Neophytos' diary (1821-1841)', *Journal of Palestine Oriental Society*, volume XVIII, Jerusalem 1938

Sukenik, E.L., *Ancient Synagogues in Palestine and Greece*, London 1934

Tibawi, A.L., *British Interests in Palestine, 1800-1901: A study of Religious and Educational Enterprise*, London 1961

Underwood and Underwood, *Jerusalem Through the Stereoscope*, New York 1905

Undique and Terram Sanctam Cartographic Exhibition from the Eran Laor Collection, Jerusalem 1976

Vester, Bertha Spafford, *Our Jerusalem*, Beirut 1950

Vilnay, Zev, *Legends of Jerusalem*, Philadelphia 1973

Watson, Colonel Sir S.M., *The Story of Jerusalem*, London 1912

Weizmann, Chaim, *Trial and Error*, London 1949

Weblowsky, R.J. Zwi, *Jerusalem: Holy City of Three Religions*, Jerusalem 1976

Wilson, Major-General Sir C.W., *The Water Supply of Jerusalem*, London 1902

Wright, J.E., *Round About Jerusalem*, London 1918

PHOTOGRAPHIC SOURCES

Royal Archives (Copyright reserved. Reproduced by gracious permission of Her Majesty the Queen): photographs on pages 5 (top), 5 (bottom), 24, 45, 61, 70, 82–83 (panorama), 111 (top), 114, 115 (bottom left), 144 (top right), 197 (right), 199 (top)

Bartlett, *Jerusalem Revisited*, 79, 82 (bottom)

Bartlett, *Walks About the City and Environs of Jerusalem*, 39

Bibliothèque de l'Arsenal, Paris, 169

Bodleian Library, 21, 55

Central Zionist Archives, 16, 64, 113 (bottom), 142, 199 (bottom), 224 (top left)

Elia Photo-Service, Jerusalem, 207

Graham, *With the Russian Pilgrims to Jerusalem*, 202, 210 (top right)

Israel Government Press Office, Photographic Department, 133 (left), 133 (right), 150 (left)

Israel Museum, 75

Jerusalem Municipality, x, 21 (bottom), 52, 67, 77, 89 (bottom left), 89 (bottom right), 91, 95, 97, 132 (far left), 132 (top left), 201 (left), 147, 191 (top left), 201 (left), 210 (bottom), 218, 226 (top left), 226 (top right), 226 (bottom)

Jewish Agency Photographic Service, 107, 175, 201 (middle), 201 (right), 224 (top right)

Martin Gilbert (photographs taken in 1984), 10, 26, 30, 42, 66, 72 (top right), 72 (bottom left), 72 (bottom right), 89 (top right), 103, 121 (top), 124, 127 (right), 142 (bottom), 150 (right), 151, 170, 189 (left), 189 (right), 191 (top right), 191 (bottom), 194

Kroyanker and Dror, *Jerusalem Architecture, Periods and Styles*, 84

Mishkenot Sha'ananim, Montefiore Album, 127 (left)

Palestine Exploration Fund, xiv, 13 (top), 21 (top), 38, 60, 72 (top left), 102, 121 (bottom), 135 (left), 163 (left), 181, 210 (top left).

Pierotti, *Jerusalem Explored*, 111 (bottom).

Private collections, ii–iii, xv, xviii, 3, 17, 50, 56, 89, 104, 113 (top), 115 (top), 115 (bottom right), 117, 138, 144 (bottom), 155 (bottom), 163 (right), 187, 200

Realistic Travels Publishers, Stereoscopic Slides, 13 (bottom left), 206

Reiner, *The Yochanan Ben Zakkai Four Sephardi Synagogues*, 183

Schiller, *The Heritage of the Holy Land*, 162 (top), 162 (bottom)

Underwood and Underwood Stereoscopic Slides, 9, 13 (bottom right), 32 (bottom), 144 (top left), 157, 192, 197 (left), 215

Vincent, *Earthly Footsteps of the Man of Galilee* (1894), 32 (top), 155 (top)

Warren, *Underground Jerusalem*, 164

Warren and Conder, *The Survey of Western Palestine* (1884), 129 (top), 129 (bottom), 130

Wilson, *Picturesque Palestine*, 132 (right)

BIOGRAPHICAL INDEX
compiled by the author

INDEX OF PLACES
compiled by the author